Advaitic Mysticism of Śaṅkara

Other Books by the Author

- Advaita — A Conceptual Analysis
- The Central Philosophy of the Ṛgveda
- Indian Philosophy of Religion
- Philosophy of Brahman
- The Philosophical Foundations of Hinduism
- Vedānta and its Philosophical Development

Advaitic Mysticism of Śaṅkara

A. Ramamurty

DK PRINTWORLD
Publishers of Indian Traditions

Cataloging in Publication Data — DK
[Courtesy: D.K. Agencies (P) Ltd. <docinfo@dkagencies.com>]

Ramamurty, A. (Aryasomayajula), 1935-
Advaitic mysticism of Śaṅkara / A. Ramamurty.
– 2nd ed.
p. cm.
Originally presented as the author's thesis (PhD)
– Andhra University.
Includes bibliographical references (p.) and index.
ISBN 9788124606797

1. Mysticism – History. 2. Advaita – History.
3. Śaṅkarācārya. I. Title.

DDC 181.482 23

ISBN 13: 978-81-246-0679-7 ISBN 10: 81-246-0679-X
First published in India, 1974
Second edition published in 2013

Printed and published by:
D.K. Printworld (P) Ltd.
Regd. office : *"Vedaśrī,"* F-395, Sudarshan Park
(Metro Station: Ramesh Nagar)
New Delhi - 110 015
Phones : (011) 2545 3975, 2546 6019; *Fax* : (011) 2546 5926
E-mail : indology@dkprintworld.com
Web : www.dkprintworld.com

Preface

THE Advaita Vedānta is one of the most important systems of Indian philosophy, from the point of view of its content as well as its influence. Although he had a number of eminent predecessors and successors, Śaṅkara is by far the greatest thinker of this school. The classical exposition of the Advaita doctrine in its fullness is to be found in his great commentaries on the Upaniṣads, the *Bhagavad-Gītā* and the *Brahmasūtra*s. There are also a number of monographs (*prakaraṇa grantha*s) expounding the Advaita doctrine, which are traditionally believed to be Śaṅkara's works. They are the *Vivekacūḍāmaṇi*, *Upadeśasāhasrī*, *Aparokṣānubhūti*, etc. Some modern scholars, however, doubt whether the author of all these *prakaraṇa grantha*s was the great Śaṅkara himself!

Although there are many books on Advaita Vedānta in modern languages dealing with its various aspects, there is none which deals with *brahmānubhava* (the experience of *Brahman* by being It) as is described and discussed in Śaṅkara's works. It is well known that Advaitins who came after Śaṅkara interpreted and developed the master's ideas in different ways. Similarly, there are some differences between Śaṅkara and his predecessors.

This book attempts to elaborate and clarify Śaṅkara's understanding of *brahmānubhava*, in all its aspects, relying exclusively on his own writings. For this, not only the commentaries, but also the *prakaraṇa grantha*s have been taken into account. In the final chapter, *brahmānubhava* is compared with what was said about the mystic experience by two of the most authoritative exponents of Christian and Islamic mysticisms, namely St. John of the Cross and Jalālu'd-Dīn Rūmī, mainly to understand Śaṅkara's position without any ambiguity. I am aware of certain repetitions here and there, but I hope they are not out of context.

This was originally submitted as a thesis for PhD, at the Andhra University. I am grateful to K. Satchidananda Murty of Andhra University under whose guidance my research work was carried out. I am also grateful to Santosh Chandra Sengupta, Director, Centre of Advanced Study in Philosophy, Visva-Bharati, for publishing this book.

Santiniketan A. RAMAMURTY
June 1973

Contents

Abbreviations

AiUB	*Aitareya Upaniṣad Bhāṣya*
BGB	*Bhagavad-Gītā Bhāṣya*
BṛUB	*Bṛhadāraṇyaka Upaniṣad Bhāṣya*
ChāUB	*Chāndogya Upaniṣad Bhāṣya*
GKB	*Gauḍapādakārikā Bhāṣya*
ĪUB	*Īśa Upaniṣad Bhāṣya*
KaUB	*Kaṭha Upaniṣad Bhāṣya*
KeUB	*Kena Upaniṣad Bhāṣya*
MaUB	*Maitreyī Upaniṣad Bhāṣya*
MāUB	*Māṇḍūkya Upaniṣad Bhāṣya*
MuUB	*Muṇḍaka Upaniṣad Bhāṣya*
PrUB	*Praśna Upaniṣad Bhāṣya*
SūB	*Sūtra Bhāṣya*
TaiUB	*Taittirīya Upaniṣad Bhāṣya*

Introduction

THE main purpose of an enquiry into the nature of Reality or *Brahman*, according to Śaṅkara, is to have direct and immediate experience of It (*paramārtha darśanam*), which is the highest state (*parā gati*) a man can attain and the supreme consummation (*parākāṣṭhā*) of human life. The real purpose of the important Upaniṣadic statements like "That thou art" and "I am *Brahman*", on which the mystical metaphysics of Śaṅkara is primarily based, is not only to present the truth as revealed, but also to make everyone realize it for oneself directly (*avagati niṣṭha*). Accordingly, Śaṅkara conceives philosophy as a means to attain the highest end of life or a preparation for the attainment of immortality (*amṛtattva sādhanam*) — the realization of one's own self in its real nature — and is pursued by those who are desirous of attaining it (*amṛtattva kāma*). Thus the starting-point of a metaphysical enquiry, according to Śaṅkara, is one's own self (*ko va mama svabhāva*), and by discovering the true nature of it, it should culminate in direct realization of it. "The true ideal of philosophy, according to Śaṅkara," says S. Radhakrishnan, "is not so much knowledge as wisdom, not so much logical learning as spiritual freedom."[1]

The greatness of Śaṅkara does not lie in his ability to construct a sound system of metaphysics only, but also in his realization that no system of metaphysics can penetrate into the depths of Reality. His thought is not so much metaphysical

[1] S. Radhakrishnan, *Indian Philosophy*, London: George Allen & Unwin, 1956, vol. II, p. 447.

as mystical. It is direct experience, but not reasoning that is given supreme importance in it. It is primarily based on the scripture, which, according to Śaṅkara, is a repository of truth as experienced, and logic is used as an auxiliary to support and strengthen his main standpoint. His main concern is not to construct, on the basis of reason, a system of metaphysics, but to present in a coherent and systematic manner the nature of *Brahman* as experienced. His writings are mystical and religious rather than logical, and their main purpose is not to make us understand, in a rational way the nature of Reality which is not possible, but to make us realize Reality directly for ourselves. His is a philosophy of the Upaniṣads (*aupaniṣadam darśanam*) and a doctrine of liberation (*mokṣa śāstra*). "With Śaṅkara," says Otto, "one has first to break through the dry husk of his speculative system and disclose, embedded in his *Brahman* and *ātman*, the living features of ancient Indian mysticism as it survives in the Upaniṣads and the Purāṇas."[2]

Śaṅkara is neither apologetic nor dogmatic, but fully comprehensive in his approach to the problems of philosophy. He has not underestimated the value of reasoning, nor does he dogmatically uphold the authority of the scriptures. In his search for truth, the direct realization of which is the supreme end of life, he has tried to understand critically the worth of both reasoning and revelation, but realizing that they are inadequate for that purpose, he tried to transcend them both in the end. He treated reason with the dignity it deserves and appreciated fully the value of free enquiry. But in the end he was compelled, on rational grounds, to reject reason as he found it to be inadequate in realizing the truth or in attaining the perfect knowledge of Reality. Instead of ending in scepticism or landing in contradictions and antinomies, which

---

[2] Rudolph Otto, *Mysticism East and West*, New York: Meridian Books, 1957, pp. 36-37.

the different systems of metaphysics based on pure reason present, he tried to transcend metaphysics conceived as a speculative activity and attempted to construct a meaningful one on the basis of intuitive insights of revelation. In that, his values differ from the values of speculative metaphysics. For him, nothing less than the direct awareness of Reality in its complete objectivity is the goal of metaphysics, while for many others it may be an intellectual understanding of Reality, whether it is possible or not. This is the true significance of the concepts of *adhyāsa* (superimposition) and *avidyā* (ignorance), and the goal of metaphysics is to transcend all the limitations imposed on Reality because of them, and to attain perfect knowledge of it. The important point to be noted in this connection is that in so far as he handled the problems of speculative metaphysics, he showed utmost independence and made full use of reason.

However, in conformity with his objective of attaining the perfect knowledge of Reality, which he realized could not be achieved by following reason, he invoked revelation. But the acceptance of revelation and subordinating reason to it are not done for reasons other than philosophical. Because of his firm commitment to truth, he was not disturbed in compromising reason for its realization. If it is a question of compromise between reason and truth, he would prefer to compromise the former. Philosophy does not rest ultimately on the claims of reason. Its basic concern is not to uphold dogmatically the sanctity of reason even when it is found out to be wanting. If the chief concern of philosophy is not simply to uphold the claims of reason, but to know things correctly and perfectly, there is no valid reason why it should resist to accept rich insights from whatever source they may come from.

No doubt, Śaṅkara is not simply a mystic. He is a metaphysician at the same time. While the aim of metaphysics is to achieve an intellectual understanding of Reality, a mystic passionately longs for a direct experience of it. He is not so much concerned with the formulation of intellectually plausible theories of Reality, nor in demonstrating the rationality and logical validity of his experience. His is mainly an approach of involvement. The concern of a metaphysician, on the other hand, is to construct a meaningful theory of Reality which is logically sound and can be rationally demonstrated. In Śaṅkara, we find that both these roles are merged into one.

The office of reason is to analyse and evaluate critically the facts of experience or to interpret them with a view to discover the underlying principle or principles that govern them. In performing these, its functions are not cognitive, but analytical and interpretative. As such when reason becomes indifferent to facts of human experience, the conclusions based on it turn to be empty. The facts of experience should be critically examined before they are accepted or rejected. Philosophy should not reject arbitrarily some of the facts of human experience. It should not pre-judge any facts or treat some of them as untouchables. To be comprehensive in its inquiries, it should keep open its doors to all the facts of human experience. Revelation is one such fact or at least points out to the possibilities of human experience, which many may have not realized, and for that reason philosophy should not be blind to such human possibilities. In so far as it offers valuable insights in understanding the problems of philosophy, its evidence should be carefully judged. On the other hand, if philosophy accepts revelation for reasons other than philosophical, it loses its distinction from theology. It is equally unphilosophical to reject revelation without ever examining its philosophic worth. Revelation may not be meaningful in terms of empirical experience and hence in terms of reason, but if by accepting it the latter can gain better significance, it should be accepted hypothetically whose confirmation lies in one's own direct experience. Thus in accepting certain revealed truths, in so far as they are not anti-rational and do not contradict empirical experience, one does not become unphilosophical in his approach. This was the exact predicament in which Śaṅkara finds himself placed in his search for truth.

Śaṅkara accepted what he considered as the cardinal teachings of the Upaniṣads. He rejected from the scriptures all that is contradictory to empirical experience. The few intuitive insights of revelation, which he accepted, were considered by him to be fruitful and relevant in deciding the transcendental problems of philosophy. He followed reason to where it led him and when he realized that thereby the perfect knowledge of Reality cannot be attained, he left off pure reason, accepted revelation and employed reason in the service of revelation. In doing so, he did not try to subvert reason because of his jealous commitment to revelation. He was fully aware of the supremacy of reason as far as the empirical experience is concerned. He was also aware of the fact that the rejection of reason is itself based on reason. It should not be rejected because of its faulty use by some philosophers, for the possibility of its future perfection is always there. He also has realized the efficiency of reason in achieving unity and cohesion of human thought, especially within the empirical realm. Moreover, he was fully convinced that what was constructed on the basis of revelation could also be constructed on the basis of reason. But, as thereby the highest end of life, which according to him is the goal of philosophy, cannot be accomplished, he rejected it. The mutual contradictions into which speculative philosophy based on reason lands showing whereby that reason lacks finality of judgement when applied to transcendental problems of philosophy, and if applied results in unsubstantial conclusions, led him to the rejection of reason and acceptance of revelation mainly for its experiential value. Thus to base his inquiries on sure grounds, so as to reach meaningful and substantial conclusions, he invoked revelation.

The philosophy of Vedānta is a critique of revelation as much as it is a critique of reason. Such that we find not one interpretation of it, but as many as its interpreters. The various commentaries and commentaries over commentaries exhibit an excellent zeal for philosophy and a capacity to philosophize. They leave behind such an impression of freedom which could not have been achieved if they never wanted to exercise their freedom of enquiry, but simply wished to follow the original faithfully. If in accepting revelation what they sought to achieve was only a rationalization or justification of it, there could have been no different systems of Vedānta philosophy. Using reason and assimilating the various arguments of their opponents, they constructed substantially different systems of philosophy. Thus what Śaṅkara presented was not completely there in revelation, for which he was later suspected as a crypto Buddhist. He who could reject much of revelation as philosophically irrelevant could have rejected it in total had he not found it rationally irresistible to do so.

Revelation too, according to him, has its own limitations. Based on duality and operative within the sphere of ignorance, it cannot present Reality as it is in itself. It can only point out in an indirect manner what Reality is, but cannot present it positively. For instance, when it says, "That thou art", it does not mean to say that the "thou" is directly identical with "That". It only indicates that the notions of "thou" and "That" are pointers to Reality. Reality is the substratum on which these notions are superimposed, and therefore to realize it is to transcend the duality of "That" and "thou". What is realized thereby cannot be presented and described positively.

Faith also has an important place in Śaṅkara's mystical doctrine. It is essential to realize the highest, but unclarified and untested by reasoning, it fails to help us in attaining the highest end of life. Thus reason, revelation and faith have their appropriate places in his mystico-metaphysical system.

Brahman is not a metaphysical postulate logically arrived at. It is pure experience or pure knowledge; and its realization, which is possible only by being It, liberates the individual self from ignorance, and the bondage and suffering caused by it. It is a "saving actuality" as Otto puts it.[3] As the true Self of everyone, It is self-evident to all and irrefutable. Its existence cannot be denied without denying one's Self. As pure experience — subject–objectless experience — *Brahman* is never an object of our knowledge or exprience. It transcends all the sources of knowledge, including the scripture, and at the same time It is the basis of them all. It is the very experience itself (*avagati mātra*) or pure knowledge (*kevala jñāna*).

However, from the standpoint of ignorance which makes one see an undifferentiated and non-dual reality as differentiated and dualistic, *Brahman* appears as something "other" (*anya*) than one's own Self. For this reason, an ignorant person looks upon *Brahman* as an object of his higher realization or the ultimate goal of his spiritual life. This objectification of *Brahman* is inevitable as long as one is not able to transcend one's individuality. As revealed in deep sleep and in the fourth state (*turīya*), individuality or selfhood is not intrinsic to the Self; it is only adventitious and is caused by the wrong understanding of the Self. Therefore, *brahmānubhava* is regarded as liberation by an individual self. In realizing *Brahman*, the individual self may seem to have become liberated from the bondage of ignorance and its effects like finiteness. But all

[3] Rudolph Otto, *Mysticism East and West*, p. 17.

this has no meaning from the standpoint of absolute truth, because in reality there is no individual self. It has no objective existence, and therefore its bondage and liberation are not ultimately valid. Bondage as well as liberation are notions that are superimposed on the Self, which in reality has no such states. In fact, there is no one who is under bondage and is to be liberated. This type of thinking tries to understand what Reality is in itself or as free from all superimposition, instead of as what It appears from the standpoint of an individual self.

Thus *Brahman* in Itself, which is essentially non-dual and is no other than the true being of the knower, cannot be known objectively through any of the sources of knowledge, including the scripture. The various sources of knowledge, which are based on a distinction between the knower and the known, can reveal a reality which is other than the knower. The "other" that is revealed through them is necessarily conditioned by the categories of human understanding; and what Reality is in itself cannot be known through them. Scriptures, which have their significance for a knower, can reveal Reality indirectly as "That" which until it is realized directly is looked upon as something other than the knower. Thus there can be no positive understanding of what *Brahman* in Itself is. In other words, whatever that can be said of *Brahman* in positive terms cannot be true of it. It can be true and meaningful only from the standpoint of human understanding. But at the same time, our understanding and experience always point out to *Brahman* in Itself which is the basis of all that we know and experience. As pure consciousness, It is the basis of our understanding and experience. Thus we find in Śaṅkara's philosophy a distinction between *Brahman* as revealed by the scriptures and understood by the human mind, which he considers as the conditioned *Brahman* or *Īśvara*, and *Brahman* in Itself which is the substratum on which all our understanding is based. It cannot be known in the subject–object way either through empirical means of knowledge, including the scripture, or through some mystical faculty. It can be known only by being It; and that is the only way of knowing what *Brahman* in Itself is. Strictly speaking, there can be no knowledge of It in the ordinary sense of the word "knowledge", but that is the only way how we can present the highest realization in language. Such knowledge of *Brahman*, that is, by being It, is the direct and unmediated knowledge of It, and it alone can destroy ignorance and liberate the individual. It is this knowledge which is the goal of one's life; and it is only when such knowledge is attained, but not otherwise, that everything else is realized to be unreal or illusory. The possibility of such absolute experience or *brahmānubhava* is not only vouched by the scriptures, but historically attested by the actual experiences of the mystics like Vāmadeva.

Brahman in Itself is none other than one's own self in its true nature. To realize *Brahman* is to realize one's own Self. Self is pure consciousness and undifferentiated. When It is actually realized, the Self cannot be said to belong to this or that person. It is the Reality, not of this or that person, but of everyone and of everything. It is absolute and ultimate. Thus Self-realization does not mean realizing one's empirical self which is peculiar to oneself, but to realize the Self of empirical self or *Brahman*. Self and *Brahman* are only names given to that which is ineffable, when it is viewed from the standpoints of an individual self and the world, respectively. Thus in realizing one's identity with *Brahman*, nothing new is attained; only the wrong notions that one is not *Brahman* and that It is not already realized are shed.

Thus Advaitic mysticism differs from what it ordinarily means, both in its nature and in its approach. It is not seeking to encounter a reality which is not already realized, nor is it to sacrifice something which is real. It is simply to become free from the veil of ignorance or to break through all the conceptions of Reality and discover for oneself what is eternally present and revealed. It is not to attain something which is not already attained. It is to become liberated from something which is not really there, but which one thinks is there.

> Indian religion in its early stages is not so much concerned with God as with immortality, and by immortality is understood a condition in which time itself is transcended.[4] It is yearning for a changed condition not for a person.[5]

In the case of Śaṅkara, we can modify this remark by stating that immortality is not a change of condition, but the realization of the truth that one is immortal by nature and that mortality is only an illusion. The change which realization brings forth is not an objective and positive one. It is mainly negative in its significance in that it only destroys ignorance, transforming thereby one's vision of differences into one of oneness or identity, which is the nature of Reality. "Unio Mystica" is meaningless where there is one only without a second; and that is the standpoint of Śaṅkara's mysticism.

Since Śaṅkara's doctrine is mainly mystical, for it is primarily based on revelation and mystic experience, but not on natural reason, his doctrine is compared with those of St. John of the Cross and Jalālu'd-Dīn Rūmī, representative thinkers and mystics of two great mystical traditions, namely Christianity and Islam. The main purpose of this comparison is not to criticize the doctrines compared, but to understand the position of Śaṅkara clear. However, criticism is inevitable if one wants to express one's preference for the one over the others.

---

[4] R.C. Zaehner, *Hindu and Muslim Mysticism* (Jordan Lectures in Comparative Religion, 1959), London: University of London, 1960, p. 7.

[5] Ibid., p. 11.

1

The Point of Departure

Knowing Brahman

THE Ultimate Reality or *Brahman*, according to Śaṅkara, is self-existent and self-evident. It is undifferentiated pure consciousness or knowledge, that is, free from subject–object distinction. It is absolutely immutable and remains so eternally. *Brahman* alone has an objective (*vastu*) existence and everything else is only an appearance of It. It is the basis or substratum (*adhiṣṭhāna*) of everything that is known through all the possible means of knowledge, whether empirical (*laukika*) or scriptural (*vaidika*). It is the Self of everyone and the essence of everything that is manifested and unmanifested. Therefore, things cannot exist without It; without It they become selfless (*anātma*) and void. The supreme end of life or liberation is connected with the perfect knowledge of It, for in knowing *Brahman* as it is in Itself man is freed from ignorance, the root cause of human bondage and suffering. Negatively, ignorance means the absence of perfect knowledge of *Brahman*, and positively the fragmentary and conditioned knowledge of It.

The empirical self (*jīva*), the phenomenal world of differences and the Lord (*Īśvara*) who creates, sustains and finally dissolves it into Himself have no objective reality. As their existence is based on ignorance, they are ultimately unreal. They are merely imagined (*kalpita*) to exist in *Brahman* or it is *Brahman* which appears as these from the standpoint of ignorance. They are relatively true; true from the standpoints of empirical and scriptural knowledge. As such, the knowledge of them is not absolute and hence cannot liberate the individual self from ignorance and the bondage caused by it. On the other hand, perfect knowledge of *Brahman* in Itself is absolutely true and completely free from ignorance, and in attaining it man is liberated from ignorance and the supreme end of his life is accomplished.

Now the problem is how to know *Brahman* in Itself. We shall discuss in this chapter the nature and scope of the various sources of knowledge such as sense perception, inference (*anumāna*), reasoning (*tarka*), intuitive knowledge (*ārṣa jñāna*) and scripture (*śruti*) in order to understand: whether it is possible to know *Brahman* in Itself through these sources of knowledge, and if it is proved that It cannot be known through them, how can It be known?

Sence perception

Brahman in Itself cannot be known through sense perception. It is wholly beyond the ken of our senses. Sense perception is the primary source of valid knowledge within the empirical realm, and it arises when the senses come into direct contact with their respective objects. By illumining (*dyotana*) their respective objects, the senses reveal them to the self through the mediation of the internal organ.[1] By their nature and constitution, the senses are capable of apprehending particular qualities of things, as for instance, the eye can perceive the colour and form of a thing, the ear can perceive the sound, and so on.[2] Thus through sense perception it is possible to know those things only, which possess certain qualities like form, colour and taste, and anything that is devoid of them cannot be perceived by the senses. As *Brahman* is

[1] *ĪUB*, IV.

[2] *BṛUB*, II.4.11; *SūB*, II.3.18, II.4.11.

undifferentiated consciousness having no attributes and qualities, It cannot be perceived by the senses.[3]

According to Śaṅkara, all the senses, being constituted of fine matter — they are made up of the same elements which they perceive — are, like wood and clod, insentient or unintelligent.[4] Therefore, by themselves or independent of a conscious principle they cannot illumine and reveal the objects. Whereas they are able to do so; and this, according to Śaṅkara, is made possible because they are illumined by the consciousness of the Self. Conscious illumination of the senses means the superimposition on them of the consciousness which is the nature of the Self. The nature of the Self is primarily superimposed on the internal organ and in its turn, the internal organ makes the senses appear to be conscious.[5] Sense-activity thus presupposes the presence of the Self, for it is the conscious principle which by inspiring (*preraṇā*) or illumining the senses enables them to perceive. It is the essence of all the senses and the basis of their activity, and the senses are merely its instruments (*kāraṇa*) in knowing things.[6] It is the capacity of all the senses to perceive, as for instance, it is the seeing of the eyes, the hearing of the ears, and so on; and therefore without it the senses cannot perceive. For this reason, Śaṅkara says that the senses cannot operate on their own basis, or their own self, or their own activity. They cannot perceive that consciousness by which they are able to perceive. For example, the eye is able to see the form of a thing only when it is illumined or inspired by the Self and fails to do so when it is not illumined; and therefore it cannot perceive the Self which is its very capacity to see; the seeing cannot be seen.

---

[3] *SūB*, II.1.6, II.1.11; *Upadeśa-sāhasrī*, IX.9; *BṛUB*, III.9.26.

[4] *BṛUB*, IV.4.18.

[5] Ibid., IV.3.7.

[6] *KeUB*, I.2; *BṛUB*, III.8.11, III.7.23.

Moreover, by their nature the senses are outwardly directed, that is, they can apprehend those things only which are external to them and are presented to them as objects (*viṣaya*).[7] Hence it is not possible for them to turn their vision inward and perceive *Brahman* which, as the Self of all, is inward. Besides, as pure knowledge or pure consciousness, *Brahman* is always that which knows and never an object of knowledge.[8] And as the nature of a thing is co-eternal with it, the possibility of the Self ever becoming an object of sense perception cannot be conceived. Now, one may question as to how *Brahman*, which is objectively real and present everywhere as the Self of all, is not perceived by the senses. To this Śaṅkara's reply is that though *Brahman* is objectively (*vastu*) real, It is never an object (*viṣaya*) of knowledge, because It is essentially non-dual; and though It is all-pervasive, Its nature is extremely subtle to be perceived by the senses.[9]

On the contrary, if it is supposed that the senses are capable of perceiving *Brahman*, then there would be no scope for conflicting opinions about Its existence and nature, as the knowledge acquired through sense perception is universally valid. It is acceptable to all and no one would disregard the authority of sense perception.[10] But the fact that different philosophers disagree and even contradict each other with regard to the existence and nature of ultimate reality clearly indicates that *Brahman* cannot be known through sense perception. According to Śaṅkara, even a semblance or reflection of the Self cannot become an object of our senses.[11]

---

[7] *SūB*, I.1.2; *KaUB*, II.1.1; *BṛUB*, IV.3.6.

[8] *AiUB*, II.1, Introduction.

[9] *Brahman* is *aviṣaya*, *ChāUB*, VIII.6.3; *BGB*, XIII.15.

[10] *BṛUB*, I.1, Introduction.

[11] *ĪUB*, IV.

Inference

Śaṅkara accepts inference as a source of valid knowledge.[12] By means of it, it is possible to know a thing that is not directly perceived through the mediation of a characteristic feature of that thing, which is directly perceived, on the basis of cause and effect relationship (*kārya–kāraṇa saṁghāta*) that is known to exist between them.[13] For instance, the existence of fire on a hill top, which is not directly perceived, can be known inferentially through the mediation of smoke which is directly perceived, on the basis of previous experience that fire and smoke are causally related. But, there is no rigid rule, according to Śaṅkara, that an inference should be based on causal relationship only; it can also be based on the experience of similarity.[14] Much of human activity is based on this type of inference. For example, people who have experienced that hunger and thirst are satisfied by eating and drinking proceed to act accordingly, for they infer on the basis of their past experience of similarity that eating and drinking would satisfy hunger and thirst. Thus the direct knowledge of a mark (*liṅga*) and some necessary relationship between it and the thing characterized by that mark (*liṅgī*) are essential to get knowledge through inference; and these are known through perception. Sense perception is therefore the basis of inference, and where the former fails there the latter too proves ineffective.[15] In other words, when we can know nothing about a thing directly through sense perception, we cannot know it through inference also. To become a source of valid knowledge, inference must be based on perception.

---

[12] *SūB*, I.1.2.

[13] *BṛUB*, IV.3.6.

[14] Ibid.

[15] Ibid., I.2.1, IV.3.6.

Now, if inference is to be employed to know *Brahman*, some characteristic feature of It, which is necessarily related to It, must be directly known or, on the other hand, a causal relationship between the directly perceived universe and *Brahman* must be established to exist. But as nothing is known about *Brahman* through sense perception, there is no basis for inference also.[16] And as we perceive the universe only, it is not possible on that basis to establish any causal relationship between it and *Brahman*, for we do not know whether the universe is caused by *Brahman* or something else. Therefore, our direct knowledge of the world cannot be a valid ground to conclude inferentially the existence of *Brahman*.[17] Besides, inference is possible only when the duality of one who infers and the thing inferred exists, and such duality exists within the empirical realm only. *Brahman* is essentially non-dual, and therefore, It cannot become an object of inference.[18]

Reasoning

Brahman cannot be known through reasoning also. Śaṅkara does not often distinguish between reasoning (*tarka*) and inference (*anumāna*), but treats them as almost synonymous. According to him,

> reasoning (*yukti*) enables us to infer something not actually perceived in consequence of its having certain equality of attributes with what is actually perceived.[19]

Besides this definition, at various places he uses the two words without discrimination.[20] Nevertheless, he does to some extent distinguish them by assigning a wider scope and meaning to

---

[16] *BGB*, XII.3, II.25; *SūB*, I.1.2, II.1.11.

[17] *SūB*, I.1.2.

[19] *AiUB*, II.1, Introduction.

[19] *SūB*, II.1.4, tr. Thibaut (Sacred Books of the East), Indian edn., vol. I, p. 299.

[20] See *SūB*, II.1.11 and II.1.6.

reasoning. Reasoning, according to Śaṅkara, is capable of performing more functions than trying to conjecture the unknown through the known, whereas the scope of inference is limited to the function of inferring the directly unknown through the directly known.[21] But, in so far as there is an attempt in both reasoning and inference to know the directly unknown through the directly known, they do not fundamentally differ from each other. Therefore, to be valid in its conclusions, reasoning, like inference, should be firmly based on facts known through direct experience. In the absence of such facts, reasoning becomes unfounded or baseless.[22] As the scope of sense perception is limited to the empirical realm, reasoning, like inference, proves ineffective in trans-empirical matters. If still it is employed to know that which transcends the empirical sphere, reasoning for want of ground or basis results in speculative opinion.[23] Such unfounded (*apratiṣṭhita*) reasoning is to be considered, according to Śaṅkara, as mere imagination of one's mind (*svabuddhi parikalpita*) having no objective validity. For this reason, knowledge based solely on reasoning varies from man to man depending largely upon the intellectual capacities of those who use it. This fact, according to Śaṅkara, is amply testified by the history of philosophy.

There can be found no agreement between any two philosophers with regard to what they postulate about ultimate reality. Even they contradict each other. If someone assumes that reality is subtle, another thinks it to be more subtle, and some other may claim it to be most subtle.[24] While some philosophers try to establish its nature to be purely spiritual, others

---

[21] The nature of reason is fully discussed in the Chapter 5.

[22] *SūB*, II.1.11.

[23] Ibid.

[24] *KaUB*, I.2.8.

may prove it to be purely material. Even concerning its existence, there can be found no agreement of opinion among various thinkers, for certain philosophers, like the nihilists, deny its existence. Likewise, about the nature of Self also there is no unanimity of opinion. Different people understand it differently as body, mind, vital force, etc. Thus what one postulates as ultimate and absolute is repudiated by the other, and the latter's position is rejected by some other, and so on.[25]

Here, it may be contended that the reasoning of certain eminent philosophers like Kapila and Kaṇāda, the founders of Sāṁkhya and Vaiśeṣika systems of philosophy, respectively, may be free from defects like unfoundedness and therefore it may be relied upon in knowing the ultimate reality. But Śaṅkara observes that even among those persons of undoubted intellectual eminence there is no unity of opinion.[26] They too have contradicted each other, for what is postulated by them is not one and the same. This shows that there can be no finality (*niṣṭhā*) in reasoning when it is used to know the ultimate reality.[27] The process of mutual contradiction in the field of metaphysical speculation clearly indicates that what is postulated by various philosophers is only their imagination, but not true and objective. As such no one can claim objective validity to one's own reasoning when there are others who oppose it and contradict it. Śaṅkara, therefore asks, "how can knowledge, which is founded on reasoning, and whose object is not something permanently uniform, be perfect knowledge?"[28] Perfect knowledge, on the other hand, is the knowledge of an objectively existing reality.[29] It does not

---

[25] *SūB*, II.1.11.

[26] Ibid.

[27] *KaUB*, I.2.8.

[28] *SūB*, II.1.11, tr. Thibaut, vol. I, p. 316.

[29] *SūB*, II.1.11.

depend on the ingenuity of the human mind, but rests solely on the nature of the object. Such objective knowledge does not vary from person to person, but is universally valid. The knowledge that fire is hot is uniformly valid to all and no one would dare to contradict it. *Brahman*, according to Śaṅkara, is an objective reality and so, knowledge about It does not depend on the creative imagination of anyone, but similar to the knowledge of a pot rests entirely on the object, that is, *Brahman*.[30] No doubt, knowledge depends also on the mind, for things are to be reflected in it if they are to be known. But it does not solely depend on the mind as in the case of meditation.[31] Before *Brahman* is directly known by being It, It is known indirectly through the scriptures, and such knowledge is mental in the sense that *Brahman* is reflected in the mind as if It is an object. But this knowledge of *Brahman* is not the true knowledge which is identical with *Brahman*.

The champions of reason may further argue that uncontradictable knowledge can be achieved through reasoning, if it is perfected or if fallacies are avoided.[32] The fact that the reasoning of some is ill-founded or unfounded is not a sufficient reason to condemn all reasoning as ill-founded or unfounded, just as there is no valid reason to maintain that a man must be stupid because his elder brother was stupid. Besides, the condemnation of reasoning as unfounded is itself unfounded, because reasoning is efficient and valid in empirical life; in fact much of empirical life is based on it.[33] Further, the assertion that reasoning has no foundation is itself based on reasoning. But these arguments do not refute the position of Śaṅkara. Even if it is supposed that uncontradictable

---

[30] *SūB*, I.1.4., I.1.2.

[31] Ibid., I.1.4.

[32] Ibid., II.1.11.

[33] Ibid.

knowledge can be achieved through perfect reasoning, man is not liberated thereby.[34] The ultimate goal of man, which is liberation from the bondage of ignorance, and for the attainment of which the enquiry into the nature of *Brahman* is primarily undertaken, cannot be attained through speculative knowledge based on reasoning. Through reasoning one cannot realize one's immortal nature. The perfect knowledge of *Brahman*, which is the only way to attain liberation from ignorance, cannot be attained through reasoning. Those who are adept in the art of reasoning are seen to be entangled in ignorance and suffer from its consequences. The arguments such as "the clay is the cause of a pot", "atoms form the cause of clay", which are based on reasoning, says Śaṅkara, cannot save man from the dread of death.[35]

The incapacity of reasoning to make us know *Brahman* becomes further clear if the nature of intellect, the seat of reasoning, is understood. The intellect is prone to think of those things only which are within the empirical realm and have some practical value to an individual.[36] Hence it assumes the non-existence of those things which are trans-empirical (*vyavahārātīta*).[37] As *Brahman* is trans-empirical and is not considered to serve the worldly needs of man, the intellect may assume the non-existence of *Brahman* also. The intellect or the internal organ of which the former is a functional aspect is made up of fine matter.[38] Being purely material in nature it cannot by itself "perform the functions like thinking and reasoning unless it is illumined by the inner light of

[34] *SūB*, II.1.11; *aparokṣānubhūti*, *śl.* 41.

[35] *Śivānandalaharī*, *śl.* 6.

[36] *TaiUB*, II.6.1.

[37] Ibid.

[38] *BṛUB*, II.1.9; *ChāUB*, VI.5.1.

consciousness".[39] The intellect appears to be conscious, because consciousness which is the nature of Self is superimposed on it. The intellect is that which is illumined and the Self is that which illumines it.[40] It is because of the Self the mind or internal organ is able to think of everything, for the Self is the capacity of the mind to think; it is the mind of the mind.[41] Therefore, the mind cannot operate on its own self or essence, or think of that by which it is able to think, just as fire which can burn everything cannot burn its own essence of burning.

The Self is the witness of the intellect (*buddhirdraṣṭa* or *dhīsākṣī*) and its functions.[42] As such, the Self cannot be witnessed by the intellect, as the witness cannot be witnessed by that which is an object of witness. What is witnessed is always an object and can never become the subject. Further, thinking — presupposing a thinker for thinking — is not possible in the absence of a thinker; and he who is a thinker will always remain so and never become an object of thought.[43] It is not possible for a thing to give up its nature, since it is co-eternal with the thing. On the contrary, if the thinker were to become an object of thought, then there would be no thinker to think of the thinker.[44] To posit a thinker to think of the thinker naturally results in infinite regress.[45] Śaṅkara, therefore, avowedly states that that which is the essence of thought cannot be thought of, and that which is the essence or basis of all knowledge cannot become an object of knowledge.[46] Thus

---

[39] *KeUB*, I.2.

[40] *BṛUB*, IV.3.7.

[41] *KeUB*, I.2, I.3, I.6.

[42] *BGB*, III.42.

[43] *AiUB*, II.1, Introduction.

[44] *BṛUB*, II.4.14, I.4.7; *KeUB*, II.1; *TaiUB*, II.1.1.

[45] *Upadeśasāhasrī*, part I (prose, p. 99).

[46] *BṛUB*, III.4.2.

the validity of inference and reasoning is limited to the empirical sphere; and notwithstanding this fact, if they are employed to know *Brahman*, which is trans-empirical, they utterly fail, just as a sharp knife becomes blunt or loses its capacity to cut when it is used against a hard stone.[47] For this reason, those who in trying to understand the nature of ultimate reality rely on reasoning only get themselves entangled in contradictions; and as long as they cannot go beyond reason, they cannot see it directly, though it is self-evident and self-revealing.

Smṛti

The place of the Smṛtis in knowing *Brahman* is discussed by Śaṅkara. The Smṛtis consist of Purāṇas, Itihāsas and the works on Yoga, Sāṁkhya, etc., which are composed by celebrated authorities like Vyāsa and are based upon the personal experiences of the sages.[48] According to Śaṅkara, the sages are capable of perceiving supersensible things through intuition (*ārṣa jñana*).[49] They acquire the capacity to intuit by virtue of their supreme religious merit which they attain as a result of their practising the religious duties (*dharma*) as enjoined in the scriptures.[50] Śaṅkara, therefore, considers Smṛti-knowledge as well-founded and accepts its authority in supernatural matters. Nevertheless, as the intuitive experiences of the sages are based on the practice of religious duties as enjoined in the scriptures, the validity of Smṛti-knowledge is not independent of the scriptures.[51] As the scriptures to be authoritative do not depend on anything else, their authority in supernatural

---

[47] *SūB*, I.1.4.

[48] *SūB*, II.1.1-3.

[49] *SūB*, II.1.11.

[50] Ibid., II.1.1.

[51] Ibid.

matters is regarded by Śaṅkara as equivalent to the authority of perception, while the authority of Smṛtis is equivalent to that of inference, for they depend for their validity on the scriptures.[52] For this reason, Smṛti should conform to Śruti if it is to become authoritative. It should not contradict the scriptures, and when there is a contradiction between Smṛti and Śruti, the authority of the former should be rejected.[53] Those Smṛtis that contradict the scriptures are to be considered as independent creations of the sages based on their own experience and understanding. Even when they are apparently based on the scriptures, the way the scriptures are interpreted in them may be subjective, but not true to the real import of the scriptures. In interpreting the scriptures the sages may have drifted away from the real significance of the scriptures. Therefore, such subjective interpretations of the scriptures fail to comprehend the real and objective meaning of the scriptures. This is substantiated by the fact that the experiences of the sages or accomplished persons (*siddha puruṣa*), though based on the scriptures, vary from person to person.[54] There are many such persons or sages whose experiences differ. Moreover, as their experiences are caused by the practice of religious duties, they are conditioned by those causes that produce them, and those causes may vary from person to person depending largely upon the type of religious instruction one receives. Thus the relative nature of these experiences indicates that *Brahman* in Itself cannot be known through them. A Smṛti is not an independent source of *Brahman*-knowledge; it becomes so only when it is in accordance with the scriptures.

---

[52] *SūB*, I.3.28.

[53] Ibid., II.1.1.

[54] Ibid.

Śrutis

According to Śaṅkara, scriptures (Śrutis) are the only source of knowledge in matters that are not within the reach of the empirical means of knowledge.[55] As *Brahman* is beyond the reach of all the natural sources of knowledge, It can be known only through the scriptures.

> *Brahman* rests exclusively on the holy texts (*śabdamūlam*), and regarding which the holy texts alone are authoritative (*śabdapramāṇa*) — not the senses, and so on — and must be accepted such as the texts proclaim It to be.[56] Through the Upaniṣads only *Brahman* is known, but not through any other means of knowledge (*na anyapramāṇa gamyam*).[57]

According to Śaṅkara, perfect knowledge — the knowledge of an objectively existing reality in its true nature — of *Brahman* is not possible outside of the Upaniṣads.[58] They have as their object firmly established things, and hence the perfection of Upaniṣadic knowledge.[59] The philosophy of Advaita is entirely based on the Upaniṣads (*aupaniṣadam darśanam*), and the highest truth is that which is in accordance with what the scriptures reveal.[60]

Although Śaṅkara accepts the absolute authority of the scriptures in knowing *Brahman*, he never considers that *Brahman* is an object (*viṣaya*) of scriptural knowledge. He says:

> Even in the scriptures the Self is not presented as an object, like heaven or Mount Meru, for it is the very

---

[55] *BGB*, XVIII.66; *SūB*, II.3.1.

[56] *SūB*, II.1.27, tr. Thibaut, vol. I, pp. 350-51.

[57] *BṛUB*, III.9.26, IV.4.20.

[58] *SūB*, II.1.11.

[59] Ibid.

[60] *aupaniṣadam darśanam, — BGB*, XIII.31; *satyamiti yathā śāstrārthata — BṛUB*, I.4.14.

> self of those that present it. A presentation by someone has for its object something to be presented and this is possible only when there is difference.[61]

To know *Brahman* as an object is possible only when there is the duality of subject and object, but as *Brahman* is one only without a second, there is no second entity that can know *Brahman* or to which *Brahman* can become an object of knowledge. By nature *Brahman* is self-revealing and self-evident. Just as the sun needs no other light to illumine it, *Brahman*, which is pure knowledge, does not depend on any means of knowledge for Its revelation. By Its nature It is eternally revealed. Contrary to this, if the scriptures are to be accepted as the means of knowing *Brahman*, the absolute oneness of *Brahman* must be given up, and the duality of subject and object should be accepted as ultimately real.

The scope of the scriptures, like that of the other sources of knowledge, is limited to the realm of differences which are the creation of ignorance. The scriptures can impart knowledge only when there is someone to receive it. They are meant to serve the purpose of an individual who seeks liberation. In other words, as long as one, due to ignorance, thinks of oneself as an individual self (*jīva*), scriptures find their scope in removing such wrong identity.[62]

> The existence of objects such as the scriptures (the teacher and the taught) is based on empirical experience (*saṁvṛtti*) which is imaginary and is imagined as a means (*upāya*) for the attainment of the highest. Therefore they have no real existence.[63]

---

[61] *BṛUB*, IV.4.20, tr. Swami Madhavananda, Almora: Advaita Ashrama, Mayavati, p. 746.

[62] *SūB*, II.3.39; *BGB*, XIII.2.

[63] *GKB*, IV.73, I.18.

Being ultimately unreal, the scriptures like other sources of knowledge cannot function when the differences cease to exist.

The function of the scriptures is to remove ignorance (*ajñānam nivartaitum śāstram*). They remove the obstacles to Self-realization like false identity, and direct one's attention to one's own Self which is by nature self-evident and self-revealed. "The knowledge of *Brahman* means only the cessation of the identification with extraneous things."[64] As such the scriptures obtain their authority regarding the Self only in so far as they serve to eliminate the non-self superimposed on it. This removal of the non-self from the Self (*anātmabhāva nivṛtti*) is what is known as the realization of the Self (*ātmabhāva*).[65]

> The scriptures describe *Brahman* merely through negation of the differences like the knower, the means of knowledge, and so on, in such terms as these: "When everything is the Self, what should one see . . . and know, and through what?" and not by resorting to the usual function of a sentence in which something is described by means of names.[66]

Even the great scriptural sentences like "That thou art" and "I am *Brahman*" do not try to establish anything about *Brahman* positively; they only try to remove the duality which the words "That" and "thou" present.

Like the other sources of knowledge, the scriptures also presuppose the presence of the Self, for one is able to negate the wrong identity caused by ignorance because of it. Therefore the scriptures cannot know that by which they are able to negate the wrong identity. Besides, the knowledge which the scriptures

---

[64] *BṛUB*, IV.4.20, tr. Swami Madhavananda, p. 746.

[65] *BṛUB*, IV.4.20.

[66] Ibid., tr. Swami Madhavananda, pp. 745-46.

generate is only mental (*manovṛtti*).[67] This type of knowledge (*vṛttijñāna*) which is capable of destroying ignorance will also be dissolved along with ignorance without ever making *Brahman* its object.[68] The existence of the mind and its functions are caused by ignorance and when the latter is destroyed, the mind and the knowledge based on it will also be destroyed.

The earlier discussion clearly points out that all the sources of knowledge, whether empirical or scriptural, fail to comprehend *Brahman*, i.e. we cannot attain a positive knowledge of *Brahman* as we can of an object like pot. The same becomes more evident if we understand the basis of all the sources of knowledge and the nature of *Brahman* which they try to know. According to Śaṅkara, all the sources of knowledge, both empirical and scriptural, are based on subject–object duality which is the creation of ignorance. The knower (*pramātā*) which is presupposed by all the sources of knowledge has no objective existence. Its existence is due to the wrong identification of the Self with the body, mind and the senses; and this wrong identification is ultimately based on ignorance. The body, mind and the senses are essential for the attainment of knowledge. While the senses and the mind are instruments of knowledge, the body is the seat of them. But as these are physical in nature knowledge cannot be attained without the help of a conscious principle. Whereas, the Self which is pure consciousness is free from all relations and is devoid of activity. Nevertheless, because of their failure to discriminate between the Self and the non-self (the body, mind and the senses) people superimpose the nature of the one on the other. Because of this process of superimposition, the pure Self appears to have become the

---

[67] *SūB*, I.1.4; *BṛUB*, I.4.7; *ChāUB*, Introduction: *advaita jñānam manovṛtti mātram*; *Upadeśa-sāhasrī*, XVIII.205.

[68] *Aparokṣānubhūti*, *śl*. 137.

knower and the instruments of knowledge appear to be conscious. This is what Śaṅkara means when he says:

> The mutual superimposition of the Self and the non-self which is termed ignorance is the presupposition on which are based all the practical distinctions — those made in ordinary life as well as those laid down by the scriptures — between means of knowledge, objects of knowledge (and knowing persons) and all the scriptural texts whether they are concerned with injunctions and prohibitions or with final release.[69]

In other words, all the means of knowledge, including the scriptures, presuppose differences, like that between the knower and the known, which are based on ignorance, and as such those means cannot operate without differences. Whereas to realize *Brahman* is to transcend all such differences by freeing oneself absolutely from ignorance.

The Upaniṣadic statement, "through which instrument should we know the knower because of which all this universe is known and who else is there to know it?" is of fundamental importance to Śaṅkara in understanding the problem of knowledge.[70] *Brahman*, which is pure knowledge, is the basic source of all knowledge. All the means of knowledge are based on It or they presuppose Its presence and can function because of It. As such it is impossible for them to know that which, as their source and basis, is their very capacity to know. Another Upaniṣadic statement, "that *Brahman* is surely different from the known, and It is above the unknown" is also significant in this context.[71] It means that *Brahman* is something different from all that is known, for It is not an object of knowledge; and at the same time, It is known to all for It is the self of everyone.

---

[69] *SūB*, I.1 Introduction, tr. Thibaut, vol. I, p. 6.

[70] *BṛUB*, II.4.14.

[71] *Kena Upaniṣad*, I.4 and Śaṅkara's commentary on it.

Therefore, the quest to know *Brahman* as if It is an object of one's knowledge must be given up before It is realized as one's own self in its true nature. However, from the standpoint of ignorance, that is, when one thinks that *Brahman* is something different from oneself, *Brahman* is said to be known. So, according to Śaṅkara, if anyone asserts that "he knows *Brahman*" it is certainly not true and meaningless, for it is impossible.[72]

Because of Its unknowability in the sense that It is not known as an object, Its existence cannot either be doubted or denied, for *Brahman* is the self of the one who tries to deny It.[73] Its existence is beyond all doubt, and to deny It is to deny oneself. If we consider It at the subjective level Its existence is the surest of all facts, for It is the Self of all. At the objective level, It is the ultimate ground of everything that is manifested and known through all the sources of knowledge. As such one cannot deny It without denying one's own self and the empirical reality which is experienced by all at every moment. The failure to know *Brahman* through the natural means of knowledge does not result in scepticism. As, according to Śaṅkara, the problem of knowledge is intimately connected with the problem of liberation, to remain sceptical about *Brahman* is worse than continuing in ignorance. Pure knowledge is pure bliss, and in knowing *Brahman* the supreme end of man is accomplished. To know *Brahman* is to know the supreme good and one attains absolute peace (*paramaśānti*) thereby. Freedom from ignorance and the bondage caused by it and the attainment of immortality are possible only through perfect knowledge of *Brahman*. Therefore, if *Brahman* remains unknown for ever, the possibility of attaining the highest end of life should be denied permanently. Then man becomes destined to live amidst unreality and suffer from ignorance and its effects unceasingly.

---

[72] *KeUB*, II.1.

[73] *SūB*, I.1.4, II.3.7.

Anubhava

Śaṅkara's position is far from any type of scepticism and despair. According to him, although all the means of knowledge fail to comprehend *Brahman*, It is not an unknowable reality, for It can be known by being It.[74] *Brahman* is known by being *Brahman* (*brahmabhūta*) and that is the only way of knowing what *Brahman* in Itself is. In no other way can a non-dual reality be known. It is by being it the supreme reality is known *tattvena tattvataḥ*.[75] The significance of the Upaniṣadic statement, "the knower of *Brahman* attains the highest", according to Śaṅkara, is that one becomes the supreme Self through Its knowledge.[76] "One who knows *Brahman* becomes *Brahman* indeed."[77] "He who knows the Self . . . as the fearless *Brahman* becomes the fearless *Brahman* and this is the purport of the whole Upaniṣad in a nutshell."[78] This is the direct and unmediated knowledge of *Brahman* in which the differences of the knower, the known and the knowledge are completely absent. This direct experience of *Brahman* (*aparokṣānubhūti* or *brahmānubhava*) is known variously as *brāhmī sthiti*, the state of being *Brahman*, *brahmaniṣṭha*, the state of being established in or as *Brahman* and *brahmanirvāṇa*, the blissful state of being *Brahman* which is the highest and perfect state of human realization.[79] It is pure experience or experience in itself (*anubhūti mātram*). It is pure knowledge (*kevala jñāna*) which is self-revealing, self-evident, unborn and eternal. This direct experience of *Brahman* by being It is the supreme end of

---

[74] *TaiUB*, II.1.1; *MuUB*, III.2.9.

[75] *BGB*, XI.54.

[76] *TaiUB*, II.8.5.

[77] *MuUB*, III.2.9.

[78] *BṛUB*, IV.4.25, tr. Swami Madhavananda, pp. 769-70.

[79] *BGB*, II.74, V.24.

man (*parama puruṣārtha*). According to Śaṅkara, the chief aim of an enquiry into the nature of *Brahman* is to realize this supreme end of life (*paramārtha darśanam*), and in its realization lies the fruitful culmination of philosophy.[80] The avowed purpose of the Upaniṣadic statements that deal with *Brahman* like "That thou art" and "I am *Brahman*" is to make everyone realize *Brahman* directly by being It (*avagati niṣṭha*).[81] *Brahmānubhava* is not an unattainable spiritual ideal, but a possibility which all can have, for it is to realize one's own true nature. Besides Upaniṣadic evidence, its possibility has been historically attested by the experiences of the sages like Vāmadeva and Triśaṅku.[82] Janaka, the emperor of Videha, had attained it by realizing his oneness with *Brahman*.[83] Indra had attained the same through a sage-like perception.[84] Commenting on the *Vedānta-Sūtras*, Śaṅkara states that *Brahman* in Its true nature can be experienced directly during *samaradhana*, the state of perfect conciliation or trance, and this fact according to him, is acknowledged by both Śruti and Smṛti.[85] He also presents a vivid description of such an experience in his *Vivekacūḍāmaṇi*.[86] The different words like, *aparokṣānubhūti*, *sākṣātkāra*, *samyagdarśana*, *anuvedanā*, *avagati*, *anubhāva* and *avabodha* are used by Śaṅkara to express it.

---

[80] *SūB*, I.1.2.

[81] Ibid., III.2.21.

[82] Ibid., I.1.4, I.1.30; *BṛUB*, I.4.10; *TaiUB*, I.10.1.

[83] *BṛUB*, IV.4.23.

[84] *SūB*, I.1.30.

[85] Ibid., III.2.24.

[86] *Vivekacūḍāmaṇi*, *ślsi*. 481-485 and 488.

2

Description of Brahmānubhava

Brahmānubhava transcends subject–object duality

BRAHMĀNUBHAVA is peculiarly unique and differs fundamentally from empirical experience. Experience, in its empirical sense, is not possible without a distinction between the knower and the known, and involves the activity of knowing. These two factors, the knower and the known, are so inseparably commingled (*saṁkīrṇa*) in empirical experience, in the absence of anyone of them, empirical experience is not possible. An object may exist independent of a knower, but to be revealed it should come into contact with a knower; and the knower becomes self-conscious while revealing something which may be an external object or an internal idea or feeling. Thus, according to Śaṅkara, the existence of each one of these factors is dependent on or conditioned by the other and hence they are not absolutely real.

The knower and the known are based on ignorance (*avidyā*).[1] The pure Self in itself is not the knower or the subject that knows objects. Although the Self's nature is pure knowledge, it cannot on that account be regarded as the knower, because the non-dual nature of the Self precludes the possibility of anything existing beside it which can become an object to it. The absolute oneness (*ekatva*) of the Self denies

[1] *SūB*, I.1, Introduction.

the possibility either of its knowing others or of its being known by others. The Self in itself cannot be differentiated into subject and object, for It is an undifferentiated mass of pure consciousness.[2] Besides, knowing, which is an activity, is alien to the nature of the Self, for there is nothing different from the Self which it may seek to know or attain. On the contrary, if activity is to be accepted as natural to the Self, then it becomes liable to change or modification, because activity causes change in that in which it inheres.[3] Thus the existence of the knower cannot be explained in terms of the pure Self. According to Śaṅkara, the mind which by its nature is inert (*acetana*) cannot also be the knower. In his words, "the intellect has no consciousness and the Self no action. The word 'knows' can therefore reasonably be applied to neither of them".[4] Yet empirical experience, which is the result of subject–object contact, is an undeniable fact and needs explanation.

Empirical experience, according to Śaṅkara, is based on ignorance, because of which people fail to discriminate between the Self and the intellect. This non-discrimination between the Self and the intellect leads to the superimposition of the nature of the one on the other. This mutual superimposition is the basic reason for the existence of all empirical differences such as the knower, the known and the knowledge.[5] Thus the non-dual and undifferentiated Self appears to be an active agent and knower, and seems to experience things with the help of the mind which, though inert by nature, appears to be conscious and to reflect objects. Moreover, the fact that these empirical differences are

---

[2] *TaiUB*, II.1.1, II.5.1; *SūB*, II.2.10.

[3] *SūB*, I.1.4.

[4] *Upadeśasāhasrī*, XVIII.54, tr. Swami Jagadananda, p. 234; see also XVIII.65 and *SūB*, I.2.12.

[5] *SūB*, I.1, Introduction; *BGB*, XIII.26.

witnessed by the Self proves that they are not inherent to the Self, that is, they do not constitute the essential nature of the Self. What is witnessed is something different from the witness and cannot form the nature of the witness. The empirical self (*jīva*) which experiences the empirical reality is witnessed by the pure Self.[6] The pure Self, as mere witness, witnesses the empirical self and all its activities. Such witnessing on the part of the Self does not indicate any activity in it, because it takes place by the mere presence of the Self, just as the presence of the sun is sufficient to illumine the objects.[7] As against this, if it is supposed that the Self is not really free from the empirical differences, then it cannot witness them, and one can never know these differences to be empirical and unreal. Therefore, viewed from the standpoint of the Self, these differences are phenomenal or illusory and, as based on ignorance, they are not ultimately real. They have no objective (*vastu*) existence, but are imagined to exist in the Self due to ignorance; and when that ignorance is removed they cease to exist.

As compared with empirical experience, which is ultimately based on ignorance, *brahmānubhava* is absolutely free from ignorance, the source of all the differences. It is not an experience in the empirical sense, as it is free from the subject–object relationship.[8] It has no object and is not the experience of a subject. It is pure consciousness or pure knowledge in which there is no awareness either of oneself as "I am so and so" or "I am finite or happy", or of objects other than oneself. It is beyond the empirical experience of differences (*lokātītam*).[9] Further, knowledge in its empirical sense is relative and transitory. It originates and vanishes along with the objects

[6] *SūB*, I.1.4, II.3.40; see also *MuUB*, II.1.1.

[7] *BṛUB*, IV.3.23; *ChāUB*, VIII.12.5.

[8] *GKB*, IV.88.

[9] Ibid.

known. When we know a particular object we will have knowledge of that object and in the absence of that object there can be no knowledge of that object. Whereas, *brahmānubhava* is timeless and uncaused, for it is of the nature of *Brahman*, and *Brahman* is eternal and uncaused. As the very nature of the Self, pure consciousness or *brahmānubhava* is never absent from the Self, as heat and light are never absent from fire and the sun respectively. Śaṅkara describes:

> Pure knowledge and pure bliss, not smitten with suffering like sense perception, but serene (*prasanna*), supremely good (*śiva*), matchless or unique, spontaneous (*anāyāsa*), ever content and homogeneous or undifferentiated (*ekarasa*).[10]

This pure knowledge is not different from the knowledge of the wise (*paramārtha darśino jñānam*) or those who have realized *Brahman* directly by being It.[11] Śaṅkara says that the fourth state (*turīya*) in which *Brahman* is directly realized is nothing but pure knowledge which is the essence of the Self (*ātmapratyayasāram*).[12]

Brahmānubhava is an experience, although the subject–object duality is completely absent in it. It is pure experience (*avagati mātra*) or pure knowledge (*kevala jñāna*). Pure experience is the nature of *Brahman*. Śaṅkara uses the word knowledge (*jñāna*) also to express *brahmānubhava*, but thereby he means the knowledge in itself as opposed to that which is acquired as a result of the activity of knowing. The word *jñāna* in this context signifies the abstract sense (*bhāvarūpa*) of the word *jñāna*, but not the noun form of the verb "to know" in which sense it is empirically used and understood.[13] It is the basis of

---

[10] *BṛUB*, III.9.28.7, tr. Swami Madhavananda, p. 563.

[11] *GKB*, IV.99; *BṛUB*, IV.3.33.

[12] *MaUB*, VII.

[13] *TaiUB*, II.1.1.

all empirical knowledge, or at the empirical level, it manifests itself in and through all knowledge.

This position of Śaṅkara may give rise to a legitimate doubt whether experience as such is possible in the absence of subject–object duality. When there is none to experience and nothing to be experienced in what sense can one establish the fact of such experience? Does it not amount to pure void? To this objection Śaṅkara's reply is as follows. Experience is of two kinds, empirical (*laukika*) and transcendental (*pāramārthika*).[14] Out of the two, the former arises through the activity of the mind and the senses. It occurs when there are objects to be experienced and ceases to exist when there are no objects to experience. It is therefore not a permanent experience. In contradiction to empirical experience, transcendental experience or *brahmānubhava* is uncaused and eternal. As the very nature of the Self, it is co-eternal with the Self and is never absent from it. It is wrong to think that in the states of deep sleep and the fourth state the Self is devoid of knowledge although all knowledge based on subject–object duality is absent then. For the reason that one is not aware of oneself or of something other than oneself in these states one may wrongly conclude the absence of knowledge as such in these states. But, according to Śaṅkara, the absence of knowledge based on subject–object duality does not warrant the absence of knowledge as such in those states. It is absent in deep sleep, because ignorance, the source of such knowledge, recedes back to its potential state or unmanifested condition. Therefore, the absence of such knowledge in deep sleep is not a sufficient reason to deny knowledge as such in that state, for the fact that one is aware of the absence of such knowledge in deep sleep, after it is over, clearly indicates the existence of knowledge then.[15] If this pure awareness were to be really absent

---

[14] *AiUB*, II.1, Introduction; *BṛUB*, III.4.2.

[15] *Upadeśasāhasrī*, part I (prose) 93; *BṛUB*, IV.3.23; *MaUB*, VII.

in deep sleep, none would be able to know the absence of knowledge based on subject–object duality also.

In the fourth state, the duality of the subject and the object on which the empirical experience is based is completely absent. The mind and the senses which are instrumental in causing empirical experience also cease to exist. During the states of waking and dream, these things appear to be distinct from the Self due to ignorance and with the removal of ignorance the Self realizes its true nature, that is, its being the self or essence of everything. Then these things are no longer seen to be different from the Self. They are realized to be identical with the Self or their oneness with the Self is realized.[16] Thus when everything is realized to be one with the Self there exists nothing different from the Self either to experience the Self or to be experienced by the Self. Because of such realization, all knowledge based on distinctions is absent in the fourth state. As discussed earlier, pure experience or the Self witnesses the empirical self and its activity (empirical experience). People, therefore, wrongly attribute the characteristics of empirical experience like origination and cessation to pure knowledge, because of their non-discrimination between the two.

> The eternal vision witnesses the transitory vision (the experience gained through the senses and the mind), but since the latter has characteristics like origination and cessation, the vision of the Self that witnesses it appears accordingly and seems to be transient owing to the delusion of man.[17]

Commenting on the *Praśna Upaniṣad*, Śaṅkara by way of answering a possible criticism explains that the absence of

[16] *BṛUB*, I.4.7, II.4.14, IV.3.23; *MuUB*, III.2.7.

[17] *AiUB*, II.1, Introduction, tr. Swami Gambhirananda, vol. II, pp. 52-53.

knowledge as such cannot be established on the basis of the absence of objects and their knowledge, just as it is not possible to imagine the absence of the eye from its failure to perceive colour in darkness.[18] The sun shines whether there are things to be illumined or not; and from the absence of the objects to be illumined absence of sunlight cannot be inferred. Likewise, the absence of knowledge based on distinctions in deep sleep and in the fourth state does not indicate the absence of knowledge as such, but only the absence of all distinctions. Moreover, it is not possible to argue away the existence of that knowledge by which one is able to know the non-existence of knowledge in the absence of knowledge based on subject–object duality. The non-existence of knowledge based on subject–object duality cannot be known if there is not that pure awareness. This sort of argument may lead to infinite regress, but at the same time, it indicates the existence of pure awareness. Thus even for the sake of argument, the non-existence of pure knowledge cannot be established. The very attempt to deny it establishes its existence.

Another doubt may arise in this connection. Whether the Self is aware of itself or not in the absence of the awareness of objects? Is not the Self conscious of itself in the absence of object-awareness? To answer this positively is to contradict the absolute oneness of the Self. If it is admitted that the Self is aware of itself in the absence of object-awareness, it should be accepted that the Self becomes an object to itself, and that means a split in the undifferentiated nature of the Self into subject and object.[19] But no such split or differentiation in the nature of the Self is possible. There is no possibility of the Self becoming a subject as well as an object at the same time. So also, the man who has realized *Brahman* does not experience

[18] *PrUB*, VI.2.

[19] *BṛUB*, III.9.28.7.

Brahman as an object, nor does he experience his own Self as if it is an object. In other words, *brahmānubhava* is neither *Brahman*-consciousness nor Self-consciousness; it is pure consciousness without subject–object duality. It will be meaningless to assume self-awareness on the part of *Brahman* when awareness is its very nature. Illustrating this point, Śaṅkara adduces the example of fire and points out that fire in the absence of something to burn cannot be said to burn itself.[20] Likewise when there are no objects to be illumined light does not illumine itself. Burning is the very nature or essence of fire and it is self-contradictory and meaningless to assert that fire burns itself or light illumines itself. In the same way, *Brahman* which is pure knowledge cannot be said to know Itself. "*Brahman* is eternally aware of this bliss for that is Its nature and hence there is no sense in maintaining that *Brahman* enjoys Its own bliss."[21]

The view that *Brahman* is aware of Itself would have been significant if the possibility of *Brahman* not being aware of Itself at any time or an interruption in Its awareness of Itself is ever conceivable.[22] For instance, a man is aware of himself and others, but during the time when he is aware of others there is an interruption in his awareness of himself. Whereas in the case of a man who is completely and uninterruptedly absorbed in an object, it is not possible to make a distinction between a state of awareness and a state of unawareness. On the other hand, if it is assumed that there are interruptions in *Brahman*'s awareness of Itself, then in those intervals *Brahman* must know something other than Itself, because knowing, which is Its essential nature, is never absent from It. This would make *Brahman* finite and mutable. Also by this, duality would be admitted. As against this, if it is asserted that *Brahman* is never

[20] *BṛUB*, II.4.14.

[21] Ibid., III.9.28.7, tr. Swami Madhavananda, p. 567.

[22] Ibid., III.9.28.7.

unaware of Itself, or that there is no interruption in Its awareness of Itself, it amounts to saying that *Brahman* retains Its nature always which is but natural. Nothing new is asserted thereby. Hence Śaṅkara emphatically states that "the text 'knowledge bliss etc.' must be interpreted as setting forth the nature of *Brahman*, but not as signifying that the bliss of the Self is enjoyed by itself", or that the Self knows itself.[23]

However, at some places *Brahman* is said to be the eternal "knower" (*vijñātā*) or the "witness" (*sākṣī*). It is considered to be the witness of the empirical self and its activities. But all this is significant only from the empirical standpoint of differences. Strictly speaking, "witness" or "knower" is meaningful only when there is something different from the Self which can be witnessed or known by the Self. This is possible only at the empirical level, for then the empirical self and its activities are witnessed by the Self. In itself the Self is pure knowledge, and there is nothing different from itself which it can witness. Thus we cannot properly apply any word like, "knower" or "witness" to *Brahman* in Itself. However, as we try to understand *Brahman*, before It is directly realized, in relation to the world which is ever an object, we think of It as the eternal knower or the witness. Therefore, when *Brahman* is said to be the knower, it is to be understood figuratively. It does not imply the duality of the knower and the known, but indicates pure knowledge.

> The word "knower" is figuratively used to indicate pure knowledge.[24] The immutable consciousness that is *Brahman* is spoken of as the eternal knower by a figure of speech (*upacāra*), just as by virtue of its heat, fire is regarded as the agent of heating.[25]

---

[23] *BṛUB*, III.9.28.7, tr. Swami Madhavananda, p. 567.

[24] Ibid., III.4.2.

[25] *BGB*, XIII.2.

It is like saying that a hill stands or the sun shines. These expressions are significant only figuratively. Śaṅkara generally uses the words "knowledge", "consciousness" and "experience" not as they are understood empirically, but in their abstract sense to indicate *Brahman*, and the word "knower" is very rarely employed for that purpose. Even then the usage is metaphorical. It is therefore more appropriate and significant to speak of *Brahman* as pure knowledge rather than to call It as the "knower". Thus, to be precise, *brahmānubhava* does not mean experiencing *Brahman*, as objects are experienced, nor is it *Brahman* experiencing Itself. The Self knowing itself or being known by something other than itself is possible only when the Self has not realized its true nature or when it is identified with the various limiting adjuncts like the intellect.

> But when the Self realizes its true nature of absolute oneness free from the limitations of intellect, there can be no awareness of the Self by itself (*svasaṁvedyata*) nor is there awareness of it by others (*parasaṁvedyata*).[26]

Brahmānubhava is immediate and direct

Brahmānubhava is immediate and direct.[27] Its attainment is neither through the mediation of the senses and the mind, nor is it in any sense indirect. *Brahmānubhava* is not in any sense a product or something that is attained through effort. Empirical experience is mediate, for it is attained through the mediation of the senses and the mind. Although empirical experience is of independently existing objects, to be known they should be illumined by the senses and reflected in the mind. Even the self-luminous objects like the sun are to be reflected in the mind if they are to be known. Thus all empirical knowledge, including scriptural knowledge, comes through

---

[26] *KeUB*, II.4.

[27] *BṛUB*, III.5.1., III.4.1, I.4.10.

mediation; it is not self-revealing and direct. For its origination, empirical knowledge depends upon the activity of knowing, and things are known only when they come into direct contact with a knower. If the mind and the senses are absent or are not functioning, empirical knowledge cannot be attained, because at the empirical level an object of experience is different from the subject that experiences it, and an effort is required to bridge the gulf between the subject and the object. In this sense, the knowledge of *Brahman* is also mental (*manovṛtti*), since in being known through the scriptures, *Brahman* seemingly becomes an object of the mind. However, such knowledge of *Brahman* is not the direct experience of It in which the activity of the mind or of the senses is not involved, but its prior state of knowing *Brahman* indirectly through the scriptures.[28]

Brahmānubhava is unobstructed (*avyavahita*). It is attained without any mediating principle, as it is to realize one's own self in its true nature. Illustrating this Śaṅkara gives the following example.[29] Some people after crossing a river wanted to be sure that all of them safely arrived. So, one of them counted all the others in the group, but failed to count himself. Therefore a person was found missing. While searching for the missing person he at last came to realize that he himself was the missing person for whom he was searching. In such a realization that he is the missing person, no effort is involved, nor is there any intervention or mediation of some other factor, because the missing person was not different from the one who searched for him. Likewise, in the case of *brahmānubhava*, the object of realization or *Brahman* and the self which aspires to realize It are not different, but identical.[30] It is only when the object of realization is something different from the Self,

---

[28] *ChāUB*, I.1, Introduction; *SūB*, I.1.4; *Upadeśasāhasrī*, XVIII.205.

[29] *TaiUB*, II.1.1.

[30] *GKB*, III.33.

some effort is meaningful and also a mediating principle is required for its realization.

> The knowledge of objects is mediate, for it depends on an intervening reflection in the mind. But as *Brahman* is the Self of the empirical self, It is immediately known.[31]

Thus Self-realization or *brahmānubhava* is neither indirect nor figurative, for it is to realize one's own self as the Self (*ātma ātmatvena*). If the Self were to realize something other than itself as *Brahman*, there would have been every possibility of such realization being either figurative or indirect.[32]

Brahmānubhava is ineffable

Another essential characteristic of *brahmānubhava* is its ineffability (*anirvacanīyatva*). The description of *brahmānubhava* is an impossibility.[33] Within the empirical realm, any experience, however subtle it may be, can be described through some appropriate medium of expression. The description may not be exact and clear, but still it is possible to describe any empirical experience since the experiencer is different from what is empirically experienced. The description of *brahmānubhava*, on the other hand, is not possible simply for the reason that its nature is essentially non-dual and undifferentiated. It is because of the mind and its activity, the Self in its empirical predicament seems to experience things other than itself, and again it is the mind that is responsible for the description of the same experience, since it has the capacity to remember what has been experienced. But in *brahmānubhava* the oneness of the mind with the Self is realized, and therefore it does not exist as something different from

---

[31] *Upadeśasāhasrī*, XVIII.40.

[32] *ChāUB*, VI.16.3.

[33] *BṛUB*, II.3.6.

Brahman. In the absence of the mind and its activity there can be no dualistic experience and its description.

It is only to objects of knowledge that a word can be applied.[34] What can be known through the various sources of knowledge can also be communicated through speech. As mind and speech, ideas and words move together everywhere, Śaṅkara says that what can be known through the instruments of knowledge can alone be represented through speech and what cannot be known cannot also be expressed in language.[35] And *Brahman* is beyond the reach of all the sources of knowledge; It is unperceivable (*atīndriya*) and unthinkable (*acintyam*). Therefore, language also fails to describe It. Moreover, *Brahman* is the revealer of the words and ideas, for It is the self or the essence of the mind and the organ of speech.[36] It is because of *Brahman* the mind is able to think and the organ of speech is able to speak, and therefore the mind cannot comprehend It and speech cannot describe It. Only those things whose nature is determinable (*savikalpa*) and which possess attributes can be described. Whereas *Brahman* has no attributes nor can Its nature be determined. A thing can be defined when it can be distinguished from other things, because of its distinguishing characteristics. But there is nothing different from *Brahman* from which It can be distinguished, nor can anything be said about *Brahman*, so that It can be distinguished on that basis.

Nevertheless, the Upaniṣads try to define *Brahman* as truth (*satyam*), knowledge (*jñānam*) and infinitude (*anantam*). But, according to Śaṅkara, no definition of *Brahman*, including the above one, is valid and meaningful from the standpoint of

[34] *Upadeśasāhasrī*, XVIII.24.

[35] *MāUB*, VII.

[36] *KeUB*, I.3.

brahmānubhava. He says that *Brahman* is defined not from the intrinsic point of view, but merely with reference to the limiting adjuncts that are superimposed on It. If, however, we wish to describe It as It is in Itself free from all that is superimposed on It, then it is an utter impossibility.[37] *Brahman* is defined as truth, knowledge and infinitude by way of superimposing these notions on which is really undefinable and undescribable. Even the words *Brahman* and *Ātman* fail to describe it.[38] The definition of the undefinable is meant to serve the practical needs of an individual self. As the knowledge of *Brahman* in itself cannot be communicated to a seeker of *Brahman* in any positive way, nor is meditation on it possible, all these things are imagined in it or superimposed on it as means to its realization, which is the highest end of life.

Such undifferentiated and non-dualistic experience, according to Śaṅkara, may however be described negatively, so as to make one understand the all-inclusive nature of *Brahman*. "It is the saying of the traditionists", says Śaṅkara, "that which cannot be elucidated is elucidated by way of superimposition and negation."[39] And still supreme is the way of silence. This is the significance of the answer given by the Sage Bhava when he was questioned by Vāshkalin about the nature of *Brahman*. When Vāshkalin requested the Sage Bhava to explain him the nature of *Brahman* the latter asking Vāshkalin to know *Brahman* became silent. Not able to understand the significance of the silence of the sage, Vāshkalin asked the sage repeatedly to instruct him about *Brahman*. The sage then replied that all the while (through silence) he was explaining him about *Brahman*; and *Brahman*

---

[37] *BṛUB*, II.3.6; *GKB*, IV.61-62; *KeUB*, II.2.

[38] *SūB*, I.1.24; *BṛUB*, I.4.7.

[39] *BGB*, XIII.13.

is absolute silence (*upaśānti*).[40] In other words, there can be no positive understanding of *Brahman* and hence It cannot be described positively. Any positive description of *Brahman* fails to describe It.

All that is said about *Brahman* in Vedānta is a mere approximation or an attempt to describe the undescribable, and this attempt is significant only from the empirical standpoint. From the standpoint of absolute truth there is no possibility of describing It. What can be described positively is not the ultimate experience as such, but that which is conditioned by our understanding of it. Even to say that it is non-dualistic is only to prevent wrong understanding about it, but not to affirm anything about it positively.[41] Words stand for the conditioned objects and therefore if they are applied to the unconditioned reality, i.e. *Brahman* in Itself, they become despoiled of their power and turn back without apprehending It. It is the conditioned *Brahman* or *Brahman* on which the categories of our understanding are superimposed, that is described as "*Brahman*", "*Ātman*", "knowledge", "bliss", "infinitude", etc., while the unconditioned reality or *Brahman* in Itself is simply undescribable and inexpressible (*niruktam*).

Yogic experience

In this part the various experiences like *nirvikalpa samādhi* of Yoga which are apparently similar to *brahmānubhava* are discussed, in order to distinguish *brahmānubhava* from them and also to make our understanding of *brahmānubhava* clear. These experiences seem to resemble *brahmānubhava* in so far as they are distinct from and go beyond the normal experience of differences and distinctions. They are the experiences of yogic *samādhi*, swoon, deep sleep and death. Although in all

---

[40] *SūB*, III.2.17.

[41] *ChāUB*, VII.24.1; *GKB*, II.18, II.36.

these experiences, the subject–object duality is absent and they seem to be undifferentiated, they are not the emancipating experience of Advaita. Advaitic experience, according to Śaṅkara, is fundamentally different from these experiences, and whatever similarity there seems to exist between them and *brahmānubhava* is only superficial and apparent, but not real. Śaṅkara analyses and explains these experiences in order to avoid confusion between them and *brahmānubhava* and also to set forth clearly the unique nature and significance of *brahmānubhava*.

The supreme end of man, according to Yoga, is to attain the indeterminate state of experience (*nirvikalpa samādhi*) in which there is no awareness either of oneself or of something other than oneself. The *yogī*s or the followers of the Yoga system of philosophy, look upon the mind as an entity different from the Self and yet related to it.[42] According to them, the pristine purity of the Self, in which state it is free from all suffering, is obscured by its connection with the mind, and because of this relation the Self experiences fear and misery. Since all suffering and bondage are due to the Self's relation with the mind, the *yogī*s think that the ultimate goal of absolute happiness is achieved solely through the practice of Yoga, whereby the mind is gradually controlled and finally dissolved. In the case of the *yogī*s, explains Śaṅkara:

> The destruction of misery and the attainment of fearlessness are dependent on the perfect control of the mind. So also, the knowledge of the Self and the attainment of the eternal peace known as liberation are due to the control of the mind.[43]

---

[42] *GKB*, III.40.

[43] Ibid.

When the mind is dissolved (*laya*) through its gradual control, the Self becomes free from the obscuring influence of the mind and shines in its true nature of purity, fearlessness and bliss. In other words, human suffering and freedom from it are explained by Yoga in terms of the mind and its dissolution.

According to Śaṅkara, the indeterminate experience of Yoga (*samādhi*) is not the same as *brahmānubhava*. He emphatically states that the seekers of *brahmānubhava* should shun from tasting the bliss which the *yogīs* seek to experience through *samādhi*.[44] Liberation (*kaivalya*) as conceived by the Yoga is essentially different from the liberation (*mokṣa*) as conceived by Śaṅkara. Śaṅkara never accepts the view that the highest end of man or liberation can be achieved through the complete control of the mind or through its dissolution. According to him, the mind is ultimately unreal; it has no objective (*vastu*) existence. Its existence is imagined in the Self as an illusory snake is imagined to exist in a rope. Thus from the standpoint of absolute truth there exists nothing different from the Self which can obscure its nature, so that its control or dissolution may lead to the liberation of the Self. As the existence of the mind is based on ignorance, the realization of the Self has nothing to do with the control of the mind. If at all it is connected with anything, it is connected with the annihilation of ignorance. According to Śaṅkara, the mind is known to exist in relation to the objects it reflects, and the objects are known to exist through the mind. As one is known to exist through the other, in the absence of any one of them the other cannot be known to exist. For this reason, when the mind is completely withdrawn from the objects, realizing them to be ultimately unreal, the mind becomes quiescent like the still flame of light kept in a windless place and does not manifest (*anavabhāsa*) itself; it then cannot modify itself into the form of

[44] *GKB*, III.45.

objects.[45] It is the objectless state of the mind in which it is neither dissolved nor is it distracted by the sense-objects, but remains serene like fire without fuel to burn. It then becomes one with the Self and attains the state of pure existence (*sattāmātra*) and remains as pure consciousness (*citsvarūpa*).[46]

Although Śaṅkara accepts the existence of the mind at the empirical level, he never admitted any real relationship between it and the Self. There cannot exist any sort of real relationship between an illusory reality like the mind and an absolute reality like the Self. As long as the mind is active and manifests itself, the Self is not realized and when the Self is realized the mind ceases to exist. However, there seems to exist some sort of relationship between them before the Self is realized. Any such relationship is due to the superimposition of the nature of the one on the other. When the cause of super-imposition, viz. ignorance, is removed there can exist no relation between them.

The state of oblivion or the dissolution of the mind, according to Śaṅkara, is as harmful (*anartha*) and undesirable as unbridled indulgence in sense enjoyment.[47] Therefore, one should refrain from the state of oblivion or the dissolution of the mind as well as from the objects of enjoyment. The wise should not go in for either, as the supreme end of life cannot be realized either through extreme control of the mind or by allowing it unrestricted freedom to enjoy the sense objects. Self-realization is through right discrimination between the Self and the non-self, but not through the suppression of the mind and its activities. Trying to achieve complete control of the mind is like trying to empty the ocean with the help of a blade of grass.[48] It is far from possible, and even if it is supposed

---

[45] *GKB*, III.46.

[46] Ibid., III.45, 46.

[47] Ibid., III.42.

[48] Ibid., III.41.

to be achieved by the *yogīs*, still there is every possibility of the mind becoming active when once the state of *samādhi* is broken up. When once the mind becomes active the Self experiences pain and pleasure again. The *yogī* then suffers like others. Because the *yogīs* look upon the mind as the source of experience of pain and pleasure, they endeavour to check it, the source of experience, so as to avoid the experience of pain and pleasure. But such a cessation of suffering achieved through the discipline of the mind is temporary, for it is caused.

Even the metaphysical position of Yoga is different from that of Śaṅkara. According to Yoga, the individual self is different from God (*Īśvara*) and the supreme end of man, according to it, is not to realize the oneness of the self with God, but to regain its original purity which is obscured because of its coming into contact with the mind.[49] As against this, Śaṅkara maintains the absolute oneness of the Self and *Brahman* and denies objective reality to the individual self. The *yogīs*, therefore, shun Advaita which teaches the illusoriness of the individual self. In the words of Śaṅkara:

> The undiscriminating *yogīs* for want of the knowledge imparted by the Upaniṣads cannot understand the doctrine of Advaita, which teaches absolute fearlessness, but apprehend in it the cause for fear as they see in it the destruction of their own individuality (*ātmanāśa*).[50]

Thus *brahmānubhava* has nothing to do with *nirvikalpa samādhi* of Yoga and the former cannot be attained through the practice of Yoga. "The highest end of man cannot be attained by the path of Yoga."[51]

---

[49] *SūB*, II.1.3.

[50] *GKB*, III.39.

[51] *SūB*, II.1.3.

There is a possibility for misunderstanding the position of Śaṅkara on *nirvikalpa samādhi* of Yoga, since in his *Vivekacūḍāmaṇi* and at other places, he speaks that the highest end of man (*mokṣa*) can be attained through *nirvikalpa samādhi.*

> When the non-dual Self is realized by means of *nirvikalpa samādhi*, the heart's knot of ignorance is totally destroyed.[52] By *nirvikalpa samādhi* the truth of *Brahman* is clearly and definitely realized, but not otherwise.[53]

These and many other statements of Śaṅkara seem to contradict what Śaṅkara said about Yoga and its ultimate goal elsewhere. This contradiction, however, is not real since the words "Yoga" and *nirvikalpa samādhi* as employed by Śaṅkara carry a different meaning from what they mean in Yoga. For instance, *samādhi*, according to Śaṅkara, is complete forgetfulness of all mental activity (*vṛtti vismaraṇam*) by first making the mind changeless (*nirvikāra*) and then identifying it with *Brahman* (*brahmākāra*). This is also known as pure knowledge (*samādhi jñānasaṁjñakah*).[54]

In understanding this passage one should remember what Śaṅkara means by *Brahman*. Here the process of identifying the mind with *Brahman* is the same as the process of negating everything in the first instance to identify everything with *Brahman* finally. In the *Bhagavad-Gītā Bhāṣya*, he identifies *samādhi* with "discriminative" wisdom (*viveka prajñā*) which one attains through discrimination between the Self and the non-self.[55] In the *Kaṭha Upaniṣad Bhāṣya*, Yoga is defined as the state in which the Self, becoming free from ignorance, is established in its own nature.[56] In the *Vivekacūḍāmaṇi*, it is said

---

52 *Vivekacūḍāmaṇi*, *śl.* 353.

53 Ibid., śl. 365, tr. Swami Madhavananda, p. 161.

54 *Aparokṣānubhūti*, *śl.* 124.

55 *BGB*, II.53.

56 *KaUB*, II.3.11.

that *samādhi* destroys all the tendencies born of ignorance, puts an end to all actions and makes the Self shine spontaneously in its true nature (*svarūpa visphūrti*), both within and without, everywhere and at all times.[57] Such a state of *samādhi* is attained by those whose minds are transparently pure and subtle. It is attained through hearing, reflection and meditation of the scriptural texts.[58] *Samādhi* so attained is tranquil, eternal and fearless. It is identical with the Self, as *turīya* is.[59] Thus, *samādhi*, according to Śaṅkara, is not different from *turīya* in which state the Self is directly realized.

Swoon

Śaṅkara explains the nature of swoon (*mugdha* or *mūrchā*) in his *Sūtra Bhāṣya*.[60] It is a state of utter darkness or total unconsciousness in which one is not aware of anything, including oneself. Then the awareness of one's finitude as well as the sense of good and bad, pleasure and pain is completely absent, and one becomes free, as it were, from all limitations. Swoon is not a separate state distinct from the three empirical states of experience — waking, dreaming and deep sleep; nor is it death. It is not waking state, as there is no awareness of anything in it. Here one may point out that the absence of awareness of objects, in the case of a swooning person, may be due to his intense concentration on the pain caused by the blow, the cause of swoon, just as a person who is completely absorbed in an object is not aware of things, though he is awake. This is not valid for the obvious reason that the man who is absorbed in an object is at least aware of that particular object upon which his mind is intensely fixed, whereas a man in the state of swoon is not aware of anything. The very

---

[57] *Vivekacūḍāmaṇi*, *śl*. 363.

[58] Ibid., *śl*. 364.

[59] *GKB*, III.37, 38.

[60] *SūB*, III.2.20.

fact that one is completely unconscious in swoon excludes the possibility of his dreaming then. One is aware of dream objects while one is dreaming. Swoon is not deep sleep. Their natures are different and the causes that produce them are also different. The swooning person "sometimes does not breathe for a long time; his body trembles; his face has a frightful expression and his eyes are staring wide open".[61] The countenance of a sleeping person, on the other hand, is peaceful. He breathes regularly; his eyes are closed and his body does not tremble. It is not easy to bring the swooning person to consciousness, while a gentle stroke will suffice to wake up a sleeping person. Sleep is natural and all people desire it. Swoon, on the other hand, is not a natural one and is desired by none. While deep sleep is caused by fatigue, swoon is caused accidentally either by drugs or by a hard blow on the head with a club. Moreover, it is the common opinion of all that deep sleep and swoon are not one and the same. Finally, swoon is not death, for the swooning person breathes and his body continues to be warm. While the possibility of regaining consciousness is present in the case of a swooning person, there is no such possibility in the case of a dead person.

As the knowledge of good and evil is absent and there is no experience of pain and pleasure in the state of swoon, as in the case of *brahmānubhava*, some people may think that in the state of swoon complete union between the Self and *Brahman* takes place. But according to those who have realized *Brahman*, says Śaṅkara, swoon is not *brahmānubhava*. In it, ignorance, the root cause of all dualistic experience and suffering, is not destroyed. It is purely temporary as it is caused. It cannot be identified completely with any state of normal experience or with *turīya*. At the same time, it is not completely distinct from them. It closely resembles deep sleep and death. It is similar to deep sleep, as there is no consciousness of pain and pleasure,

[61] *SūB*, III.2.10, tr. Thibaut, vol. II, p. 151.

good and evil in it, and as a doorway to death, it is very near to death. Thus it is compounded of all the states, but not a distinct state of experience.

Deep Sleep

Deep sleep is another state of experience which is apparently similar to *brahmānubhava*. It is an undifferentiated state of consciousness free from all the distinctions like the knower, the known and the knowledge. In deep sleep, one neither experiences the phenomenal world as in the waking state, nor does one dream. Deep sleep is said to be an undifferentiated or unified state (*ekībhūta*) of experience, because in it the subject–object duality which characterizes the other two states of empirical experience is absent.[62] In deep sleep, the differences are not apprehended, not because they are not present, but because the senses and the mind through which they are apprehended cease to be active, just as the differences are not perceived during night because of the presence of darkness. The senses and the mind through which the differences are apprehended during the states of waking and dreaming, stop functioning in deep sleep. Everything then becomes an undifferentiated mass, as it were. For this reason, the state of deep sleep is known as the "mass of undifferentiated consciousness", as it were. Deep sleep is a state of bliss, for in it the suffering and misery caused by the activity of the mind are absent. Nevertheless, it is not pure bliss which *brahmānubhava* is. The very word *suṣupti*, according to Śaṅkara, indicates that the Self in deep sleep has become one with the supreme Self or has realized its own nature, for the word *suṣupti* means attaining one's own true Self (*svam-apita*).[63]

---

[62] *MāUB*, V.

[63] *SūB*, I.1.9; *BṛUB*, II.1.17.

Though in deep sleep the individual self seems to have become one with the supreme Self, ignorance, the source of all differences, is not destroyed in deep sleep. Ignorance then persists in its potential state or unmanifested condition, as youth is potentially there in boyhood and a tree in a seed.[64] Therefore, it does not appear to exist or seems to have been destroyed, and for that reason people wrongly think that in deep sleep man is freed from bondage caused by ignorance. Deep sleep is not real freedom, because in it ignorance is not annihilated; it only reverts to its potential state of existence. It re-manifests itself when the deep sleep is over. Thus if *Brahman* is misapprehended during the waking and dream states, in deep sleep *Brahman* is not apprehended.[65] While ignorance in its manifested condition makes one wrongly understand *Brahman*, in its unmanifested condition or in deep sleep there is no understanding at all. The waking and dream states are causally related to deep sleep, for they proceed from it in the sense that ignorance which is latent in deep sleep manifests itself during the waking and dream states. So, deep sleep is not free from ignorance. Also the fact that one returns to the state of ignorance or waking experience after the deep sleep is over proves that the latter is a state of ignorance.

On the other hand, *brahmānubhava* is absolutely free from ignorance and when once it is attained there is no return from it into a state of ignorance. While *brahmānubhava* is uncaused and eternal, deep sleep is a caused state and temporary. The undifferentiated state of consciousness, which is attained in deep sleep, is due to one's inability to apprehend the differences, but not due to the realization of their oneness with the Self which is *brahmānubhava*.

---

[64] *SūB*, II.3.31, III.2.9.

[65] *GKB*, I.12.

Death

Brahmānubhava is not death, the disembodied condition of the Self or the passing away of the Self from the body. In death the Self seems to have been liberated from the bodily limitations, and for that reason some may consider death as liberation. But, according to Śaṅkara, there is no embodied condition of the Self in reality, so its attainment of the disembodied state of existence is not meaningful. To accept that the Self attains the disembodied state of existence, the embodied condition of it should first be admitted; whereas the Self is eternally free from all conditions. It is in its true nature never bound by anything as there exists nothing beside it. The embodied condition of the Self is just an imagined one. It is due to superimposition of the illusory entities like the body, mind and the senses on the Self.[66] Because of this superimposition, people wrongly think that the Self is embodied. In no other way, the embodied condition of the Self can be established. Therefore, it is possible for the person who has realized the Self to become free from the bodily limitations even while he is alive.[67] Even otherwise, death only means a change of body for the Self, but not the end of ignorance, the cause of Self's embodied condition. Death is a natural happening, and if it is to be regarded as the supreme end of life or liberation, then there will be no meaning in striving to attain liberation by understanding the scriptures and following an ardent spiritual discipline.

Thus *brahmānubhava* is essentially different from yogic *samādhi*, swoon, deep sleep and death. The former three states of experience, in general, represent an intense passivity of the mind or psyche, which may be due to its withdrawal from the world of experience or due to the stopping of its activity. In

[66] *SūB*, I.1.4.

[67] Ibid.

these states, there is no awareness that the mind and the experience of differences caused because of it are illusory and have no objective existence. Instead of trying to achieve an awareness of oneness of everything with the Self or the realization that there is nothing different from the Self or *Brahman*, which culminates in perfect bliss and liberates the individual from ignorance, the cause of all differences, we observe in these states an attempt to suppress the experience of differences. The approach of yoga is negative, in that the mind, which is the source of attaining knowledge, is sought to be dissolved through its gradual control, so that the painful experience of differences is avoided, instead of realizing the unreality of all differences. This may be due to the wrong understanding that the experience of pain can be stopped by stopping the experience as such. So, the *yogī*s endeavour to dissolve the mind, the source of all experience. Though the mind as mind is unreal, it is not different from the Self in reality. Therefore, it is not the mind that causes human suffering, but ignorance because of which the mind and everything else are seen as different from the Self. It is ignorance that projects differences on an undifferentiated reality, and the mind is its seat only. Therefore, it is not by suppressing or dissolving the mind, but by conquering ignorance that one is able to overcome the differences and the suffering caused by them. By conquering ignorance, one realizes the oneness of everything with the Self and then the differences cease to exist.

These states mark the absence of understanding, whereas *brahmānubhava* is attained through perfect understanding of Reality. There is no place, in these states, for right discrimination and Self-knowledge, through which alone *brahmānubhava* is attained. These are the states in which the problem of human suffering is evaded instead of understanding it correctly and then solving it. They are the states of utter darkness, but not of perfect knowledge. In all these states, ignorance, the root cause of all suffering, is present. While *brahmānubhava* is natural and uncaused, all these states are caused and hence have a beginning and an end. While there is no return from *brahmānubhava* into the state of ignorance, one falls back into the state of ignorance and suffering the moment these states are over. In all these states, the Self's attainment of its nature of undifferentiated consciousness is only seeming. Because ignorance is not destroyed, the old state of differences re-establishes itself as soon as the Self returns from these states into the state of waking experience.

Although the state of non-duality is literally attained in all these states, one is not aware of it. Śaṅkara says that all the creatures become one with *Brahman* every night in deep sleep and at the time of death and cosmic dissolution, but as they are not aware of the same fact, it is of no significance to them.[68] But *brahmānubhava* is pure awareness. In it there is awareness, but it is not the awareness of differences and distinctions. It is the awareness of absolute oneness or identity of everyting.

Experiencing Brahman is experiencing one's own Self

What distinguishes Advaita Vedānta from other schools of Indian philosophy is its primary concern with the knowledge of the Self. It is primarily an enquiry into one's own true nature (*pāramārthika svarūpa*) rather than an attempt to understand the nature of ultimate reality objectively. An enquiry into the nature of Self does not mean trying to know the Self as if it is an object (*viṣaya*) of our knowledge, but to understand the true nature of the inquirer himself (*vedituḥ svarūpa*).[69] Thus the

[68] *ChāUB*, VIII.3.2, VI.9.2.

[69] *TaiUB*, II.1.1; *KeUB*, II.1.

purpose of Vedānta is to make one directly realize the real nature of one's own self.

The existence of the knower is presupposed in our entire empirical experience. Without the knower it is not possible to have any knowledge, and for that reason our knowledge remains incomplete and imperfect as long as the nature of the knower remains unknown. One's knowledge of anything is not as sure and certain as the awareness of one's own self. This knower or the self that knows everything is an ever-abiding and unchanging principle in all empirical experience, and therefore its knowledge can provide us a firm ground for higher knowledge and speculation. Generally, man thinks of knowing everything except his own self (*svātma*). In his effort to know everything man may succeed and also he may be able to achieve anything and everything, including moral perfection and omniscience, but if the self is not realized nothing significant is attained. The achievement of everything and the understanding of the whole universe are only instrumental in realizing the Self, and hence nothing of ultimate significance is achieved, in achieving all these, if the Self remains unrealized. They are not in themselves the end, but the means for the final end, that is, Self-realization.

Further, if one is ignorant about oneself, or if one does not realize what one is, then there will be no basis for one to speculate and conclude about the absolute and its nature. Śaṅkara asks, "how can a fool who does not know his own Self know its unity or difference with the absolute".[70] As the unchanging principle in our empirical experience, the self or the knower can become the starting point of a meaningful metaphysical enquiry. Thus the philosophy of Advaita is based on the irrefutable and self-evident fact of one's own self, and its purpose is fulfilled when the true nature of one's own self is directly realized. According

[70] *BṛUB*, II.1.20.

to Śaṅkara, there is no greater danger to man than indifference to knowledge of the self in its true nature, for a distorted knowledge of one's own self or a fall from it (*svarūpa vibhraṁśa*) is at the root of all suffering and misery.[71] Therefore it should be the ultimate aim of man to arrive at the right knowledge of his own self. Hence to understand Advaita is to understand and realize directly one's own real nature (*svasvarūpa vedanam*). "In all Vedānta," says Śaṅkara, "it is the inner self which is put forward as the reality to be known, as 'I (am *Brahman*)' and never any external object like 'sound' saying, 'that is *Brahman*'."[72] The significance of the Upaniṣadic statement "let no man try to find out what speech is; let him know the speaker" is, according to Śaṅkara, to direct one's attention towards the realization of the inner self as the supreme reality.[73] "The inner self (*pratyagātma*) is the subject of study in higher knowledge."[74] Direct realization of one's own Self (*svānubhūti*) is the single purpose of all the Upaniṣads and, according to Śaṅkara, they are unanimous in proclaiming that the true nature of every inquirer is the ultimate reality, and that to attain the supreme end of life one should realize one's own true nature.[75]

In the following passage Śaṅkara clearly expresses the nature of *brahmajñāna* which, according to him, is the same as *ātmajñāna*.

> *Brahmajñāna* is of the same nature as *ātmajñāna* (Self-knowledge) and *ātmajñāna* is of the nature of the Self.[76]
>
> Self-knowledge means the knowledge of one's own Self.[77]

---

[71] *Vivekacūḍāmaṇi, śl.* 328.

[72] *BṛUB*, II.1.20, tr. Swami Madhavananda, p. 294.

[73] *SūB*, I.1.3.

[74] *BṛUB*, II.4.1, Introduction.

[75] *KeUB*, II.1; *BṛUB*, III.5.1.

[76] *BGB*, XVIII.50.

[77] Ibid., II.69.

Some more passages which expressly state that the realization of the Self is the highest realization or *brahmānubhava* may be cited:

> The state of being *Brahman* is the same as the realization of the Self.[78]

> Perfect knowledge is to realize the innermost self as *Brahman*.[79]

> No man who knows *Brahman* as something other than one's own Self is a knower of truth.[80]

If, on the other hand, the realization of the Self is not to be deemed as *brahmānubhava*, the scriptural statements like "it knew itself as I am *Brahman*" and "That thou art" will become meaningless. These statements can be consistent and significant only if there is no supreme reality other than the Self. Therefore, according to Śaṅkara, the words *Brahman* and *Ātman* are synonymous (*ekārtha*) and are so used in all the scriptures.[81] He, accordingly, has nowhere made any distinction between Self-realization (*ātmadarśanam*, *ātmānubhava*, *ātmāvabodha* and *ātmāvagati*) and *brahmānubhava* or *brahmāvagati*. "My Self is pure consciousness, free from all distinctions and suffering":[82] this is the nature of *ātmānubhava* and *brahmānubhava* is likewise described as pure consciousness free from all differences. Thus *brahmānubhava*, *ātmānubhava* and *mokṣa* indicate the same experience.

While the starting point for a seeker of truth is an enquiry into the real nature of the Self, the Self by its nature is self-evident and ever revealed. As the self of all, it is never

---

78 *GKB*, IV.85.

79 *Vivekacūḍāmaṇi*, *śl.* 202; *KeUB*, II.4.

80 *Upadeśasāhasrī*, XVI.70.

81 *BṛUB*, I.4.10.

82 *SūB*, IV.1.2.

unknown to anyone at any time. Now, as the Self is self-evident, an enquiry into its nature may appear to be superfluous and meaningless. But it is not so, as there are many opinions about its existence and nature. Different people understand it differently as body, mind, vital force, etc., and some even consider It to be pure void. There are some who even deny its existence. In the presence of such conflicting opinions about its existence and nature, an enquiry to determine its real nature will not be superfluous. As the Self is objectively real, there should be no scope for diversity of opinion about it; its knowledge should be uniform to all, that is, it should be known by all as one and the same. Nevertheless, the fact that the Self is known differently by different people may indicate either that the Self has no permanent and immutable nature of its own or that our understanding of it is erroneous. The former position is untenable, as the nature of a thing, being co-eternal with the thing, is not liable to change; it remains the same always. The latter one is correct according to Śaṅkara. The differences in the understanding of the Self are due to the presence of ignorance, but not because the nature of the Self is always changing. Ignorance conceals, as it were, the true nature of the Self and makes us know it wrongly. Śaṅkara says that though people are seeing the Self every moment, yet they do not see it, inasmuch as they see it wrongly (*viparīta*), just as those suffering from an eye disease known as *timira* see more than one moon.[83] Thus all people know the Self, but their knowledge of it is not objective (*vastu*) and perfect.

Our experience of the Self, at the empirical level, is not direct and immediate as it is in the fourth state (*turīya*). At the empirical level, the Self is known indirectly in its relation to the mind and its various modifications. It is that which knows, thinks and acts. The Self as conditioned by the mind, that is,

[83] *BGB*, XIII.27.

as the empirical self or the subject, knows the mind and all its modifications as its objects, and in knowing them, it also becomes known (*pratibudhyate*).[84] At some places, Śaṅkara even says that, at the empirical level, the Self is always known inferentially through the various functions which it seems to perform.[85] The nature of the Self manifests itself through such functions like hearing, seeing and thinking which are superimposed on it, and at the same time, the nature of the Self is revealed in and through them. Thus the Self is known as the knower when knowing is superimposed on it, as thinker when thinking is superimposed on it, as hearer when hearing is superimposed on it, and so on. In this way, the Self is known at the empirical level as the knower, thinker, enjoyer, sufferer etc., and otherwise it cannot be known. Śaṅkara says that before the Self enters, as it were, into the differentiated universe as the individual self, it is not known; it is known only when it enters the universe. The entrance of the Self into the differentiated universe merely means its being perceived as a reflection within the intellect, just as the reflection of the sun is perceived in water.[86]

> Before the manifestation of the universe, the Self is not perceived. It is only after the manifestation of the universe, the Self is perceived within the intellect like the reflection of the sun in water and the like.[87]

For this reason, the Self is described, at the empirical level, as that which is perceived in and through the intellect and also as that which perceives through the intellect.[88] It is revealed through the intellect and all its functions, just as the lamp that

---

[84] *KeUB*, II.4.

[85] *BṛUB*, I.4.7, IV.3.1, Introduction, IV.4.18.

[86] Ibid., I.4.7.

[87] Ibid., I.4.7, tr. Swami Madhavananda, p. 121.

[88] Ibid., II.1.10.

is kept inside a perforated dome gets itself revealed by its light emanating through the holes of the dome. If the Self does not reveal Itself in this way, as what is reflected in the intellect, there can be no knowledge of the Self at the empirical level. As the modifications of the intellect are not known without the knower, the knower also will not be known in the absence of these modifications, for each reveals the other.[89] If this is not true, then the possibility of realizing the Self directly at the empirical level cannot be denied and the same possibility cannot be established in the fourth state.

What is known indirectly and mediately at the empirical level is not the Self. It is the Self in its empirical predicament or self (*jīva*) which acts, knows, enjoys and suffers. At the empirical level, the Self is known either as the individual self or as a mere witness (*sākṣī*). When the Self becomes identified with the body, mind and the senses or when the latter are superimposed on the Self, it appears to be the individual self which knows, acts and enjoys, while it appears as mere witness and witnesses the activities of the individual self, when the mind or the internal organ alone is superimposed on it. As such, when the process of superimposition is completely stopped or when the Self abides in its own nature of pure consciousness, there will be no duality; and in the absence of duality, the Self cannot be known either as the individual self or as mere witness. Therefore, what is commonly known by all as the self is not the real Self, or what the self in itself is.[90] Our empirical understanding of the Self is conditioned by various factors of superimposition and therefore, it is relative, imperfect and subjective. As the factors of superimposition vary from person to person, depending upon the intellectual and spiritual maturity of the person concerned, the

---

89 *Upadeśasāhasrī*, XVIII.74; *SūB*, II.3.29.

90 *KaUB*, II.1.1; *ChāUB*, VI.8.7.

understanding of the Self also varies from person to person. Though our understanding of the Self varies, it remains the same throughout. Therefore, the purpose of the scriptures is not to teach us about the empirical self, which is known to all in the aforesaid manner without any instruction, but to direct our attention towards the Self which is the self of the empirical self.

The empirical self has no objective existence. Because of ignorance, it is imagined to exist (*avidyā kalpita*) in the Self, like the snake imagined in a rope. It is only an object of illusion (*mithyā vastu*) and does not exist outside the sphere of ignorance. It appears to exist as long as there is ignorance and when ignorance is destroyed, it ceases to exist. The empirical self is only an appearance of the real Self or what the latter appears as when it is viewed in relation to the non-self. Thus as long as one is under the influence of ignorance, one's empirical nature (*vyāvahārika svabhāva*) is a fact, but the moment ignorance is destroyed one's empirical nature comes to an end.[91] Since the empirical nature (*saṁsāritva*) of the Self is only due to ignorance or wrong apprehension (*viparīta darśana*), it is not the true and essential nature of the Self. While the Self is non-dual, unconditioned, immutable and eternal, the empirical self is conditioned, finite, illusory and transient. While the Self is self-existent and self-evident, the empirical self depends for its existence on ignorance and is known indirectly through the mind and its modifications.

As the empirical self is nothing but the distorted condition of the Self, the empirical self in its intrinsic nature is not different from the Self. This means, the Self is not different from the empirical self if the latter is seen in its real nature (*tāttvika svabhāva*). In other words, when the empirical self gives up its empirical nature, which is only illusory, it becomes the Self.

---

[91] *SūB*, II.3.30.

Thus Self-realization, which is the same as *brahmānubhava*, means the empirical self realizing its intrinsic or true nature. "The state of being *Brahman* is the same as the realization of the Self and it is the *summum bonum* of life also."[92]

This is also the purport of the great Upaniṣadic statements like "That thou art" and "I am *Brahman*". They first prove the Self's empirical nature to be unreal and then establish the identity of the Self with *Brahman*. The purpose of the statement "That thou art" is to remove the idea of "Self" with regard to the empirical self (*jīva*) and then to establish without the slightest restraint that the "thou" (the empirical self) in its real nature is absolutely and entirely the same as the highest reality or *Brahman*.[93] Again it is said that "by the purest understanding that one is *Brahman*, one should realize one's own Self which is undifferentiated pure knowledge".[94] Thus, according to Śaṅkara, the purpose of the Upaniṣadic statements like "That thou art" and "I am *Brahman*" is to "present the true nature of the Self (*ātmavastu samarpaṇa*)".[95]

The empirical self expressed by the words "thou" and "I" in the above sentences is not directly identical with *Brahman* or "That", for they possess contradictory attributes. The empirical self or "thou" is finite and limited, whereas *Brahman* or "That" is the creator of the universe and also the ruler of individual selves. Therefore, there can be no identity between "That" and "thou" if their direct meaning is taken into consideration. But the contradiction in their natures is only apparent, but not real. According to Śaṅkara, the two realities known as "That" and "thou" are not ultimately real; they are

---

[92] *GKB*, IV.85.

[93] *ChāUB*, VI.16.3; *SūB*, I.1.31.

[94] *Vivekacūḍāmaṇi*, *śl.* 387.

[95] *BṛUB*, I.4.7.

illusory. They are imagined to exist in the supreme reality which cannot be conceived and is beyond the reach of all words. Though It is one only without a second, it appears as many due to superimposition of various limiting adjuncts on it. In the present case, its appearance as the individual self and as *Brahman* is due to the difference in the limiting adjuncts superimposed on it. When the mind and its functions are superimposed on the supreme reality, it appears as the individual self, while the superimposition on it of the cosmic functions, like the creation of the universe, makes it appear as *Brahman* or "That". In other words, the same reality when it is viewed in relation to the mind is known as the individual self or "thou" and as *Brahman* or "That" when it is viewed in relation to the universe. Thus, though both "That" and "thou" are the appearances of the same reality, as appearances, they are not identical, because the superimposed factors that are responsible for their existence are different. In the case of *Brahman*, the conditioning factor or the limiting adjunct is illusion (*māyā*) while in the case of an individual self, it is ignorance (*avidyā*). While *Brahman* is known through the scriptures, the self is known through the intellect. *Brahman* appears as something different from the individual self or the individual self looks upon *Brahman* as an object of its higher realization.

But as superimposition cannot take place without there being something which is real and forms the substratum of it, the illusory realities like "That" and "thou" point out to a reality on which these notions are superimposed or of which these are the appearances. As appearances, "That" and "thou" presuppose the existence of something of which these are the appearances. Therefore, when the superimposition is negated, the "thou" and "That" are realized to be unreal and the reality on which these are superimposed stands self-revealed in its undifferentiated nature. Nevertheless, what is imagined is not objectively (*vastu*) different from that in which it is imagined. "That in which something is imagined to exist through delusion is that thing itself when rightly understood, and not different from it."[96] When ignorance, on which is based the difference between "That" and "thou", is removed their oneness is revealed or they cease to be different. In other words, the "thou" in its intrinsic nature is the same as "That" in its intrinsic nature. The two words, "That" and "thou" in their indirect sense indicate the same reality, as in the sentence "I am the tenth" the words "I" and "the tenth" point out the same person.[97] The following example given by Śaṅkara may clarify this point further. A kingdom is the symbol of a king and a shield of the soldier, but when the king is deprived of his kingdom and the soldier of his shield, there will be no king and no soldier. Then they will remain as men only.[98]

Here, an objection may be raised as to how the Self in itself which by its very nature is eternally self-revealed (*svayamlabdha svabhāva*) and free from all limitations and attachments, can be said to have been realized as if it was not realized at any time. This is not a valid objection, for the view that the Self is really attained or realized is never endorsed by Śaṅkara. Though from its own standpoint, the Self is ever attained or realized, from the standpoint of an individual self, it appears as if it is not attained, and therefore its attainment is quite significant from the standpoint of an individual self. Śaṅkara says, "to whom *Brahman* appears as unattained owing to his ignorance, the realization of it as none other than one's own Self is quite significant".[99] For the ignorant person who imagines himself to be finite and different from the supreme

---

[96] *Vivekacūḍāmaṇi, śl.* 387.

[97] *Upadeśasāhasrī,* XVIII.172, 192.

[98] *Vivekacūḍāmaṇi, śl.* 244.

[99] *TaiUB,* II.1.1.

Self, and for whom the Self appears as something to be attained, but not already attained or realized, realization of the Self by way of removing such wrong understanding is meaningful. Thus viewed from the state of ignorance or the previous state of non-realization, the realization of the Self is not a contradiction; however, this has no meaning from the standpoint of the Self.

To realize Brahman to attain identity with all

Till now the identity of the Self with *Brahman* (*ātmaikatva darśana*) has been discussed. Now, the identity of "all" with *Brahman* (*sarvātmaikatva darśana*) will be discussed. Following that it will be considered whether the Self's identity with *Brahman* and the identity of all with *Brahman* are two different experiences, or they are one and the same experience.

There are several passages both in the Upaniṣads and in the commentaries thereon by Śaṅkara in which the identity of "all" with *Brahman* is established. According to Śaṅkara, "all" (*sarvam*) means the whole of the differentiated universe or whatever that is manifested and known through the various means of knowledge. It is that which is extended all over in the form of an effect having name and form as its substance. It is that which appears to be different from the individual self and *Brahman*. Here some of the statements may be given in which the oneness of all with *Brahman* is established.

> The knowers of *Brahman* after turning away from the world of differences, see the same Self in all beings, moving and unmoving, and attain the state of non-duality by realizing the oneness of all with the Self (*sarvātmaikabhūtamadvaitam*). That is immortality.[100]

> The identity of all with the Self is the highest state and it is

[100] *KeUB*, II.5, tr. Swami Gambhirananda, vol. I, p. 72.

> the natural and the real state of the Self.[101]
>
> The attainment of the highest is to realize the identity of all with *Brahman*.[102]
>
> The result of *Brahman*-knowledge is to realize *Brahman* directly and that means realizing the identity with all.[103]
>
> When ignorance is destroyed, the knowledge of the Self arises, then one attains the identity with all, and that is liberation.[104]

According to Śaṅkara, the nature and significance of the scriptural statement, "all is *Brahman*" are similar to that of the statement "That thou art".[105] Both the statements seek to establish the non-dual nature of the ultimate reality by way of pointing out the illusory nature of all the differences. Just as the sentence "That thou art" establishes the undifferentiated nature of Reality by proving the illusory nature of things ordinarily denoted by the words "That" and "thou", the sentence "all is *Brahman*" also aims at establishing the absolute oneness of Reality by proving the differentiated universe or "all" to be ultimately unreal. Its aim is not to establish the multiformity of *Brahman*, nor does it indicate that the universe of differences is directly identical with the undifferentiated reality. Both unity and multiplicity cannot form the nature of the same reality. The true import of the sentence is to indicate that the reality of "all" is due to the superimposition of the world of differences on the supreme reality, just as the existence of the empirical self is due to the superimposition of the mind and its functions on the Self. In other words, the undifferentiated reality is seen as the differentiated universe because of ignorance, just as a rope is seen as a snake. Thus the "all", like

---

101 *BṛUB*, IV.3.20.

102 *BṛUB*, IV.3.32.

103 *TaiUB*, II.1.1.

104 *BṛUB*, IV.3.20.

105 *SūB*, I.3.1.

the empirical self, has no objective reality. It is merely imagined to exist in *Brahman* because of ignorance. But as that which is imagined in *Brahman*, the universe can have no existence apart from *Brahman*, for "what is superimposed cannot have existence apart from its substratum".[106] Therefore, it is the supreme reality that appears as the universe. Accordingly, Śaṅkara says:

> Whatever a deluded person perceives through an error is *Brahman* only. The silver is nothing but the shell objectively. So it is *Brahman* that is always perceived as this universe, and what is superimposed on *Brahman* is merely a name.[107]

According to Śaṅkara, if a thing cannot be known apart from something else, the latter forms the essence of that thing. For instance, when a musical instrument, like a drum, is played upon, one cannot separate the various particular notes from the general sound, for they cannot exist apart from it. Any particular note cannot exist apart from the general sound, for in the absence of the general sound the particular notes are not known to exist.[108] Similar is the case with the things perceived. They are not perceived, during the waking and dream states, apart from or independent of pure knowledge or the Self, and therefore they are to be considered as non-existing apart from the Self.[109] Thus while things are seen, at the empirical level, as dependent on the Self, in *brahmānubhava* they are seen as one with the Self. Śaṅkara says that "on knowing the supreme Self, the source of everything, there arises the realization that the Self alone is all this and there is nothing besides it".[110]

---

[106] *Vivekacūḍāmaṇī*, śl. 231; see also *GKB*, II.33.1.6.

[107] Ibid., *śl*. 236.

[108] *BṛUB*, II.4.7.

[109] Ibid.

[110] *MuUB*, II.1.10, tr. Swami Gambhirananda, vol. II, p. 127.

Self-Brahman realization is the same as all-Brahman realization

The realization of the Self's identity with *Brahman* and the realization of the identity of all with *Brahman* are not in any sense different. The realization of the Self's identity with *Brahman* is the same as the realization of the identity of all with *Brahman*. However, the distinction between them is meaningful from the standpoint of an individual self. As an individual self thinks that it is different from *Brahman*, before it has realized its identity with *Brahman*, it also thinks that the universe is different from *Brahman*. At the empirical level, the differences between the self and *Brahman*, *Brahman* and "all" and therefore between the self and "all" are real. Such that an ignorant person looks upon the differentiated universe as different from *Brahman*, and as he thinks of himself to be different from *Brahman*, he naturally thinks that he is different from the universe. But as these differences are ultimately based on ignorance, they seem to be real as long as one is ignorant; and when ignorance is destroyed they cease to be real. Then the Self realizes its oneness with *Brahman* and simultaneously it also realizes its oneness with all, for in reality the Self is *Brahman* and *Brahman* is all.

> Even before knowing *Brahman*, everybody, being *Brahman*, is really always identical with all, but ignorance superimposes on him the idea that he is not *Brahman* and not all.[111]

This, he says, is not only in accordance with the scriptures, but is also testified by the actual experiences of the sages. He points out to the experience of the Sage Vāmadeva who by realizing his identity with *Brahman* realized at the same time his oneness with Manu, the sun, etc., that is, with everything.[112] Therefore, Śaṅkara explains that the realization of the Self's

---

[111] *BṛUB*, I.4.10.

[112] Ibid.

identity with all is simultaneous with the realization of its identity with *Brahman*.

Nevertheless, some of the statements of Śaṅkara may appear to mean that "all-*Brahman*" identity realization follows "Self-*Brahman*" identity realization. He says, "at first springs up the experience that "I am *Brahman*" and then follows the realization that "all is *Brahman*".[113] "Before the realization of oneness of all with the Self (*ekatva vijñāna*) is attained, *Brahman* is to be realized as identical with the Self."[114] But these statements do not indicate any cause and effect relationship between "Self-*Brahman*" identity realization and "all-*Brahman*" identity realization. One does not produce the other. They refer to the same experience. Causation of any sort is impossible in *brahmānubhava*. Self's realization of its oneness with *Brahman* is an end in itself and is never observed to fulfil any other purpose. It is never seen to remove something which is real or to create something anew. It only dispels the wrong notions that one is not *Brahman* and that one is not all. Therefore, the realization of the Self's identity with *Brahman* cannot make one realize the identity of all with *Brahman*, if the "all" is not really identical with *Brahman*. And if "all" is in reality not different from *Brahman*, when the Self realizes its identity with *Brahman*, it also realizes its identity with all simultaneously. The identity between the Self and *Brahman*, and between *Brahman* and all is an objective and eternal fact. If, on the other hand, "all-*Brahman*" identity realization is to be regarded as a consequence of "Self-*Brahman*" identity realization, the former realization cannot be eternal, for it will be a caused one — caused by the latter realization.[115] Things cannot be eternal and at the same time be caused. Moreover,

---

[113] *Śataślokī*, *śl*. 3.

[114] *KaUB*, II.1.11, tr. Swami Gambhirananda, vol. I, p. 187.

[115] *BṛUB*, I.4.9-10.

when the "Self-*Brahman*" identity is realized, there will remain no scope for further realization, since the individual self loses its identity then, and in its absence there will be none to have any further realization like "all is *Brahman*". Besides, in realizing its oneness with *Brahman* the Self realizes its oneness with all or becomes all, for *Brahman* is everything. Then there remains nothing different from the Self which it can realize. Then the idea of "all" will not be there, as everything becomes one (*ekam*) and undifferentiated (*abhinnam*) or everything becomes one with the Self (*ātmaiva sarvam bhavati*).[116]

Nevertheless, the statements differentiating "all-*Brahman*" identity realization from "Self-*Brahman*" identity realization are significant from the standpoint of an individual self. As an ignorant person thinks that the Self, *Brahman* and the universe are three different realities, it is essential to establish the identity of all the three. So, both the statements, "I am *Brahman*" and "all is *Brahman*", are necessary to remove all the notions of difference.

Brahmānubhava is negative in significance

Brahmānubhava is negative in significance. In it nothing positive or new is gained or attained. What is realized in the fourth state (*turīya*) is an already attained and self-evident reality. As *brahmānubhava* is pure knowledge, it never depends for its revelation on things other than itself, just as light does not require another for its illumination. "The Self is of the nature of what is always attained."[117] The attainment of a thing is meaningful and also possible only when the thing to be attained is different from the attainer. Whereas in realizing the Self one is not realizing anything that is not already realized. One realizes one's own true nature in realizing the Self. Contrary

---

[116] *BṛUB*, IV.4.6, I.4.7.

[117] *Upadeśasāhasrī*, XVII.6.

to this, if the Self were to be attained, as if it were an object of attainment, there should be some other thing to attain it. But as the Self is non-dual, there exists nothing besides it. Besides, as the very Self of the one who wants to attain it, *Brahman* is not something that is not already attained, but by nature It is eternally attained. The reality of the Self is not something that can either be accepted or rejected depending upon the choice of an individual. It is objectively real, and as the true nature of everyone, it can never be denied. *Brahman* never gets Itself transformed or modified or changed into something other than Itself; so the problem of It attaining Its original state or the unmodified condition does not arise. Its nature is absolutely immutable. As *Brahman* is the inner self of everyone and the essence of everything, It is present everywhere. As such It cannot be attained as a limited thing is attained.[118] As the inner self of all, It is always that which knows and attains, but never an object of knowledge and attainment. It is eternally a non-object (*aviṣaya*). Lastly, if *Brahman* is to be considered as an object of attainment, Its attainment cannot be eternal, for what is attained is transient and may be lost in course of time.

Although in itself the Self is always attained, an individual is not aware of that fact, for its attainment is veiled, as it were, by ignorance. "its non-attainment is but the ignorance of it."[119] Even before one realizes one's identity with *Brahman*, one is *Brahman*. Everyone is *Brahman*, in reality, whether one is aware of it or not. It is ignorance that makes one forget one's real nature or one's identity with *Brahman*. As such, there is no real and objective difference between the realized and unrealized. The only difference between them is the absence and the presence of ignorance.

---

[118] *SūB*, I.1.4.

[119] *BṛUB*, I.4.7.

> Ignorance is of the nature of illusion; it is a universal sleep in which are lying the individual selves destitute for the time being of the real knowledge of themselves (*svarūpa pratibodha*).[120]

Ignorance is not total absence of knowledge; it is wrong knowledge (*anyathā jñāna*).[121] It is non-realization of one's own true nature.[122] There is always the awareness of the Self, but the real nature of it is not known due to the presence of ignorance. Because of it, people are deluded and think of themselves as finite beings different from the highest reality. As they view it as something other than themselves and hence unattained, they aspire to attain it. On the other hand, if the Self is really different *Brahman*, then there will be no possibility of the Self attaining its identity with *Brahman*, for a thing cannot become some other thing.

Since the non-attainment of the Self or *Brahman* means ignorance about it, the removal of ignorance is tantamount to its attainment.[123] To realize the Self is to become free from ignorance which obscures its true nature, just as to know the objects enveloped by darkness is to dispel the darkness. Here it may be pointed out that besides the removal of darkness, objects should come into contact with a conscious principle, if they are to be known. But this is true only with regard to empirical experience which is dualistic. In the case of the Self mere removal of ignorance is sufficient, for in Self-realization there is no difference between the one who realizes and the thing realized. Just as cutting simply splits the wood into two and does not effect any further change in the wood, the

---

[120] *SūB*, I.4.3, tr. Thibaut, vol. I, p. 243.

[121] Ignorance is *anyathā jñāna*. This is quoted from a minor work of Śaṅkara. In his major works, he defines ignorance as *viparīta grahaṇa*.

[122] *TaiUB*, II.1.1.

[123] Ibid., I.1, Introduction; *BṛUB*, I.4.7.

knowledge acquired through the scriptures simply removes ignorance, and has no other purpose to fulfil.[124] Knowledge removes the idea of non-self (*parātmabhāva nivṛtti*) superimposed on the Self, and when this is done the Self becomes self-revealed without any further effort.

> To be one's own Self in its true nature on the removal of ignorance is what is meant by the attainment of the highest.[125]

> Realization of the Self means the removal of its identification with the non-self.[126]

> The attainment of the Self is simply the removal of the obstruction of ignorance by knowledge.[127]

Moreover, "the knowers of *Brahman*", says Śaṅkara, "accept that only as liberation which consists in the removal of ignorance, the source of bondage and suffering, but not anything which is a product".[128]

> The word "attainment" (*saṁkramaṇa*) is used figuratively with regard to this removal of delusion caused by ignorance, for in no other way it is possible to establish the attainment of all-pervading Self.[129]

Brahmānubhava is thus not to experience *Brahman* as an object, nor is it the experience of the Self by itself, but it is to shed the wrong knowledge that one is different from *Brahman*. This has been illustrated by Śaṅkara through some parables. One such parable is the story of a prince who was, from his childhood, brought up by a hunter.[130] As he was brought up

---

[124] *MāUB*, VII.

[125] *TaiUB*, I.1, Introduction.

[126] *BṛUB*, IV.4.20.

[127] Ibid., I.4.7.

[128] *MuUB*, III.2.6, tr. Swami Gambhirananda, vol. II, p. 166.

[129] *TaiUB*, II.8.5, tr. Swami Gambhirananda, vol. I, p. 382.

[130] *BṛUB*, II.1.20.

by a hunter, the prince thought of himself to be a hunter, but later when he was informed that he was not really a hunter, but a prince, he at once realized his real identity. Now, his realization that he is a prince makes no objective difference in his person, for in reality he is a prince even before he knew it. Here the significance lies in what he has given up, namely the wrong notion that he was a hunter. He has not gained anything new thereby. Similar is the case with one's realization of one's own Self. Śaṅkara has given some other examples to illustrate the same.[131]

Brahmānubhava is Liberation

From the standpoint of an individual self *brahmānubhava* is known as liberation (*mokṣa*). It is the highest end and the supreme consummation (*parā gati* and *parākāṣṭhā*) of human life. It is to be in one's own immutable nature.[132] "Liberation is the same as *Brahman*."[133]

The significance of liberation is also negative. It is just to become free from the ideas of bondage and suffering caused by ignorance. In reality, one is always free, immortal and free from all suffering, but one is not aware of this truth because of ignorance. One imagines oneself to be finite, limited and mortal, and consequently suffers, though in reality one is absolutely free from all these. As such there is no real bondage to the Self and it never suffers. The conditions that produce bondage are superimposed on the Self, and hence liberation

[131] Śaṅkara gives the example of a crystal. Because of non-discrimination, a pure crystal may appear to be red or green according to the objects placed nearby it. But as soon as one is able to discriminate between the nature of the crystal and the objects placed nearby it, the crystal is found out to be colourless (*SūB*, I.3.19). Another example is given in *ChāUB*, VIII.3.2.

[132] *BGB*, XVIII.55; *TaiUB*, I.11.4.

[133] *SūB*, I.1.4.

means the abolition of these superimposed conditions. "The cessation of ignorance alone is commonly called liberation."[134] On the other hand, if bondage were to be real, liberation would not be possible, for what is real or natural cannot be removed or avoided. Liberation is looked upon as a result only in a figurative sense, in so far as it is the cessation of all bondage and suffering, but not as implying the obtainment of something new.[135]

Brahmānubhava is not limited to turīya

Brahmānubhava is not limited to the fourth state only. "The statement 'That thou art' shows that the fact of *Brahman* being the Self of all is not limited by any particular state."[136] In Advaita, the entire human experience is distinguished into waking, dreaming, deep sleep and *turīya*. The purpose of such a distinction, according to Śaṅkara, is not to show that the Self, like the four feet of a cow, has parts or states corresponding to the four states of experience, but only to help understanding the experience. It is like dividing money into various units or parts.[137] One and the same experience, which is continuous and indivisible, is distinguished into different states on the basis of the nature of objects experienced. While the objects of experience during the waking state are gross, the impressions left by them are the objects of experience during dream state. Though there is no object-experience in deep sleep, it is the potential or causal state of waking and dream states. And what is distinct from these three states of experience is known as the fourth state. Thus from the point of view of one state, the other states are looked upon as different from itself, and so from the point of

---

[134] *BṛUB*, IV.4.6.

[135] *SūB*, IV.4.2.

[136] Ibid., II.1.14, tr. Thibaut, vol. I, p. 323.

[137] *MāUB*, I.2.

view of the three empirical states of experience, the fourth one is regarded as a different state of experience. But the same consciousness, which has no states, is uniformly present throughout these states. The only distinction that can be made between the three empirical states of experience and the fourth one is that while the Self is known indirectly and imperfectly during the former states of experience, it is known directly and perfectly in the fourth state. Our knowledge of the Self, during the three states of empirical experience, is conditioned by various factors of superimposition. But when these states of experience are merged, as it were, into the fourth state on the destruction of ignorance, the Self is known directly in its unconditioned and pure nature. In other words, while the three empirical states are instrumental in revealing the Self, the fourth state is the Self itself, that is, it is identical with the Self.[138] In it the Self is realized directly and immediately. Thus viewed from the three states of empirical experience, the state in which the Self is directly realized is called the fourth state, while from its own standpoint, the Self is ever revealed. Moreover, it is not possible to maintain the eternity of that which has states or which passes on from one state to the other. Besides, that which emerges in a particular state cannot be permanent. So, the Self is not attained only in the fourth state; it is always attained. But this fact is veiled, as it were, by ignorance during the three empirical states and that veil of ignorance is just removed in the fourth state.

The Significance of Brahmānubhava

The discussion in the earlier parts clearly shows that *brahmānubhava* is not merely an undifferentiated state of unconsciousness wherein all the distinctions and limitations are literally absent for a time. It is pure knowledge in which the empirical distinctions like the knower, the known and the knowledge are completely absent.

[138] *MāUB*, I.2.

They are absent in the sense that their oneness with the Self is realized. They are unreal in themselves, but are real as one with the Self. The absence of multiplicity in *brahmānubhava* is due to the realization of the identity of everything with the Self. In contrast to this, the absence of all dualistic experience in the states of yogic *samādhi*, deep sleep and swoon is not because of Self-realization, but due to the suppression of the mind, the source of such knowledge; and it may be due to deliberate dissolution of the mind as in the case of yogic *samādhi* or may be accidental as in the case of swoon and deep sleep. In these states, the dualistic experience is sought to be avoided, instead of realizing its illusory nature by way of realizing the oneness of everything, including oneself, with *Brahman*.

In *brahmānubhava*, nothing that is real is abolished or anything that is new is attained. It also does not bring forth any change anywhere. It is pure knowledge and knowledge is never observed to alter or modify the nature of things. It is observed to be effective in removing ignorance only. While empirical knowledge removes the ignorance concerning empirical things, revealed or scriptural knowledge annuls basic ignorance. And as ignorance is in no way related to *Brahman* in Itself, the removal of it has no significance whatsoever from the standpoint of *Brahman* in Itself. Nevertheless, its removal is of liberating significance to an individual self. It is for this purpose the whole of philosophical enquiry is undertaken. Thus before and after its realization, the Self remains the same. To give up ignorance is to remove a basic error from our understanding. A jaundiced person, though seeing, does not see things in their true colour. Similarly when our understanding is stained with ignorance, the Self, which is never unknown to anyone, is known wrongly. Therefore, to realize the Self is to attain perfect vision (*samyag darśana*) by freeing our understanding from ignorance.

According to Śaṅkara, attainment of the Self means the realization of it. "The attainment (*labdha*) means mere realization (*vijñānamātram*)."[139] "Attainment does not mean anything but direct realization of the Self."[140] "There is no real difference between realization and attainment."[141] As defined by Śaṅkara, realization (*vijñāna*) means the direct and immediate realization of the knowledge got through the scriptures.[142] "Realization (*anuvedana*) means the supreme consummation of knowledge (*paripāka*) or ripening of knowledge, in which the results of knowledge (like the destruction of ignorance) are fully realized."[143] It is like the sense of complete satisfaction which one gets after eating.[144] Before the Self is realized, one sees differences and so suffers from bondage, finiteness and mortality. "Illusion causes differences, the cause of all suffering."[145] With the realization of one's identity with all, the differences cease to exist and one attains the state of absolute fearlessness. Cessation of differences does not mean reducing the differences to oneness as all the pots made of clay can be reduced to dust, but to realize the unreality of all the differences in the light of their oneness with the Self. In other words, the differences are not literally destroyed nor is one unconscious of them as in swoon and in deep sleep. Though they are seen, they are not seen as having any existence of their own; they are seen as one with the Self or *Brahman*. Thus Śaṅkara says that one should see the universe as filled with *Brahman* (*brahmamayam*) or as not

---

139 *TaiUB*, II.8.5.

140 *KaUB*, I.3.11; *BṛUB*, I.4.7.

141 *MuUB*, I.1.5; *BṛUB*, I.4.7.

142 *BGB*, VI.8; *TaiUB*, II.4.1; *MuUB*, II.2.7.

143 *BṛUB*, IV.4.8, tr. Swami Madhavananda, pp. 732-33.

144 Ibid.

145 *Svātmanirūpaṇam*, *śl*. 6.

different from *Brahman*, by transforming the vision of differences and distinctions into one of perfect knowledge.[146] Reality remains the same before and after it is realized, but the experience of it differs. It may differ from man to man and it may even differ from time to time in the life of a particular person. It all depends on what we superimpose on Reality in understanding it. Depending upon our understanding of it, we may identify it with this or that or think it to be this or that. Now, an ignorant person or one whose understanding of Reality is imperfect sees in it differences and, therefore, it becomes a source of bondage and suffering for him. But a person of perfect knowledge or one who has realized *Brahman* as It is in Itself sees in It no differences. It is one with his Self. For such a person, It is perfect bliss and peace. A rope when seen as a snake becomes the source of fear, while in itself the rope is harmless.

---

[146] *Aparkoṣānubhūti*, *śl*. 116.

3

Behaviour of a Brahmajñānī

BRAHMĀNUBHAVA is possible while one is alive and, according to Śaṅkara, all can attain it. "A *yogī* (in the Advaitic sense) attains *brahmanirvāṇa*, the bliss of being *Brahman* or liberation, by being *Brahman* here itself, that is, while he is alive."[1] Commenting on the Upaniṣadic statement, "by being *Brahman* one attains *Brahman*", Śaṅkara says that *brahmānubhava* is possible while one is alive and there is no need to wait until death for its attainment, as the results of knowledge, like the destruction of ignorance, are obtained immediately unlike the fruits of action.[2] It is impossible for ignorance to persist when knowledge arises, just as darkness cannot exist in the presence of light. Therefore, as soon as the perfect knowledge of the Self arises ignorance about it disappears and the Self in its real nature becomes revealed. This can happen anytime in the life of an individual, and so he continues to live in the world even after realizing *Brahman*. As he lives, he may mix freely with the people around him and may also participate actively in the affairs of the world. In other words, he behaves, but his behaviour, like that of an ignorant person, is not based on the experience of differences; it is based on and also reflects the realization of absolute oneness of everything, that is, *Brahman*. The only difference that can be discerned between the behaviour of such a person and that of an ignorant person is that the behaviour of the former is entirely free from basic

---

[1] *BGB*, V.24.

[2] *BṛUB*, IV.4.6; *MuUB*, III.2.9.

ignorance and its effects. His whole outlook gets transformed in the light of his realization and, accordingly, his attitude and behaviour will be based on his realization of oneness.

Now, the behaviour of a *brahmajñānī* (one who has realized *Brahman*) may help us in understanding the nature and significance of *brahmānubhava* in a clear and lucid manner. With this purpose in view, the behaviour of a *brahmajñānī* as described by Śaṅkara will now be presented. Before doing so we have to consider whether any behaviour is possible in one who has realized *Brahman* which is non-dual, and if so, how can it be explained in terms of non-dualistic experience? In what manner does one's realization of *Brahman* influence one's behaviour or how is it reflected in one's attitudes and behaviour? Whether it is possible to understand the nature of *brahmānubhava* in terms of the behaviour of a *brahmajñānī*.

Brahmajñānī and his behaviour

One may find it difficult to understand the possibility of behaviour on the part of one who has realized *Brahman* which is non-dual. A non-dualistic experience, one may point out, does not leave any scope for behaviour, because in it the sense of agent, the objects to be acted upon and the instruments with which to act are completely absent. Whereas, no behaviour is possible without them. They form the basis of all behaviour. Moreover, a *brahmajñānī* will have no desires, for in attaining *Brahman* he has attained everything, as *Brahman* is everything or there is nothing besides It. But the desire to achieve something which is not already attained is the motive for action. How is it then possible to conceive any behaviour in one who is not an agent, and has no desires? This problem arises, according to Śaṅkara, only when *brahmānubhava* is understood literally and the absence of all differences and distinctions is taken to be literally true. In other words, the problem is faced by one who thinks that in *brahmānubhava* everything would be reduced into an undifferentiated mass. This is not only absurd, but also impossible. According to Śaṅkara, the multiplicity of millions of living beings and the elemental substances will not be reduced into an undifferentiated mass in *brahmānubhava*, just as the solidity of butter melts away when it is heated.[3] This, he says, is impossible; otherwise it could have been accomplished by the first liberated person, so that there would have been no world of differences afterwards.[4]

As it was pointed out earlier, *brahmānubhava* is essentially an inward experience like that of pleasure and pain. It is pure knowledge or perfect realization (*vijñāna*) and knowledge cannot bring about any change in the nature of things; it can only remove ignorance about them. Such that the realization of non-duality does not mean the actual disappearance of the world of differences. It only means the removal of ignorance, because of which one sees differences in an undifferentiated reality. According to Śaṅkara, real liberation does not consist either in giving up of the external things, like the staff and water-bowl, or in becoming free from the body. It consists in the destruction of ignorance.[5] When ignorance is destroyed, all the differences and the experience based on them cease to be, just as when the eye disease known as *timira* is cured one does not see more than one moon. This does not mean the absence of experience as such, as in deep sleep or in swoon, but only indicates the absence of experience based on differences. Like all others, a *brahmajñānī* experiences things, but unlike them he does not see them as different from himself. In realizing his identity with *Brahman*, he also realizes his identity with all and therefore, nothing exists for him which is not one with the Self.

---

[3] *SūB*, III.2.21.

[4] Ibid.

[5] *Vivekacūḍāmaṇī*, *śl.* 558.

> Though perceiving, one who does not perceive the world of differences, during waking state, as in deep sleep, owing to the realization of non-duality, and similarly who remains actionless while acting is a man of Self-realization.[6]

Brahmānubhava does not in any way disturb the integrity of human personality. It also does not destroy the body, mind and the senses, nor their capacity to perceive and think. They remain normal and function as before, but they are not looked upon as something different from the Self when the latter is realized.[7] The sense organs of a *brahmajñānī* continue to perceive their respective objects, but the attachment (*rāga*) for them is completely absent in him, as he is free from egoism or "I"-sense which has been destroyed by the knowledge of the Self. Such detached perceptual knowledge is incapable of producing in the mind either good or bad impressions that bind an individual.[8] A diseased person, whose senses have lost their capacity to perceive, and also an ignorant fool who, by the practice of extreme austerity, is able to abstain from the enjoyment of the sense-objects, may also appear to be free from the senses. However, as their attachment for the sense-objects is not extinguished, as in the case of a *brahmajñānī*, there is no real difference between them and those who indulge in sense-enjoyment.[9] Likewise, the mind of a *brahmajñānī* does not cease to exist, nor does it stop functioning, but its oneness with the Self is realized. The existence of the mind is not known apart from its activity, which is possible when there is duality, and when that duality is realized to be illusory, the mind also ceases to exist.

---

[6] *Upadeśasāhasrī*, X.13.

[7] *BṛUB*, IV.3.23; *AiUB*, II.1, Introduction.

[8] *BGB*, II.5 and 9, IV.37.

[9] Ibid., II.59.

The person who has realized the Self acts, though it is no action in reality. According to Śaṅkara, inaction is not real freedom from action, for both action and inaction are based on the idea of agency caused by the superimposition of the activity of the mind and the senses on the Self.[10] Thus, in the one who acts seeking the enjoyment of the fruits of action, as well as in the other who abstains from action seeking to avoid the consequences of action, the sense of agency is present. Both think of themselves as agents whether they seek to enjoy or avoid the fruits of action. Thus as based on the idea of agency, which is the creation of ignorance, both action and inaction are equally binding. Whereas, real freedom consists in becoming free from both action and inaction, and it is attained when one realizes that one is not an agent. Such a man may act like others, but since the sense of agency is completely absent in him, his action is to be regarded as no action.[11] According to Śaṅkara, the one who has realized the non-agency of the Self performs no action in reality, not even the act of begging food for the sustenance of the body. "To one who has realized that all is *Brahman* there is no action."[12] But he appears to be an agent of his actions, like begging food, only from the standpoint of empirical experience wherein action implies agent. Nevertheless, from the standpoint of his own experience, he is no agent.

Brahmānubhava and the behaviour of Brahmajñānī

According to Śaṅkara, the knowledge of the Self cannot literally destroy actions in the way fire reduces fuel into ash.[13] It

---

[10] *BGB*, IV.18.

[11] Ibid., IV.22, 24.

[12] Ibid., IV.24.

[13] Ibid., IV.37.

only renders them unproductive (*nirbīja*), so that they become incapable of producing impressions, either good or evil, which may bind the Self. The liberated person, who is absolutely free from the sense of ego, the cause of attachment to actions and their results, remains like a spectator unconcerned with them. He neither directs his senses towards their objects nor withdraws them from their objects.[14] He remains in his own nature of pure bliss. Thus the observation of the external behaviour of a *brahmajñānī* may not be helpful in understanding his inward experience truly. As one's inward experience of pain, pleasure, anger, etc. cannot be known directly by others, but is to be known inferentially on the basis of one's outward behaviour, so also, the nature of *brahmānubhava*, which is also purely inward, is to be inferred from the external behaviour of one who has attained it.[15] Such an inferential understanding may not prove to be valid, as there is no necessary or causal relationship between behaviour and *brahmānubhava*. *Brahmānubhava* is uncaused, and in its turn it does not cause anything.

A further difficulty in understanding the behaviour of a liberated person is the indistinct (*avyakta*) and paradoxical nature of his behaviour.[16] As he transcends the limitations of the empirical world, his behaviour is not bound by the norms and regulations that govern the behaviour of an ignorant person. Therefore, the pattern of his behaviour, like that of a dull person (*jaḍa*) or of a child is highly paradoxical and unpredictable. He may live amidst people behaving like an ordinary person or may withdraw himself totally into calm seclusion. He may live in a palace like a prince or like a beggar in a hut. He may associate himself with children, youth or old

[14] *Vivekacūḍāmaṇī*, *śl.* 552.

[15] *BGB*, XIV.22; *Vivekacūḍāmaṇī*, *śl.* 475.

[16] *BṛUB*, III.5.1; *GKB*, IV.95.

people and may mix freely with people belonging to various cults and paths. He may be seen in unperturbed contemplation or arguing things. He may be seen behaving like a fool among fools, like a wise man among wise men, like a sufferer among sufferers and so on. He has no attachment for good nor does he hate evil.[17] Thus he may act in thousand ways, but he is not bound thereby. He is a *sthitaprajña*, the one who is firm in his realization that he is not different from *Brahman*. He does not try to distinguish himself from others by putting on certain signs, just as the monks do by putting on ochre robes. He also does not announce to the world that he is wise or has realized *Brahman*, but behaves with utmost humility.[18] This is due to the complete absence of egoism which makes one boast.

However, the behaviour of a *brahmajñānī* can be distinguished from that of others, in so far as it is characterized by the absence of ignorance and its effects. While an ignorant person's behaviour is based on the experience of differences, the behaviour of a *brahmajñānī* is based on the realization of oneness. In other words, an ignorant person considers others to be different from himself and shapes his relations with them accordingly, whereas a *brahmajñānī* does not see others as different from himself and therefore, his relations with others will be in terms of oneness. Therefore, in the case of a *brahmajñānī*, certain concepts with which human behaviour is connected take on a new meaning. For instance, the concept of equality (*samatā*) means for him supreme equality (*paramam sāmyam*) consisting in the realization of oneness and non-duality, whereas the equality conceivable within the realm of duality is inferior to it.[19]

---

[17] *BGB*, II.55-57, XII.14-19; *Vivekacūḍāmaṇī*, *śls*. 542-45.

[18] *GKB*, II.36.

[19] *MuUB*, III.1.3.

Another characteristic behaviour of a *brahmajñānī* is fearlessness. A *brahmajñānī* is absolutely free from fear. Śaṅkara says:

> Fear is caused by a second entity or by things conceived to exist as different from the Self. And when this notion of a second entity is eliminated by the realization of oneness, there will be no source of fear.[20]

Thus, for those who think that God (*Īśvara*) and his creations are different from themselves, there is no freedom from fear, for they become the sources of their fear.[21] Whereas, for a *brahmajñānī* fear is impossible, for he does not see anything as different from himself. Further, as an ignorant person thinks that he is transient and destructible, anything that may cause his destruction becomes a source of fear for him. Whereas, for him who has realized himself to be the eternal and indestructible Self, there is nothing to be afraid of.[22] According to Śaṅkara, the Self is the source of both fear and fearlessness. It becomes the source of fear for him who, out of ignorance, imagines himself to be finite and impermanent. But as the Self is fearlessness, one who has realized it becomes fearless. Even death loses its dreadful significance for him, because of his realization that he is eternally unembodied. His body may fall off, but it does not mean anything to him, as he has no attachment to it.

The most terrible calamity in life is grief (*śoka*), the mental anguish (*manastāpa*) which a man experiences when the supreme end of his life remains unaccomplished.[23] This, a person can overcome by realizing *Brahman* which is the supreme end of life (*parama puruṣārtha*), and as *brahmajñānī* has

---

[20] *BṛUB*, I.4.2; see also *TaiUB*, II.7.1.

[21] *TaiUB*, II.8.5.

[22] *BṛUB*, I.4.2.

[23] *ChāUB*, VII.1.3.

realized It, he is free from it. *Brahmajñānī* has no desires. Desire means a quest for agreeable and pleasure-giving objects of experience, and it is felt when such objects come within the range of our senses, or when they are heard of, or remembered.[24] Desires are based on the experience of differences and impel a man to action, so that a thing that is not already attained is attained. But in realizing the Self all desires are fulfilled, because in its attainment, man attains everything, for it is everything. Then there remains nothing to be attained. Śaṅkara says that by being *Brahman*, which is present everywhere as the self or essence of everything, one enjoys everything simultaneously without depending upon the instruments of enjoyment like the senses and the mind.[25] Thus desirelessness, in the case of a *brahmajñānī,* is not due to the suppression of desires, but because of his realization of *Brahman*, after realizing which there remains nothing to be desired. Such a man of wisdom remains steadfast and unaffected though desires of all sorts enter into him, just as a ocean remains undisturbed despite rivers flowing into it from all sides.[26]

The knower of *Brahman* transcends all the polarities of empirical life, such as good and evil, shame and honour, pain and pleasure, sorrow and happiness. It should be noted in this connection that moral perfection is not the supreme end of life, according to Śaṅkara, nor does he deny its importance in human life and conduct. As we shall see, it is essential for the attainment of *brahmānubhava*. A liberated person, in whom the sense of agency is absent, is free from both righteousness and unrighteousness. "For one who seeks liberation, even righteousness (*dharma*) is a sin, for it causes bondage."[27] They

---

[24] *BGB*, V.23.

[25] *TaiUB*, II.1.1.

[26] *BGB*, II.70.

[27] Ibid., IV.21.

both belong to the sphere of ignorance and are of value to an ordinary man of ignorance. They have nothing to do with a man of Self-realization. This does not, however, mean that a man of Self-realization is morally reckless or does anything evil. The realization of the identity of "all" with the Self prevents one from doing any evil.[28] He who sees the same Self in all realizes that whatever is pleasant to himself is pleasant to all the beings, and whatever is painful to himself is painful to all the beings. Thus realizing he becomes non-injurious (*ahiṁsaka*) and abstains from doing that which is repulsive to others.[29]

Although the supreme end of his life is accomplished, a *brahmajñānī* works for the welfare of others.[30] He may not have anything to achieve for himself, yet he works, so that an example is set before the world in preventing the wrong notion that inaction is freedom from action. Seeing everything as identical with the Self, he wanders the whole world teaching for the welfare of others the real nature of the Self.[31]

In realizing the Self one attains immortality (*amṛtattva*), the blessed state of being in one's own true nature.[32] Since it is to be in one's own true nature, it is not a produced state; but as this realization is obstructed by the identification of the Self with the body, through giving up that false identity, one attains immortality.[33] It is to shed the wrong notion that one is mortal with the strength that comes through the knowledge of the Self. Śaṅkara says that through knowledge of the Self,

---

[28] *BṛUB*, III.5.1; *SūB*, II.3.48; *AiUB*, Introduction.

[29] *BGB*, VI.32.

[30] Ibid., III.24-25.

[31] *TaiUB*, III.10.5-6.

[32] *KaUB*, II.1.2.

[33] *KeUB*, II.4; *BṛUB*, IV.4.17.

one gets strength superior to and uncomparable with what is gained through other means like medicine and Yoga; and through such strength alone it is possible to conquer the idea of death.[34] *Brahmānubhava* is pure bliss. The bliss that is *brahmānubhava* is not something that can be enjoyed. It is uncaused and eternal. As the essential nature of the Self, it does not involve the duality of the enjoyer and the enjoyed. "It is free from the subject–object relationship and is natural, eternal and indivisible."[35] It is beyond the reach of the senses and the mind. On the contrary, the happiness that is enjoyed is momentary and is mixed with pain. It is only an inkling of the pure bliss.

Because of its highly paradoxical nature and the lack of attachment in it to actions and their results, the behaviour of a *brahmajñānī* is likened to that of a child and to that of a mad man. This comparison should not be wrongly taken to mean that the senses and other faculties of a liberated person are undeveloped or incapacitated. The purpose of such a comparison is to point out how *brahmānubhava* is similar to the unique inward state of a child which is free from passions and attachment to the sense-objects.[36] The child has no attachment to all that it does, and there is never any attempt on its part to display itself. Likewise, the person who has realized the Self is free from passions and has no attachment to all that he does. In other words, the sense of "I" or "mine" is totally absent in a *brahmajñānī*. He cannot hate or covet anything. Since he has come to know by immediate experience what is the ground and essence of everything, he will desire to know nothing further. For such a person his body is like what a cast-off slough is for a snake.[37]

---

[34] *BṛUB*, III.5.1; *KeUB*, II.4.

[35] *TaiUB*, II.9.1.

[36] *SūB*, III.4.50.

[37] *BṛUB*, IV.4.7.

All that is said about the behaviour of a *brahmajñānī* does not really belong to him, but it is the only possible way of talking about him and his behaviour in terms of our understanding. Therefore, all that is said about him and his behaviour is said in the manner of praise (*stuti*), but not to establish that it really belongs to him.[38]

---

[38] *BṛUB*, III.5.1.

4

The Way to Brahmānubhava

As *Brahman* is self-evident, no evidence or proof is required for Its existence. So, Vedānta may be considered as a means of realizing *Brahman* directly or as a preparation to achieve *brahmānubhava*. For this reason, Śaṅkara calls it a doctrine of liberation (*mokṣa śāstra*) and its ultimate purpose, according to him, is to help and guide an individual to experience *Brahman* directly. It is a means to attain immortality (*amr̥tattvasādhanā*), the realization of one's own real nature, and "*brahmajñāna* is for those who are desirous of attaining immortality (*amr̥tattva kāmasya*)".[1] Although metaphysical speculation finds its place in the mystical doctrine of Śaṅkara, its importance is recognized to the extent it is helpful in attaining *brahmānubhava*.

How to attain such immortalizing experience, the experience that emancipates man immediately and bestows on him absolute bliss and peace is a practical problem which concerns everyone who seeks it. Before discussing the nature and scope of the various possible means of attaining *brahmānubhava*, one or two important questions should be settled. We have to consider, whether *brahmānubhava* is a caused experience, that is, attained as a result of man's endeavour, and if so can that caused experience be absolute and ultimate, and worth our striving?

---

[1] *SūB*, I.1.4.

Bhramānubhava is uncaused

According to Śaṅkara, *brahmānubhava* is eternal and uncaused. It cannot be produced either through human or divine effort. It is not something that can be effected (*asādhya*) and therefore any effort to accomplish it is meaningless. The Self's identity with *Brahman* is natural and self-accomplished (*svayam prasiddha*), but not something that is to be achieved through effort. *Brahmānubhava* is of the nature of Self and the Self is never unattained, nor can there be any means to attain it. As *brahmānubhava* is pure consciousness, it is essential for the attainment of anything, and therefore, the very attempt to attain it indicates its attainment. In other words, all the means of attainment are based on *brahmānubhava* (pure consciousness), and therefore they cannot attain that which they presuppose. On the contrary, to suppose that *brahmānubhava* can be attained through some effort is to reduce it to an effect; and any effect is transitory, because whatever is caused will also have an end.

As *brahmānubhava* is of the nature of *Brahman,* it is co-eternal with It. So, its attainment in time cannot be thought of. On the contrary, empirical experience is caused and hence it is transient. It is always of objects, which may be either external objects or internal ideas and feelings, and so will have a beginning and an end along with the objects experienced. Whereas the underlying principle of consciousness, on which the whole of empirical experience is based, *brahmānubhava* is always present and unchanging. Its absence can never be imagined. This absolute consciousness which is revealed indirectly along with the objects it reveals (*pratibhoda vidita*), during empirical experience, is in itself self-luminous and self-evident. As pure experience, it does not depend for its revelation on things other than itself. "Self-knowledge is independent of any other knowledge (*vijñānapekṣam*), because it is of the nature of knowledge (*vijñāna svarūpatvāt*)."[2]

As undifferentiated experience, *brahmānubhava* does not involve the distinction of one who experiences and the object experienced. So it is not possible to say that *brahmānubhava* is the experience of someone or of some object. Such that to talk of its attainment would be meaningless. The attainment of *brahmānubhava* would have been possible if *Brahman* were to be something different from the Self. But in reality, *Brahman* is not different from the Self. Thus, according to Śaṅkara:

> The attainment of the Self cannot be, as in the case of things other than itself, the obtainment of something that is not already obtained, for here there is no difference between the person attaining and the thing attained.[3]

On the other hand:

> If the Self has to attain something other than itself, it becomes the attainer and the non-self the object of attainment.[4]

Brahman cannot be experienced, because It is experience itself. It is always that which experiences and never an object of experience. Besides, it is not possible to think of another experiencing principle to which It can become an object of experience. Moreover, all the means and the ends which they are capable of achieving, being based on the experience of differences, fall within the sphere of ignorance.[5] The means are of use only when there are things different from the Self, and when one has the desire to attain them. Therefore, as

---

[2] *Sri Sankara's Teachings in His Own Words*, Swami Atmananda, Bombay: Bharatiya Vidya Bhavan, p. 152. See also *GKB*, III.33, IV.81; *Upadeśasāhasrī*, part I (prose), pp. 92, 97.

[3] *BṛUB*, I.4.7, tr. Swami Madhavananda, p. 139.

[4] Ibid.

[5] Ibid., I.3.28, I.4.1; *PrUB*, VI.2.

long as one is attached to means desiring to obtain through them, something different from the Self, one cannot attain *brahmānubhava*. Thus, according to Śaṅkara, there can be no means to attain *brahmānubhava* and it would be meaningless to talk of attaining *brahmānubhava* through some means. On the contrary, if means are searched for its attainment, "it would be like swimming on land under the impression that it is water or like searching in the space for the footprints of birds".[6]

Although by its nature *brahmānubhava* is always attained (*svayamlabdha svabhāva*), it seems to be unattained from the standpoint of ignorance.

> Though quite self-evident and easily knowable, quite near and forming the very Self (of everyone), *Brahman* appears — to the unenlightened, to those whose reason is carried away by the differentiated phenomena of names and forms created by ignorance — as unknown, difficult to be known, very remote, as though it were a separate thing.[7]

For example, though one is in fact perceiving a pearl-shell, one does not realize that fact and instead perceives it as silver, because of illusion. Similarly, because of the presence of ignorance, one does not realize the fact that the Self's identity with *Brahman* is natural and does not depend on man's endeavour. According to Śaṅkara, many people are not even aware of the fact that they are more than their bodies and this also provides a reason or suggests why the Self's identity with *Brahman* is not realized by many though it is natural and eternal.

Ignorance, which is comparable to a veil, conceals, as it were, the true nature of the Self. Because of it, one may apprehend reality as what it is not, or may fail to perceive the true nature of it. It may cause doubt (*saṁśaya*) about the

---

[6] *BṛUB*, IV.4.22, tr. Swami Madhavananda, p. 759.

[7] *BGB*, XVIII.50, tr. A. Mahadeva Sastri, p. 487.

existence of trans-empirical things like the Self and also about its oneness with *Brahman*.[8] Because of it, man wrongly identifies the Self with the non-self and also differentiates the Self from *Brahman*. Therefore, an ignorant person thinks that he is different from *Brahman*, and as he thinks so *brahmānubhava* means for him the experience of *Brahman*. So, he thinks that some effort is required for its attainment. But ignorance is not in any way related to the Self. It is neither an attribute of the Self, nor does it belong to its nature.[9] If at all there is any relationship between the Self and ignorance, it is based on non-discrimination and wrong knowledge. While there is no relationship between them in reality, they appear to be related for an ignorant person. Knowledge and ignorance, like light and darkness, are opposed to each other. According to Śaṅkara, the very possibility of realizing the pure Self or the Self free from ignorance indicates that the two are not really related.[10] If, on the contrary, ignorance were to form part and parcel of the Self, realization of the pure Self would become an impossibility. Besides, as what is known by the Self as an object, ignorance is essentially different from the Self and does not belong to it, for what is known is naturally different from that which knows it.[11] Therefore, ignorance does not really veil the Self; it only makes it appear as some other thing. If, on the other hand, ignorance could really veil the Self, then that very fact would remain unknown, for then the principle which knows would be completely enveloped. Whereas the fact that people are aware of its presence and strive to get rid of it indicates that the Self is not really concealed by ignorance. The existence of clouds is revealed by the sun, although they

[8] *BGB*, XIII.2; *BṛUB*, III.3.1.

[9] *BṛUB*, IV.3.20; *BGB*, XIII.2; *Upadeśasāhasrī*, XVI.37.

[10] Ibid.; *BGB*, XIII.2.

[11] *BṛUB*, IV.4.6; *TaiUB*, II.8.5; *BGB*, XIII.2.

seem to hide it. If, on the other hand, clouds could completely block the sun, then that very fact and also the presence of clouds would not be known. Likewise, the existence of ignorance is made known to us by the Self.[12]

No means to attain Brahmānubhava

From all this it is clear that no effort is required for the attainment of *brahmānubhava*, which is natural, and by its nature ever attained. Nevertheless, some effort is necessary to destroy ignorance which obstructs the fact of its attainment. As the non-realization of the Self is only due to the presence of ignorance, the only thing that should be done to realize it is to give up that ignorance. "The attainment of the highest means merely the removal of ignorance and nothing more."[13] In utter darkness objects are not perceived even though they are in direct contact with the senses and what is required for their revelation is the removal of darkness. In the example of rope–snake illusion, when the illusion of snake is got rid of, the rope becomes revealed without any further effort. In like manner, to realize the Self, no effort is required besides the removal of ignorance, and the Self is realized simultaneously with the removal of ignorance.[14] Since the wrong knowledge of the Self, that is, the knowledge of the Self in relation to the non-self, obstructs the perfect knowledge of the Self, just as the perception of silver in the pearl-shell obstructs the perception of the pearl-shell, when the obstruction of wrong knowledge is removed, the real nature of the Self becomes self-revealed. Thus, according to Śaṅkara, except the removal of the superimposition of the non-self on the Self, no effort, whether bodily or mental, is necessary for the realization of

[12] *Śataślokī*, *śl*. 32.

[13] *MāUB*, I.1.5; see also *BṛUB*, I.4.7.

[14] *MāUB*, VIII.

the Self.[15] He wonders whether there can be any regulations for the realization of one's own Self.[16]

As *brahmānubhava* is simultaneous with the removal of ignorance, some may consider it to be the result of the removal of ignorance. It is not so, because the Self is never unattained in reality. So, with the removal of ignorance only the wrong notion that the Self is something not already attained is given up, and the Self which is always attained becomes self-revealed, as it were. It is the seeming non-realization of the Self before the removal of ignorance, and its realization immediately after the removal of ignorance that make one think that the Self is realized as a result of the removal of ignorance.[17] Although, at various places, Śaṅkara says that *brahmānubhava* is attained by those means that remove ignorance, according to him, such statements are only figurative, but not literally true.

Means to remove ignorance

Now, we shall consider the various possible means of removing ignorance. They are: action (*karma*), devotion (*bhakti*), meditation (*dhyāna* or *upāsanā*), grace of the teacher (*guru prasāda*) and the grace of the Lord (*Īśvara anugraha*), prayer and renunciation. After a careful and thorough consideration of these means, Śaṅkara comes to the conclusion that the removal of ignorance cannot be effected by any one of these means. According to him, knowledge alone is effective in destroying ignorance.

Action

Human action, in any of its form, is not effective in destroying ignorance. Action proves useful in attaining (*āpti*) an object or

---

[15] *BṛUB*, I.4.7; *BGB*, XVIII.50.

[16] *svavedane ka niyamādyavasthā* — *Vivekacūḍāmaṇi*, *śl*. 529.

[17] *TaiUB*, II.1.1; *Ātmabodha*, *śl*. 44; *BṛUB*, I.4.7.

in producing (*utpatti*) a thing out of something, or in reaching a place or in bringing about a change or modification (*vikāra*) in a thing or in purifying (*saṁskāra*) a thing; and people resort to action when they want to achieve any one of these.[18] But the Self is not something that can be produced, attained, reached, modified or purified. By its nature, the Self is self-existent and always attained, immutable and ever pure. Action is based on the idea of agency and is due to non-discrimination. It operates within the realm of differences and is moved by desires. Action presupposes an agent, but the Self is not an agent. It only appears to be so when the activity belonging to the body, mind and the senses is superimposed on it. Action is based on desire, and desire is based on the experience of differences, for only when one sees something different from the Self, one gets the desire to attain it. Thus there should be some imperfection or something unattained, so that one is impelled to act either to achieve perfection or to attain that which is not attained. This is the case with all actions, whether selfish or altruistic.[19]

Thus actions and their results are confined to the empirical realm of differences, the sphere of ignorance. But to realize *Brahman* is to transcend the realm of differences, and action, which proves effective within the realm of differences, cannot make one transcend it and realize the undifferentiated reality. Moreover, the result of every action is temporary, and if *brahmānubhava* is to be considered as a result of some action, then it will also be temporary. Further, there is no contradiction (*virodha*) between ignorance and action. They are not opposed to each other in their natures. It is only when there is mutual opposition between them that ignorance can

---

[18] *TaiUB*, I.11.4; *MuUB*, I.2.12; *BṛUB*, III.3.1, Introduction.

[19] *SūB*, II.2.37.

be removed by action. But as action is based on ignorance, it cannot remove ignorance, just as darkness cannot remove darkness.[20] Actions cause bondage; and what causes bondage cannot destroy it. Therefore, "not even in a dream the realization of the identity of the Self with *Brahman* can be accomplished through action".[21] Thus action of any sort is useless for one who seeks *brahmānubhava*. Following the path of action by one whose goal is *brahmānubhava*, the highest and all-comprehensive end of life, would be like digging a well when there is a flood of water close by.[22] Who will be interested in acquiring a piece of land when a whole kingdom is at hand? The highest and all-comprehensive end of life cannot be achieved by those means which are meant for achieving limited goals.

Devotion

Devotion and meditation are also not effective in destroying ignorance. Śaṅkara defines them in similar terms, since both of them are functions of the mind. According to him, "devotion (*bhakti*) is that which never seeks any object other than the Lord, and by virtue of which no object other than Him is experienced".[23] Because of it one comes to realize that all that one sees, hears and touches is nothing but the Lord.[24] Like the rivers which naturally flow towards the sea, like the iron filings which are spontaneously attracted by a magnet and like a creeper which twines around a tree for itself, devotion is a state of mind in which it is attracted by the Lord and remains always fixed on Him.[25] In the *Bhagavad-Gītā*, four types of devotees are

---

[20] *BGB*, XVIII.66; *Bṛ̥UB*, III.3.1, Introduction.

[21] Introduction to *MuUB*.

[22] *BGB*, XVIII.66.

[23] Ibid., XI.54, tr. Mahadeva Sastri, p. 301.

[24] Ibid., XIII.18.

[25] *Śivānandalaharī*, *śl.* 61.

enumerated. "The distressed (*ārtta*), the seeker of knowledge (*jijñāsu*), the man desiring wealth (*arthārthī*) and the wise (*jñānī*) are the four kinds of good men that worship Me."[26] Commenting thereon, Śaṅkara explains that the distressed is one who is overpowered by grief caused by any particular fearful situation in life; the second type of devotee is one who seeks to know the real nature of the Lord; one who is desirous of acquiring wealth is the third type of devotee and the person who is devoted to the knowledge of the Self is the fourth type. Although all of them are devoted to God, the devotion of the first three types of devotees, as it is impelled by desires to attain something other than the Self or the highest truth, is inferior to that of the fourth type of devotee, who seeks nothing but Self-realization. In the presence of desires, man fails to discriminate between the Self and the non-self, and also imagines differences in a reality which is devoid of them. Thus except the seeker of truth or Self-realization, all others are deluded and fail to realize that Reality is undifferentiated and that it is not different from their own Self.[27]

In its ordinary sense, devotion presupposes the duality of one who is devoted and the object of devotion. Without being based on such duality, devotion is not possible. Therefore, the object of such devotion is not *Brahman* in Itself, but as It is conditioned by factors that are superimposed on It by a devotee. As such the devotion to *Īśvara* or conditioned *Brahman* is based on ignorance and hence it cannot save one from ignorance. Moreover, the fruits of such devotion are impermanent and imperfect, whereas *brahmānubhava* is absolute, unconditioned and eternal. Therefore, *brahmānubhava* cannot be attained through ordinary devotion.

---

[26] *Bhagavad-Gītā*, VII.16.

[27] *BGB*, VII.20 and 23-24.

The devotion of a *jñānī* or one who seeks Self-realization is supreme and is not different from the higher knowledge (*parā vidyā*) of Vedānta. *Parā bhakti*, the devotion of a *jñānī*, is the same as *jñāna-niṣṭhā* or *parā vidyā*, devotion to higher knowledge.[28] Through this, the Lord is known as He is in Himself (*tattvataḥ*), while through the other three types of devotion, Lord is known according to a devotee's nature and limitations, that is, as understood by a devotee. *Parā bhakti* is an inquiry into one's own real nature (*svarupānusandhāna*) and culminates in the realization that one is not different from the object of devotion.[29] Such a devotion is not motivated or impelled by any of the desires of the devotee. It is based on, or an expression of pure love (*prīti* or *snehapūrvaka*) for the Lord. Thus, among all devotees, a man of higher devotion is most dear to the Lord; he is the greatest of all men (*mahātmā*), as he is not different from the Lord.[30]

Meditation

According to Śaṅkara, meditation (*upāsanā*) is fixing the mind or thought uninterruptedly, like the flow of oil, on an object, either prescribed by the scriptures or chosen by the individual. Such an object serves as a prop (*ālambana*) to the mind in achieving concentration by not allowing other ideas to distract the mind.[31] It is also of two types: lower and higher. The object of the lower type of meditation is conditioned *Brahman*. In it a particular form or an attribute, which the supreme reality is imagined to possess, is meditated upon, and it is meant for those who look upon *Brahman* as something different from themselves. It is useful to those who are not intellectually keen

[28] *BGB*, XVIII.55.

[29] *Vivekacūḍāmaṇi*, *śl.* 31; see also *BGB*, VII.17-18.

[30] *BGB*, VII.19.

[31] Ibid., XII.3; *BṛUB*, I.3.9; *TaiUB*, I.3.4.

enough to meditate upon *Brahman* in Itself, which is infinite and devoid of attributes, and yet are desirous of attaining the supreme end of life. Śaṅkara says:

> For those who are full of faith and are of right conduct, but are unable to fix their minds on the formless *Brahman*, meditation of the formless *Brahman* as having a form should be encouraged.[32]

Though the object of such meditation is ultimately unreal, in so far as it serves the practical purpose of an individual by becoming a prop to his mind, its value is to be recognized. It helps an individual in realizing *Brahman* in Itself ultimately, just as an image of Viṣṇu helps a devotee in realizing Viṣṇu.

According to Śaṅkara, devotion and meditation do not essentially differ from action, as all of them are capable of producing results.[33] While action is more physical and outward, meditation and devotion are mental and inward. In all these one is motivated to attain something which is other than one's own Self. "The fruit of meditation like that of action is only enjoyment (*bhoga*), but not the attainment of Self-realization."[34] The results of meditation vary depending upon the objects meditated upon. They may be prosperity, gradual liberation, or success in an undertaking. But nothing absolute and ultimate can be achieved by meditation. According to Śaṅkara, meditation on conditioned *Brahman* can only lead one to relative liberation, but not to real liberation.[35] The distinction between one who meditates and the object of meditation, which is essential to meditation, stays even after the object of meditation is attained. Therefore, meditation, which is not

---

[32] *GKB*, IV.42-43.

[33] *SūB*, IV.1.6, III.3.42.

[34] *BṛUB*, I.4.1.

[35] *ChāUB*, V.10.2; *SūB*, I.3.39.

possible without duality, cannot help us in transcending duality and in realizing the highest. Moreover, the various notions superimposed on the Self should be discarded if it is to be realized, whereas meditation is based on them.[36] Thus it is not possible to attain *brahmānubhava* through meditation, for ignorance cannot be destroyed by it. *Upāsanā* is meant for those who seek fulfilment of their desires. It also may be helpful in attaining certain supernatural powers and objects, but thereby one does not become free from ignorance. The fruits of meditation like that of action fall within the empirical sphere and "the injunctions connected with meditation are not concerned with the exposition of the nature of Reality".[37] For all these reasons, Śaṅkara says that meditation does not exalt the meditator to Self-sovereignty (*svarājya*), his identification with the self-refulgent *Brahman*, which is attained by the realization of the truth contained in such scriptural statements like "That thou art" and "the Self is all this".[38]

On the other hand, higher meditation, like supreme devotion, is effective in attaining *brahmānubhava*. Its purpose is to make one attain the supportless state (*nirālambana sthiti*) of pure bliss by constant meditation on the idea that one is *Brahman*. After withdrawing the mind from all external objects, if one meditates constantly with devotion and faith, on the identity of oneself with *oṁ*, the symbol of *Brahman*, by way of superimposing the idea of *Brahman* on it, one realizes one's identity with *Brahman*.[39] *Oṁ* is a more appropriate symbol and appellation of Reality than the words *Brahman* and *Ātman*.

---

[36] *SūB*, IV.1.4.

[37] *SūB*, III.3.9.

[38] *ChāUB*, III.14.4.

[39] *BṛUB*, V.1.1.

Though action, ordinary type of devotion and lower kind of meditation are not effective in destroying ignorance, they are still useful in attaining *brahmānubhava*. Action is natural to man, but because of his sense of ego, man becomes attached to actions and their results; and this attachment causes suffering and bondage. But if they are done without attachment, or done for the sake of the Lord, they turn into means for the purification of the mind, which is a prerequisite for the attainment of the knowledge of *Brahman*.[40] Similarly, if one meditates with no attachment to its results, it also helps one in attaining tranquillity or steadfastness of the mind, which is also essential for acquiring the knowledge of *Brahman*. Thus when action, devotion and meditation are done with a spirit of detachment, instead of causing bondage they fulfil the preliminary requirements of spiritual discipline which ultimately leads one to Self-realization. These make one fit (*samartha*) to receive the knowledge of *Brahman*. Thus, though they cannot directly destroy ignorance, they indirectly do so by paving the way for the knowledge of the Self.

As ignorance alone is responsible for the non-attainment of *brahmānubhava*, perfect knowledge is the only means of attaining it, for knowledge alone can destroy ignorance. As ignorance is the absence of perfect knowledge, the presence of the latter removes the former. As ignorance is wrong apprehension (*viparīta darśana*) or seeing a thing as what it is not (*anyathā grahaṇa*), perfect vision (*samyag darśana*) alone can remove it. It is because of ignorance one has wrong knowledge of oneself, and it can be dispelled by perfect knowledge of the Self only. No amount of effort or action can make one free from the fear caused by an illusory snake. The fear of snake can be removed only by dispelling the illusion, and the knowledge of rope can alone do that. Similarly, the illusion of *saṁsāra* and

---

[40] *ChāUB*, 1.1, Introduction; *Vivekacūḍāmaṇi*, *śl*. 11; *BGB*, V.12.

its effects cannot be dispelled by anything but *brahma-jñāna*. Moreover, the very nature of ignorance suggests that its dispersion is possible through knowledge only. Like light and darkness, knowledge and ignorance are opposed to each other in their natures, that is to say, one cannot exist in the presence of the other. Because of this opposition, ignorance can be dispelled by perfect knowledge alone. "Whether ignorance means the want of knowledge, or doubt, or false knowledge," Śaṅkara says, "it is always removable by knowledge only, but not by action in any of its form, for there is no contradiction between ignorance and action".[41] And the knowledge that can remove the basic ignorance can be had from the Upaniṣads only, for *Brahman* cannot be known through any other source.

As pointed out earlier, knowledge also cannot be the cause of *brahmānubhava*, which is uncaused and eternal, for "anything that is eternal cannot be caused either by action or by knowledge".[42] Just as the function of light in knowing an object enveloped by darkness is to remove darkness, the role of scriptural knowledge in attaining *brahmānubhava* is to remove ignorance, because of which it appears as if it is not already attained. In other words, scriptural knowledge does not cause *brahmānubhava* directly; it does so only indirectly by dispelling ignorance.

Here an objection may be raised as to how the scriptural knowledge can make us realize *Brahman* by removing the wrong knowledge about It when it cannot offer us positive information about *Brahman*. To put it in the words of Śaṅkara, "If there is no effort on the part of the scriptures to make us understand the true nature of the Self, how can they remove the wrong knowledge of duality".[43] To this, Śaṅkara's reply is

[41] *BṛUB*, III.1, Introduction, tr. Swami Madhavananda, p. 451.

[42] *BGB*, XVIII.66; tr. Swami Mahadeva Sastri, p. 501.

[43] *GKB*, II.32.

as follows. There is no need to impart Self-knowledge to anyone, because the Self is self-evident to all. It is never unknown to anyone. However, its real nature is not known to anyone. However, its real nature is not known to us as it is concealed, as it were, by ignorance. Because of ignorance, the notions such as one is happy or miserable, born, embodied or an agent, enjoyer and suffer that cause the illusion of duality are superimposed on the non-dual Self. But as the substratum of superimposition, the Self follows (*anugata*) all the notions that are superimposed on it, just as a rope is present in all the notions superimposed on it. And in thus following, the nature of the Self becomes revealed for itself simultaneously. As its nature is thus comprehended invariably as the basis of every notion superimposed on it, the knowledge of the Self is not something that is to be generated by the scriptures. On the contrary, if the scriptures try to establish a self-established and self-evident reality, they lose their authority, for they are meant, according to Śaṅkara, to make us know what is not already known.[44] Therefore, the purpose of the scriptures is not to make us know the Self, but to make us know it truly, and that too not directly, but indirectly by way of eliminating the superimposed notions that seem to block the true nature of the Self. Thus the way the scriptures impart knowledge of the Self is not through positive assertion, but through negation as "not this", "not this", that is, the Self is not an agent, not an enjoyer, not a sufferer and so on. This, Śaṅkara says is in conformity with the opinion of those who have known the real meaning of the scriptures, for they say that the authority of the scriptures regarding the Self is not through positive assertion, but through negation.[45] Elsewhere, Śaṅkara says that:

---

[44] *GKB*, II.32; *SūB*, I.1.3.

[45] *GKB*, II.32.

> The scripture which is the supreme and final authority regarding the Self, obtains its authoritativeness only as serving to eliminate the superimposition of the attributes alien to the Self, but not by revealing what is altogether unknown.[46]

Now, the scriptural knowledge proves ineffective in destroying ignorance if the intellect is impure. An impure intellect fails to comprehend the meaning of the scriptures perfectly, just as a stained mirror cannot reflect things clearly. Śaṅkara explains:

> Though the intellect in all beings is intrinsically able to make the Self known, still being polluted by such blemishes as attachment to external objects, etc., it becomes agitated and impure, and does not like a stained mirror or ruffled water make the reality of the Self known, though it is ever at hand.[47]

By itself fire is capable of burning wood, but if the wood is wet, fire will not be able to burn it. Likewise, the fire of knowledge does not touch the mind that is wet with passions and attachment.[48] In other words, scriptural knowledge fails to accomplish its end if the man is not perfectly pure at heart. The capacity of the mind to discriminate between truth and untruth is weakened when it is swayed by passions and attached to sensual pleasures. This is so even with regard to empirical things. One's understanding of things is generally coloured or tainted by one's impurities and imperfections. Illustrating this, Śaṅkara gives the example of Indra and Virocana, who were equally instructed about *Brahman* by Prajāpati, but only the former could understand perfectly what he was taught. In this context, Śaṅkara observes:

---

[46] *BGB*, II.18, tr. Mahadeva Sastri, p. 39.

[47] *MuUB*, III.1.8, tr. Swami Gambhirananda, vol. II, pp. 155-56.

[48] *Śataślokī*, śl. 40.

> It is a matter of experience, that even though *Brahman* is spoken of, there is either non-comprehension or miscomprehension in the case of one who has not been purged of his sins.[49]

Thus, in spite of his scriptural scholarship, man fails to attain *brahmānubhava*, if his intellect is not pure; if his senses are not subjugated; if his passions are not subdued and if his evil ways are not mended. Knowledge of *Brahman* arises only in one who has attained the requisite holiness. It follows from this that, according to Śaṅkara, perfect knowledge is something altogether different from the mere verbal understanding of the scriptures. Ignorance is not destroyed and the bliss of Self-realization is not attained merely through ascertaining the meaning of the scripture. The man who has simply mastered the scripture is in no way spiritually superior to the unlearned, for both of them suffer from basic ignorance. The real knowledge, which immediately destroys ignorance, is not just scriptural scholarship; otherwise so many learned men will not continue to suffer from ignorance and bondage. Therefore, to be effective in destroying ignorance, the understanding of the great scriptural statements like "That thou art" should form the culminating stage of an ardent spiritual discipline (*sādhanā*). Such knowledge of *Brahman* is distinguished from the mere mastery of the scriptures and is called the higher knowledge.[50]

The spiritual preparation (*sādhanā*) which purifies the intellect and makes it fit to receive and comprehend perfectly the scriptural teaching has four components. Discrimination (*viveka*) between what is permanent and what is impermanent is the first component.[51] Until one becomes discriminative one cannot see

---

[49] *KeUB*, IV.8, tr. Swami Gambhirananda, vol. I, p. 92.

[50] *MuUB*, I.1.5; see also *ChāUB*, VII.1.3.

[51] *SūB*, I.1.1; *Vivekacūḍāmaṇi*, *śl.* 19.

the fact of superimposition or ignorance. One should feel the presence of ignorance and the bondage caused by it before one wants to become free from them. He who sees his own finiteness and mortality, the many-sided limitations and imperfections of the world and the transitory nature of the things empirically experienced, and is thoroughly dissatisfied with them becomes qualified to know the things of supreme value.[52] Through right discrimination one should understand that what is empirically experienced is ever changing and hence ephemeral, while the seer or the Self is immutable and eternal. Non-attachment to the enjoyment, here or hereafter, of fruits of actions is the second component.[53] It is indifference to all the seen and unseen results attainable by various means, whereby one becomes devoted to scriptural teaching and not carried away by one's own natural desires. This is not the state of absolute desirelessness or *brahmānubhava*, but the state where one is desirous of attaining nothing except Self-realization. Afterwards, one should become virtuous by abandoning all desires (*śama*), restraining the senses (*dama*), withdrawing from the objects of enjoyment (*uparati*), enduring patiently all the polarities of life like pain and pleasure (*titikṣā*), having implicit faith in the teachings of the scripture as well as in the spiritual competency of the teacher (*śraddhā*) and finally by fixing the mind on Reality (*samādhāna*).[54] This is the third component of *sādhanā*.

Finally, one should have an intense desire (*mumukṣatva*) to get rid of bondage. *Mumukṣatva* is not only a passionate desire to become free from ignorance, but also the pursuance of that desire till *Brahman* is directly experienced (*avagati paryantam*).[55] According to Śaṅkara, the Self is realized by those who long

---

52 *BṛUB* I.5.2, I.4.1; *KeUB*, I.1, Introduction; *KaUB*, I.1.19.

53 *SūB*, I.1.1; *Vivekacūḍāmaṇi*, *śl*. 19.

54 Ibid., 1.1.1; *Aparokṣānubhūti*, *śls*. 6-8; *Vivekacūḍāmaṇi*, *śls*. 22-26.

55 *SūB*, I.1.1.

for it deeply. One should pray (*prārthanā*) for its knowledge and realization, and *sādhanā* is meant for such an aspirant, and then alone it proves to be effective in realizing the Self.[56] A man may become morally perfect and may achieve many supernatural powers, but if the desire for Self-realization is absent in him, they will be of no real significance. Therefore, according to Śaṅkara, keeping the highest end of life or Self-realization always in view is most essential in *sādhanā*; otherwise, one's attention may be distracted by petty achievements and the supreme end of life, for which all other things are to be undertaken as means, may be forgotten. An ardent desire for liberation, thus forms the basis of *sādhanā* and prepares an aspirant to undertake any discipline that may prove effective in realizing the Self.

Now, the scriptures are meant and are also helpful for those who have pepared themselves in the above-said way. Water is of use only to those who are really thirsty, and likewise, the scriptural knowledge is for those who are not satisfied with the world of empirical experience and are in search of truth.[57] Even then, the scripture only directs a person's attention to the Self in a gentle and persuasive manner rather than in an imperative way (*niyoga*). It cannot hinder one from enjoying sense-objects, nor can it force one, who is averse to them, to go after them.[58] People choose their goals in accordance with their own natures and adopt suitable means for their achievement. If some follow the lead of their senses and become attached to sensual pleasures, the scripture is helpless to hold them back. But those who are desirous of realizing the Self may rely on its authority and attain immortality.

---

[56] *MuUB*, III.2.3.

[57] *BṛUB*, I.4.1.

[58] Ibid., II.1.20.

Grace of the teacher

After having attained purity of mind, a seeker of truth should, in an appropriate manner, approach a teacher. "A proper teacher is one who is established in *Brahman* (*brahmaniṣṭha*) or whose purpose in life is fulfilled."[59] From such a teacher alone scriptural knowledge should be received, and then alone one can have faith in the validity of scriptural knowledge. According to Śaṅkara, one should not try to understand the scripture without the guidance of a teacher, even though one is competent to understand the scripture independently. Unless there is a living example before an aspirant, it is difficult to have faith in what the scripture teaches and to follow it. In the words of Śaṅkara, "that knowledge alone which is imparted by those who have realized the truth and no other knowledge can prove effective" in attaining *brahmānubhava*.[60] Only then the real meaning of the scripture is comprehended and the Self is realized. The knowledge so received makes the student attain equality with the teacher, that is, the student also attains *brahmānubhava*. As such, a spiritual teacher is more than a father, for he confers absolute bliss and fearlessness.[61]

Now, the nature and place of *śravaṇa* (hearing), *manana* (reflection) and *nididhyāsana* (contemplation) in attaining perfect knowledge will be discussed. *Śravaṇa* is to hear the scriptural statements like "That thou art" and "I am *Brahman*" from a teacher. In the case of those who are intellectually mature and mentally pure, it is possible to grasp the meaning of these statements by hearing them once. But repetition is necessary for those who are dull.[62] Here, it may be asked that if by hearing the statements once the required result is not

[59] *MuUB*, I.2.12; see also *TaiUB*, I.3.1; *KaUB*, 1.2.8; *GKB*, I.16.

[60] *BGB*, IV.34, tr. Mahadeva Sastri, p. 149.

[61] *PrUB*, VI.8.

[62] *SūB*, IV.1.2.

produced, what is the use of repeating them? But, in daily experience we observe that when people have understood a sentence only imperfectly by hearing it once can, however, by repeating it again and again, gradually rid themselves of all misconceptions about it and understand it perfectly. So, the value of repetition in understanding the scriptural statements also must be admitted. On the other hand, if the scriptural statements are repeated for the sake of repetition, then the repetition will have no value; it is valuable only in so for as it helps understanding. The scriptural statements are not imperative and the repetition of them is not enjoined as a duty, the mechanical fulfilment of which has a ritualistic value.[63] If so understood, repetition becomes not only mechanical, but also meaningless. After hearing them through a teacher, the scriptural statements should be critically reflected upon by the seeker himself; but this reflection should be in strict conformity with the scripture. This is *manana*. The purpose of it is to fortify one's conviction of the truth received from the scripture and to rid oneself of all doubts. According to Śaṅkara, its value is superior to that of faith. If unreflective people can attain the highest by merely having faith in the authority of the scripture, Śaṅkara says, "what to speak of those who can independently reflect upon the evidence and discriminate".[64] Another important function of reflection is to make one comprehend the real meaning of the scriptural statements by consistently interpreting them, so that the apparent inconsistencies are resolved. The final step leading to the realization of the Self is steadfast meditation on the purport of the scriptural statements, namely the Self's identity with *Brahman*. This is *nididhyāsana* in which the mind is turned completely inward and is fixed firmly on the inner self and its

[63] *SūB*, IV.1.2.

[64] *BGB*, XIII.25.

identity with *Brahman*, till one's finitude and individuality are dissolved. It is repetition (*āvr̥tti*) carried on within till the Self is realized.[65] As has been stated earlier, meditation on the inner self is the same as supreme devotion (*parābhakti*). It is *jñānaniṣṭha*, the state of being established in *jñāna*. It is a continuous and uninterrupted awareness of the inner self and its oneness with *Brahman*. Through *nididhyāsana*, the knowledge of the Self got through a teacher and understood with the aid of critical reflection becomes ripened or attains maturity (*paripāka*) and leads to Self-realization.[66] These three — hearing, reflection and meditation — combine to form a single process which when completed culminates in the realization of the Self, just as the act of threshing results in freeing the kernel from the husk.[67] According to Śaṅkara, more attention should be paid to the means (*upāya*) like the purification of the mind, than to the end (*upeya*), especially in the case of Self-realization, because the end or Self-realization is by its nature ever accomplished.[68]

Grace of the Lord

According to Śaṅkara, the grace of the Lord (*Īśvarānugraha* or *Īśvara prasāda*) is also one of the effective factors in making one fit to receive the knowledge of the Self. "We must assume that final release is also effected through knowledge attained by the grace of the Lord."[69] But the grace of the Lord cannot confer on one the bliss of *brahmānubhava* directly. It can only confer fitness (*sāmarthya*) to receive Self-knowledge which alone is the means of Self-realization.[70]

---

[65] *SūB*, IV.1.1.

[66] *BGB*, XVIII.55.

[67] *SūB*, IV.1.1.

[68] *TaiUB*, I.11.4.

[69] *BGB*, II.39; see also *SūB*, II.3.41.

[70] *TaiUB*, I.11.4.

In the case of certain people, like Sage Vāmadeva, who had realized *Brahman* while he was in his mother's womb, perfect knowledge of the Self may arise directly and immediately on hearing the great scriptural statements without their following any spiritual discipline. This, according to Śaṅkara, is possible because moral perfection conducive to the rise and maturity of *Brahman*-knowledge had been attained in their previous lives.[71] In the course of many births it is possible for one to acquire moral perfection essential for the origination and maturity of knowledge. In such cases perfect knowledge may arise as soon as the scriptural statements are heard.

In this connection it should be noted that, according to Śaṅkara, there is no restrictive rule that one must either pass through all the stages of life (*āśrama*) performing the duties incumbent on them or renounce all duties and become a mendicant before one takes up the life of *sādhanā* and acquire the knowledge of the Self.[72] As both of them are equally effective in preparing an aspirant to receive the knowledge of the Self, one may choose any one of them and follow it with faith. The choice depends on one's spiritual maturity and intellectual ability. However, Śaṅkara thinks in consonance with *Gītā*, that the path of detached action (*karma-yoga*) is superior to the renunciation of actions if renunciation of actions is not due to knowledge.[73] The renunciation of all actions by the one who has knowledge of the Self and is devoted to it, so as to realize the Self is superior to detached action or *karma-yoga*.[74] Although the goal sought to be achieved through them is the same, that is, *brahmānubhava*, Sāṁkhya Yoga or

---

[71] *AiUB*, II.1.5-6; *SūB*, II.4.38; *BGB*, VI.45; *TaiUB*, I.11.4.

[72] *BṛUB*, IV.5.15.

[73] *BGB*, V.2.

[74] Ibid., V.5; *SūB*, IV.1.18.

jñānaniṣṭha leads one to *brahmānubhava* directly, while *karma-yoga* does so indirectly. The path of detached action prepares an individual to receive the knowledge of the Self (*jñāna-yoga*) and through the latter only the real renunciation of action is possible. Real renunciation or freedom from action by way of giving up of the sense of agency naturally follows the realization of the Self. Thus there is no distinction between real renunciation of action (*karma saṁnyāsa*) and giving up of the sense of agency, which is possible through *jñāna-yoga*.

Śūdras and Bhramānubhava

Even those, like śūdras, who are excluded from following the *āśrama* duties, as well as those, like widowers, who are not eligible to perform them are qualified to attain the knowledge of the Self.[75] In their case, prayer (*japa*), fasting, devotion to God, etc. prove helpful in preparing them for receiving the knowledge of the Self. Also, the spiritual merit or moral perfection acquired because of assiduous performance of *āśrama* duties in their previous births, may qualify them to attain the knowledge of the Self in the present life. The low-born or the śūdras who are not entitled to hear or study the scriptures are not, for that reason, debarred from knowing the Self. In their case, the attainment of (a) spiritual competency to receive the knowledge of the Self and (b) the knowledge of the Self is through the teachings of the Smṛtis, Itihāsas and Purāṇas, provided the other conditions, like desire for liberation, are fulfilled. This is possible because śūdras, like Vidura and Dharmavyādha, did attain the knowledge of the Self; and when once it is attained, the fruit of it, that is, Self-realization cannot be withheld, since in all cases knowledge definitely brings about its result.[76] The low-born, as they lack

---

[75] *SūB*, III.4.36, III.4.38.

[76] Ibid., I.3.38.

spiritual competency, are not fit to receive the knowledge of *Brahman* directly from the scriptures, though the desire for it may be found in them. In spiritual matters, as in the case of worldly matters, desire alone does not constitute a sufficient reason for attaining a thing. It is the capacity to attain a thing that matters much. Again, the capacity with which one achieves success in the world of differences is different from spiritual capacity or spiritual maturity, which alone proves effective in attaining spiritual goals, and this is absent in śūdras in general. For this reason, Śaṅkara explains that the śūdras are excluded from the study of the scriptures. This, however, does not mean that they are not eligible for knowing the Self and realizing it, which cannot be denied to anyone without denying the reality of the Self.

> The mere circumstance of being in a condition of desire does not furnish a reason for qualification, if capability is absent. Mere temporal or empirical (*laukika*) capability, again does not constitute a reason for qualification, spiritual capability being required in spiritual matters. And spiritual capability is (in the case of śūdras) excluded by their being excluded from the study of the scripture (Veda).[77]

[77] *SūB*, I.3.34.

5

The Place of Faith, Emotions and Reasoning in Brahmānubhava

THE philosophy of Śaṅkara is based mainly on revelation and its chief aim is to make one realize Reality directly. It is a means or a preparation for the attainment of the supreme end of life (*brahmānubhava*). As such, faith occupies an important place in his philosophy. As the possibility of *brahmānubhava* is known primarily through revelation, faith in it is essential for the attainment of *brahmānubhava*. The path leading to *brahmānubhava* is as sharp and subtle as the edge of a razor, and unless one has faith (*śraddhā*) in the existence of *Brahman*, in one's identity with It and in the possibility of realizing this identity, one cannot tread this path. Faith is essential for the accomplishment of all the objectives of life.[1] It is an essential precondition for the realization of *Brahman*. To become qualified to receive the knowledge of *Brahman* and thereby to have direct experience of It by being It, one should develop several spiritual virtues. One is required, by passing through an ardent spiritual discipline, to achieve purity of heart, detachment, etc. to acquire perfect knowledge of *Brahman* which culminates in *brahmānubhava*. In the first part of this chapter, the nature and scope of faith, its objects and sources, its need and its relation to knowledge and reasoning, and finally the consequences of unfaith and doubt are discussed.

---

[1] *MuUB*, I.7; see also *Sarvavedānta Siddhāntasāra Saṁgraha, śl.* 211.

Faith

Faith is a disposition (*vṛtti*) of the heart (*hṛdaya*) or mind.[2] Like thinking and feeling, it is a natural function of the mind. It is clearness of the mind or its tranquillity (*citta prasāda*).[3] It is a believing nature or disposition of the mind (*āstikya buddhi*).[4] It is a precondition for accomplishing all the ends of life. "*Śraddhā* is implicit faith in the teachings of the scripture and the teacher."[5] According to Śaṅkara, faith is natural to man, though its objects and sources may differ from man to man. Man is full of faith (*śraddhāmaya* or *śraddhā prāyaḥ*).[6] As faith is born of man's nature, the nature of man's faith will be in accordance with his nature which is shaped by the deeds which he had done during his previous lives.[7] "As a man's faith is, so is he."[8] The deeds done during the previous lives survive in the form of latent impressions and shape an individual's nature in the present life. Thus human nature and faith influence each other. While one's faith is determined by one's nature, one's life will be in accordance with one's faith.

The objects of faith are those that cannot be known through the natural sources of knowledge, but can be known only through the scripture and the spiritual preceptor. They are: what is good and bad, the performance of rites and ceremonies, the results of which cannot be directly perceived, the existence of divine or supernatural beings (*devatā*), the truth of what the scriptures teach, the real nature of *Brahman* and

---

[2] *BṛUB*, III.9.21; *SūB*, III.1.5, II.3.40.

[3] *MuUB*, II.1.7.

[4] *BṛUB*, III.9.21.

[5] *Aparokṣānubhūti*, *śl*. 8.

[6] *BGB*, XVII.3.

[7] Ibid., XVII.2.

[8] Ibid., XVII.3.

one's identity with It and finally the possibility of attaining that identity or *brahmānubhava*. The performance of rites, ceremonies and penance enjoined by the scriptures rests entirely on faith, without which it is impossible to perform them. Here, faith means belief in the efficacy of the rites directed towards invisible ends. Again, it is with complete faith that one should give away religious gifts; and here faith means the liberal attitude of giving (*distutvam*).[9] On the other hand, if one gives away the religious gifts, or performs the rituals and ceremonies, or does penance without faith, they are to be considered as naught though much effort has been put into their performance, for then they do not prove effective in producing their appropriate results.[10]

The ethical behaviour of man is also based on faith. Without faith it is not possible for man to devote all his energies in doing good and avoiding evil. "It is faith that inspires men to put their complete effort into doing good and avoiding evil."[11] To follow the path of righteousness is to be guided in one's conduct by the scriptural injunctions and prohibitions. To be righteous is to accept on faith the scheme of life as presented in the scriptures, that is, the caste system and the four stages of life (*āśrama*) and to abide by the laws and regulations that govern one's particular caste and stage of life.[12] On the contrary, to be led away by the instincts and the senses is to follow the path of evil, and is also demonic. If it is asked as to why one should depend on faith to know the nature of good and evil, Śaṅkara's explanation is that it is because the knowledge of what is good and what is evil cannot be

[9] *BṛUB*, III.9.21, I.5.3.

[10] *BGB*, XVII.28.

[11] *PrUB*, VI.4.

[12] *TaiUB*, II.6.1.

obtained through any means of knowledge other than the scripture. Sense perception and inference cannot provide us ethical knowledge. Moreover, the nature and validity of good and bad, being relative, change from time to time and from place to place. For example, killing in general is sinful, while in exceptional cases, like in a sacrifice, it is not sinful. As such man has to depend on faith in the scriptures to know what is good and what is evil; he cannot know them otherwise.[13]

Faith also means belief in the existence of supernatural being or beings. Those who cannot understand the scriptures, and hence what is said in them about God, but have belief in the existence of something beyond what is empirically experienced can also attain faith in the existence of God or gods. In their case, the source of faith is tradition.[14] Faith is differentiated into three types depending upon the differences in the nature of man. In accordance with the nature of their faith, different people worship different gods. The nature of a man's faith is to be inferred from the characteristic effects which it produces in his life and behaviour and also from the kind of gods he worships and the type of devotion it evokes. Those who are pure in nature will have faith in the existence of gods and worship them with devotion. Such faith is pure (*sāttvika*).[15] Those who believe in the existence of *yakṣa*s and demons (*rākṣasa*) and worship them with faith are passionate

---

[13] *SūB*, III.1.25.

[14] *BGB*, XVII.1.

[15] Ibid., XVII.2, 4.

According to Śaṅkara, apart from men there are no gods and demons. Men whose thoughts and actions are in accordance with the teaching of the scriptures are gods. Men who are guided by their instincts and passions and seek earthly pleasures are demons. Similarly, faith in scriptures and the *guru* is divine, while faith in natural inclinations and instincts is demonic (*BṛUB*, I.3.1, V.2.3).

in their nature. Such a faith is passionate (*rājasika*).[16] Lastly, those who worship the dead (*preta*) and the spirits (*piśāca*) are the utterly deluded people and their faith is demonic (*tāmasika*).[17]

Faith is also used in the sense of belief in the existence of *Brahman* or the Self as the supreme reality. "To accept as truth what the scriptures and the spiritual teacher instruct is faith; and it is through it that Reality is known."[18] The existence of *Brahman* as something beyond what is empirically experienced and the existence of the Self as something different from the body, the mind and the senses are known through faith only. This is prior to direct realization of *Brahman* or the Self. The absolute identity of *Brahman* and the Self and also the possibility of realizing it directly are also objects of faith, before such an identity is directly realized. That is to say, before one is actually liberated, the possibility of its attainment is a matter of faith. Now, one's faith in the reality of *Brahman* and in the possibility of realizing It directly, by being It, gives birth to faith in the path that leads to *brahmānubhava*. Faith in moral perfection is essential to accomplish the supreme end of life, because perfect knowledge whereby it is attained does not arise in the absence of mental purity. On the other hand, it is impossible for those, who lack faith in the existence of *Brahman* or the Self, to have faith in the path that leads to Its realization. They are the people who deny the existence of anything that is not empirically experienced and accept the reality of the body, the mind and the senses and all that is experienced through them.[19] Accordingly, they regard sense enjoyment as the highest end of life and cannot have faith in the possibility

---

16 *BGB*, XVII.2.

17 Ibid., *ChāUB*, VIII.8.5.

18 *Vivekacūḍāmaṇi*, *śl*. 25.

19 *BGB*, IX.3.

of attaining perfect bliss or liberation. In the absence of faith in liberation, it is not possible to have faith in the path that leads to it. Thus one's faith is determined by what one thinks about ultimate reality, and one's faith determines one's way of life.

As the reality of *Brahman* and the identity of the Self with It are known exclusively through the scriptures, faith in their authority is also essential for the realization of the Self. "*Brahman* rests exclusively on the holy texts and regarding which the holy texts alone are authoritative — not the senses and so on — and must be accepted such as the texts proclaim It to be."[20] According to Śaṅkara, the highest truth can be known through the Upaniṣads only, for the scriptural passages like "I now ask thee that person taught in the Upaniṣads" and "none who does not know the Veda knows that great one" indicate that.[21] Commenting on the *Muṇḍaka Upaniṣad*, he asserts that the attainment of the highest is the target of that great weapon known as the Upaniṣad.[22] Thus the philosophy of Advaita Vedānta, according to Śaṅkara, is nothing but the philosophy of the Upaniṣads (*aupaniṣadam darśanam*).[23]

Now, the scriptural texts are not the only source of *Brahman*-knowledge; experience (*anubhava*) is also a means of it. This is because, first, experience is the final outcome of an enquiry into *Brahman* and second, *Brahman* is an objective reality.[24] This position of Śaṅkara may seem to contradict his position on the scripture, that is, the scripture is the only source of *Brahman*-knowledge. But there is no such contradiction in

[20] *SūB*, II.1.27, tr. Thibaut, vol. I, pp. 350-51.

[21] *SūB*, II.1.3.

[22] *MuUB*, II.2.3.

[23] *BGB*, XIII.31.

[24] *SūB*, I.1.2.

reality. Experience is not an alternative to scripture in knowing *Brahman*. To the person who has it, *brahmānubhava* is not a proof for the existence of *Brahman* in the usual sense of the word proof, for *Brahman* is not known as an object in it. *Brahmānubhava* being *Brahman* Itself, only in a figurative sense, the former may be regarded as a proof of the latter, though in truth *brahmānubhava* is an end in itself, but not a means to anything. However, the person who has realized *Brahman* may stand as an example or proof to others. In other words by having faith in a *brahmajñānī*, one can attain knowledge of *Brahman*. Śaṅkara says that those who lack the capacity to think for themselves and therefore cannot follow the paths like *jñāna-yoga* and *karma-yoga* can also attain perfect knowledge of the Self by having faith in those who have realized *Brahman*.[25] Only in this way *brahmānubhava* can be considered as a source of *Brahman*-knowledge.

Faith in the spiritual preceptor is also essential to realize *Brahman*.[26] Even those who can discern the meaning of the scripture for themselves require the guidance of a teacher. Faith in the teacher means belief in his teachings and in his spiritual competency to guide an individual to attain *brahmānubhava*.

It is possible to raise an objection here. If *Brahman*'s existence is objective (*vastu*), how It can be considered as an object of faith, for things that are objectively real can be known through natural means of knowledge, independently of faith? This objection cannot be sustained. The existence of *Brahman* does not depend upon the faith of anyone, but to know It truly man should have faith in the scriptures. Although *Brahman* is objectively real, It is never an object (*viṣaya*) of

---

[25] *BGB*, XVII.1; *BṛUB*, I.4.2.

[26] *ChāUB*, VII.20.1; *Vivekacūḍāmaṇi*, *śl*. 25; *Aparokṣānubhūti*, *śl*. 8.

knowledge. As It is the inward self of all and non-dual, it is not even possible to think of It as an object. When It is not an object, there is no question of Its being known through any of the sources of knowledge. Therefore, It is an appropriate object of faith, and is to be known through faith in the scriptures. No doubt, at the empirical level, *Brahman* is known as the individual self, and it is not an object of faith, as it is known to all as the "I" presupposed in all activity, but the "I" is not the real Self which is not different from *Brahman*. The Self or the real nature of the empirical self is not revealed to us in empirical experience and, therefore, one has to rely on faith only to know It. In other words, *Brahman* is self-existent and self-evident, but because of ignorance, It is not known to man in Its real nature. As such until ignorance is removed, man has to depend on faith only for Its knowledge. Thus faith in the scripture is the beginning of knowledge.

But how is one to attain faith in the truthfulness of the scriptures? According to Śaṅkara, one knows the truthfulness of the scriptures on their authority only.[27] The validity of scriptural knowledge is independent of other knowledge, as all knowledge is. All knowledge, according to Śaṅkara, is valid *per se*. As long as any knowledge is viewed and judged from the standpoint of itself, it is valid.[28] Therefore, scriptural knowledge is self-evident and intrinsically valid.

Faith is not required in the case of objects which can be known through the natural means of knowledge. To know that fire burns one need not depend on faith, since it can be perceived directly. But with regard to the existence of things, of which knowledge cannot be attained through natural means of knowledge, faith is the only way of knowing them. As has been discussed in Chapter 1, *Brahman* cannot be known

[27] *SūB*, II.1.1; *BṛUB*, II.1.20, II.3.6.

[28] *ChāUB*, VIII.5.4.

through any of the means of knowledge. Nevertheless, as the basis of all the sources of knowledge, the existence of *Brahman* cannot be denied. Thus *Brahman* cannot be known and at the same time It cannot be denied. Elucidating this point we find an illustration in the *Chāndogya Upaniṣad*.[29] The core of a banyan seed is very subtle and therefore cannot be seen, but still it is the source from which springs up a huge banyan tree. One has to believe this, for the fact of the subtle and unseen essence of a banyan seed becoming a huge tree cannot be ascertained through any means of knowledge. Similarly, *Brahman* which is the source of all that is experienced is, as it were, extremely subtle in Its nature and hence cannot be comprehended. It is to be known through faith only. In this context, Śaṅkara says:

> In the case of extremely subtle things, a man who has his mind taken up by external things, and follows the natural bent of his mind finds it difficult to understand the subtle nature of things, if he were not imbued with a large degree of faith.[30]

All those who seek knowledge of *Brahman*, including those who can discern and understand things for themselves, are to depend on faith. It is not meant for those only who are not intellectually sharp and hence cannot understand the scriptures for themselves. To accept the scripture as the valid source of *Brahman*-knowledge is in itself an act of faith. However, there is a difference between a dull man's faith and an intelligent man's faith. While an intelligent person can fortify (*dārdhya*) and confirm (*sthira*) his faith with the aid of reasoning, a dull person cannot reflect upon the scriptural statements; he simply accepts them with full faith.[31] But the latter can also attain

---

[29] *ChāUB*, VI.12.2.

[30] Ibid., VI.12.2, tr. Sir Ganganatha Jha, Poona: Oriental Book Agency, 1942, pp. 347-48.

[31] *BGB*, XIII.25; *Upadeśasāhasrī*, XVI.68.

perfect knowledge with the help and guidance of a person who has realized the Self. However, the man who can independently appreciate the evidence and determine the true meaning of the scriptural-statements for himself, with the aid of reasoning, is superior to the man of mere faith.[32]

Faith also helps the mind to become fully concentrated on an object.[33] Without faith, it is not possible to fix one's attention steadfastly, for a long time, on anything, and without such concentration, it is not possible to understand and realize subtle things like the Self.

Although faith occupies an important place in realizing *Brahman*, it is not the direct means to attain it.[34] Through mere faith one cannot directly attain the highest or faith alone is not sufficient to realize *Brahman*. Like detached action, devotion and meditation, faith can only help one indirectly in attaining *brahmānubhava*. By inspiring one to study the scriptures and to follow a spiritual teacher, it helps one to acquire perfect knowledge which is the direct means of *brahmānubhava*. To be effective in producing the knowledge of *Brahman*, faith must be accompanied by certain other virtues.[35] The man of faith should not be slothful and inert, but should be always alert and be devoted to the ways of obtaining knowledge, such as the search for a spiritually qualified teacher. He should withdraw the senses from their objects and become free from passions. Such a man of faith, devotion and self-control is sure to attain knowledge which culminates in *brahmānubhava*.[36]

---

[32] *BGB*, XIII.25.

[33] *ChāUB*, VI.12.2.

[34] *SūB*, III.3.31.

[35] *BGB*, IV.39.

[36] Ibid.

Faith does not consist in doing certain outward acts like prostrating before the teacher or in wearing a particular dress.[37] As a disposition of the mind, faith is purely inward and hence there is no place in it for pretension, display and hypocrisy. The criterion of faith is not this or that act done by a man of faith, though it manifests itself through them, but it is one's own heart, as faith rests on one's heart and is one's own conviction.[38] Faith is not opposed to such knowledge and reasoning which do not contradict the scripture. While faith is essential to accept the authority of the scriptures, to understand and determine their meaning reasoning is necessary. Such rational understanding of the scriptures enlightens or clarifies faith. Thus faith gives rise to knowledge and knowledge enlightens faith. As such when it does not lead to perfect knowledge, faith is not helpful in attaining the highest end of life.

As Śaṅkara teaches, faith leads to understanding, that is to say, one tries to understand the objects of faith only when one has faith in them, but not otherwise.[39] Therefore, if one has no faith in the validity of the scriptures, one may not try to understand the correct meaning of the scriptural statements like "That thou art" and "I am *Brahman*". It is only when one has faith in the validity of the scriptures that one tries to understand their real meaning by hearing them and reflecting upon them, and reasoning helps in promoting such understanding. According to Śaṅkara, perfect knowledge is that which is based on both scriptures and reasoning, and such knowledge alone, because of its universal validity, deserves one's complete faith.[40] Simple faith in the scriptures

---

[37] *BGB*, IV.39.

[38] *BṛUB*, III.9.21.

[39] *ChāUB*, VII.19.1.

[40] *BṛUB*, IV.5, Introduction.

is not sufficient, for by it alone the true meaning of the scriptures cannot be ascertained, which is the reason why there is no agreement as to the correct meaning of the scriptures among the simple believers of them. Whereas when the correct meaning of the scriptures is ascertained with the help of sound reasoning, it acquires universal validity, and cannot be contradicted or disproved by others on any ground. Only then the scriptural meaning is grasped as clearly as an object placed on one's palm.[41] But it should be noted that faith is opposed to mere reasoning. While reasoning that is in conformity with the scriptures is acceptable to faith, independent reasoning or that which is not in accordance with the scriptures is opposed to it. Similarly, while any knowledge from any source can be accepted on faith, if it is in complete agreement with the scriptures, that knowledge which is not in conformity with the scriptures is not acceptable to faith.[42]

Unfaith

Unfaith, the opposite of faith, is general disbelief in the existence of things that are not known through the natural means of knowledge. A faithless person, therefore, does not believe in the validity of the scriptures and hence rejects the reality of *Brahman* and the possibility of realizing It.[43] He accepts the reality of things that are known only through the natural means of knowledge and rejects the existence of everything that is not empirically experienced. He does not believe in the reality of the Self as something different from the body, mind and the senses.[44] He also believes in the non-existence of God (*nāstika*). Such a person is demonic (*asura*),

---

[41] *BṛUB*, III.1, Introduction.

[42] *SūB*, II.1.3.

[43] *BGB*, IV.40, IX.3.

[44] Ibid., IX.3.

since he regards the physical body as the Self and follows the lead of the senses and accepts the enjoyment of earthly pleasures as the highest end of life.[45] More sinful than the faithless is one who is full of doubt (*saṁśaya*), for doubt ruins a man completely.[46] Born of utter ignorance, its seat is one's own intellect.[47] The sceptic not only doubts the validity of supernatural things, but also the validity of the things commonly experienced and enjoyed. Such a man fails to enjoy either the pleasures of the earth or the spiritual bliss. "Neither the world which is common to all men, nor the other, the highest (*parā*) is attained by him."[48] There is still another type of unbelievers. They think that they are one with *Brahman*, but do not give up the false identity that they are the agents and experiencers. They are the people who do not follow either the path of knowledge or of action, and therefore do not attain the fruits of either.

Emotions

The place of devotion (*bhakti*) in realizing *Brahman* makes it clear that the value of emotions is recognized by Śaṅkara. Even after *Brahman* realization, emotions have an important place. In realizing the Self, the senses and the mind are neither destroyed nor do they stop functioning. They come to be looked upon as not different from the Self. So also, other men and the world exist, but not as the "others" and the "world". They too are realized to be non-different from the Self or *Brahman*. "The absence of duality for the man who has realized the Self is due to the realization of all as the Self."[49] The

---

[45] *BGB*, IX.3.

[46] Ibid., IV.40, 42.

[47] Ibid., IV.42.

[48] Ibid., IV.40.

[49] *Upadeśasāhasrī*, X.13.

disappearance of plurality is not literally true; it is true in one's own inner realization, in the sense, that the superimposed differences are realized to be unreal, and everything is realized as one with *Brahman*. Therefore, the man who has realized the Self also sees, hears, thinks, feels, etc., but these are not directed towards things other than one's own Self, as there is nothing different from it, or the Self is realized to be all. Thus one can have emotions like love and affection even after realizing *Brahman*.

Śaṅkara describes the following emotions as belonging to a *brahmajñānī*. They are love (*rati*), affection or delight (*ramaṇam*), play (*krīḍā*) and the enjoyment of company (*midhunam*).[50] From the standpoint of empirical experience, these emotions are not possible without duality. As the reactions of the mind, they are experienced always in relation to an object or an idea. They presuppose the duality of one who experiences them and their objects. Now, Śaṅkara makes a distinction between love and play and explains that while play is dependent upon instruments like hands and feet, love is independent of any instruments. Love is a simple feeling of joy or delight (*prītimātram*) towards all agreeable objects.[51] Yet duality is involved in both of them. However, for the one who has realized everything as one with the Self, love, affection, play and enjoyment of company are not dependent on duality. He will have all these in the Self only. Śaṅkara says:

> It is the Self itself that is all and is everywhere, knowing this One which is unborn, all-pervading like *ākāśa* (space), full and without a second, the wise man reflects upon it and realizes it and thereby he comes to love the Self, that is, all his love, affection and joy are centred in the Self.[52]

---

[50] *ChāUB*, VII.25.2; *MuUB*, III.1.4.

[51] *MuUB*, III.1.4.

[52] *ChāUB*, VII.25.2, tr. Sir Ganganatha Jha, p. 408.

For such a person love means to love all as his Self. In loving his Self he loves all. Thus, for him the fulfilment of all emotions is through the realization of the Self. As the existence of "others" is a fact for those who have not overcome ignorance, the love of a *brahmajñānī* may appear to have an object from their standpoint. But from the standpoint of his inner realization, the love of *brahmajñānī* has no object, for he does not see anything as different from the Self. Likewise, he enjoys the company of others not as "others", but as the Self. In this manner only all his emotions are fulfilled, and it is not possible to explain them in any other way.

Contrary to this, if statements expressing the emotions of a *brahmajñānī* are to be taken in their literal sense, a division of the Self into one which loves and the other that is loved would have to be admitted. This is untenable.[53] For an ignorant person, all these emotions are meaningful and also possible only in relation to someone whom he likes and loves. He can love his own people only, associate and play with his friends only and can find delight in agreeable objects only. He, therefore, suffers when he cannot have them or when he loses them or if he is forsaken by them. But in the case of one who has realized everything as Self, there cannot be any such limitations, for he loves all and delights in everything.

The Place of heart in self-realization

According to Śaṅkara, one's heart is the abode or temple (*adhiṣṭhāna* or *ālaya*) of *Brahman* or the Self, and it is there that *Brahman* is experienced; it is the seat of *brahmānubhava*.[54] It is into the hearts of all living beings that *Brahman* has entered as their self (*jīva*) after creating them.[55] The heart is known as

[53] *SūB*, IV.4.6.

[54] *TaiUB*, II.6.1; *SūB*, I.3.25; *BṛUB*, III.9.23.

[55] *KaUB*, II.1.6.

the city of *Brahman* (Brahmapuram or Brahmaloka), because in it *Brahman* reveals Itself in Its essential nature of pure consciousness.[56] *Brahman* is therefore perceived within the heart as though It is abiding within it. It is also known as the sheath (*kośa*) of *Brahman*.[57] According to the Upaniṣads and Śaṅkara, the word *hṛdayam* (heart) etymologically means the place where *Brahman* resides. "This Self (*ayam*) is in the heart (*hṛdi*) and therefore, it is known as heart (*hṛdayam*)."[58] The Self reveals itself in the hearts of all as the ever-abiding conscious principle or knower, which is the centre and basis of all experience. It manifests itself in and through the heart and all its functions like thinking and feeling. The Self as pure bliss manifests itself as the worldly happiness that is enjoyed by all in their hearts. As pure consciousness, it reveals itself as the knower. Thus the Self reveals itself, at every moment, in and through empirical experience as knowledge, bliss, etc., and as the heart is the centre of empirical experience, it is known as the abode or symbol (*pratīka*) of *Brahman*.[59] Physically, the heart is a lotus-shaped (*puṇḍarīka*) lump of flesh which is in all living beings as a vital part of their bodies. But what has been said above applies only to the human heart, for men only are entitled to the study of the scriptures, but not other living beings, as the former alone are endowed with the capacity to learn and understand and have desires and goals.[60] In the *Chāndogya Upaniṣad*, its physical description is given.[61] Although by its nature, the heart is physical and hence insentient, it appears as if it is sentient (*cetanāvat*) to common understanding, because

[56] *MuUB*, II.2.7; *ChāUB*, VIII.1.1.

[57] *TaiUB*, I.4.2; *MuUB*, II.2.9.

[58] *ChāUB*, VIII.3.3.

[59] *TaiUB*, I.4.2.

[60] *SūB*, I.3.25.

[61] *ChāUB*, VIII.6.1.

of its illuminative character and its proximate relation to the Self. It inherits, as it were, the consciousness of the Self, or it may be said that the consciousness of the Self is reflected in it. It is the innermost of all the organs and is also considered to be the first-born among all the sense organs.[62] It presupposes all actions, knowledge and enjoyment.

"The heart is the seat of the intellect (*buddhi*), the internal organ (*antaḥkaraṇa*), and all the other or external organs are subject to that intellect abiding in the heart."[63] All the other sense organs are channels or means for the manifestation of consciousness which has been reflected in the heart. For this reason, at various places, the heart is identified with the intellect and the internal organ.[64] Śaṅkara also describes the functions of the internal organ and the functions of the heart in identical terms. The heart is the centre of all mental and volitional activities. It is the seat of desire, resolve, doubt, faith, want of faith, steadiness, unsteadiness, shame, intelligence, fear, anger, etc. It is through its modification into the form of things that one experiences things. Because of the intelligence that is within the heart, one sees, hears, thinks, feels, and so on. It is through the heart that memory and knowledge and also their loss are possible. In short, the heart is the seat of all empirical experience; and it is through the mediation of heart that the self knows everything. Accordingly, Śaṅkara derives the meaning of the word *hṛdaya* as that which receives the objects in the form of impressions and passes them on to the Self. The letter *hṛ* in the word *hṛdaya* means "that which receives", as the heart receives the objects perceived by the various senses in the form of impressions; and the letter, *da*

---

[62] *TaiUB*, II.5.1.

[63] *BṛUB*, II.1.19, tr. Swami Madhavananda, p. 285.

[64] Ibid., IV.3.32, IV.3.7, III.9.20, V.3.1.

mean "to give" as the heart gives or passes on these impressions to the Self.[65] The heart is dependent on the body and the body as consisting of name, form and action depends on the heart; and these along with the vital force (*prāṇa*) work together as a whole to fulfil the purpose of the individual Self.[66]

What has been said above about the nature and functions of the heart as well as the direct assertions by Śaṅkara like "heart or intellect", "heart or internal organ" shows that according to him, the words — heart, intellect and internal organ — refer to the same entity.[67] The only distinction between the heart and the internal organ is that the heart, a lotus-shaped lump of flesh, is a physical entity while the internal organ is purely a functional unit. The former is the physical basis of the latter. The internal organ is known through its functions and the heart is the physical basis of all such psychic activity, just as the physical eye is the basis of optical activity.

The heart in its pristine purity, that is, in its first-born condition is as subtle and bright as the Self. Though the Self is omnipresent, it reveals itself clearly in the heart, because of the latter's proximity to the Self and its highly illuminative character, just as objects are reflected clearly in bright mediums like mirror. In other words, the consciousness, which is the nature of the Self, is superimposed on the intellect. Therefore, the statement, "*Brahman* abides in the heart", means that *Brahman*'s nature is superimposed on the intellect. The Self is the "light within the intellect".[68] Thus the intellect is that which is illumined and the Self or pure consciousness is that which illumines the intellect; and the world gets the light of

---

[65] *BṛUB*, V.3.1.

[66] Ibid., III.9.26.

[67] *BGB*, IV.42, XIII.17 and XV.15.

[68] *BṛUB*, IV.3.7.

consciousness through the intellect and its functions. In other words, we come to know the Self, at the empirical level, in and through the intellect. Śaṅkara uses the words *buddhi, vijñāna, medhā* and *prajñā* to mean the intellect. However, he distinguishes between the intellect which performs specific functions like determination and discrimination, and the intellect in its broad sense in which it is not different from the internal organ. In the latter sense of the term, the intellect is more comprehensive and includes all psychic activity. Of this intellect, the intellect in the specific sense of what reasons out and discriminates is only a function.

An objection may be raised here. How can *Brahman,* which is omnipresent and infinite, abide in a particular place like the limited space within the heart? Does it not contradict the omnipresence of *Brahman* and Its infinitude? According to Śaṅkara, there is no contradiction in saying that *Brahman* abides within the heart, for it does not affect the omnipresence of *Brahman.* He says that contradiction can arise only when we say that a thing is omnipresent when in reality it occupies a limited space, but not when we say that *Brahman,* which is omnipresent, occupies a limited space which is possible when It is viewed from a particular standpoint.[69] Śaṅkara illustrates this with an example. An emperor whose rule extends over an entire country may also be called, without any contradiction, the ruler of the capital city.[70] To give another example, the space which is present everywhere can also be said, without any contradiction, to be present within the tiny limits of a needle's eye.[71] Likewise, though *Brahman* is present everywhere and infinite can still be said as occupying the limited space within the heart, if it is viewed from the

[69] *SūB,* I.2.7.

[70] Ibid.

[71] Ibid.

standpoint of a spiritual aspirant who wants to meditate on It. On the other hand, if it is asserted that *Brahman* is within the heart only, it will be certainly wrong and contradicts Its omnipresence, for *Brahman* is not within the heart only; It is everywhere.[72] "To attribute to *Brahman* a definite locality in spite of Its omnipresence", says Śaṅkara, "subserves the practical purpose of contemplation and therefore does not contradict reason."[73] The attention of those who think that Reality is not one, because of their dull intellect, and can understand it only in terms of space and time, cannot all at once be diverted towards the absolute reality which is infinite, undifferentiated and without space and time relations.

As the fulfilment of the supreme end of man is connected with the knowledge of *Brahman*, and since the intellectually dull cannot understand the subtle nature of *Brahman* directly, it is practically necessary, for their benefit, to localize *Brahman* and say that It is within the heart of everyone. Later, their attention can gradually be directed towards the real nature of *Brahman*. This is like projecting the idea of Viṣṇu on an image to serve the practical purpose of devotion.[74] The image in itself is not Viṣṇu, but when it is worshipped with faith and devotion, one can gradually attain Viṣṇu. Therefore, the purpose of all those scriptural statements in which *Brahman* is said to exist in a particular place is to help an individual in realizing *Brahman*, but not to show that *Brahman* has spatial limitations. Their validity is psychological rather than ontological. "Those passages which refer to a *Brahman* qualified by form do not aim at setting forth the nature of *Brahman*, but rather at enjoining the worship of *Brahman*."[75] In another

[72] *SūB*, I.2.3.; *ChāUB*, III.12.9.

[73] *SūB*, I.2.14, tr. Thibaut, vol. I, pp. 125-26; see also *SūB*, I.2.11.

[74] *TaiUB*, I.6, Introduction; *SūB*, I.2.14.

[75] *SūB*, III.2.14, tr. Thibaut, vol. II, p. 155.

passage, he says that "the attributes of limitation of abode and of minuteness depend, in *Brahman*'s case, entirely on special forms of contemplation, and are not real".[76] Hence such things like the heart wherein *Brahman* is said to reside are only means of realizing *Brahman*, for they help the mind to fix itself on *Brahman*, but are not in themselves the objects of higher realization. Therefore, when those statements in which *Brahman* is said to abide in a particular thing, contradict those statements in which the true nature of *Brahman* is indicated, the former are to be rejected.

In many of his statements, Śaṅkara says that one knows the Self in and through one's own heart, for it abides in it.[77] The wise men realize the Self or *Brahman* in their hearts.[78] At the empirical level, *Brahman* is perceived clearly in the intellect; and apart from this there can be no knowledge of *Brahman*.[79] Like Rāhu, which is known in its relation to the sun, during a solar eclipse, *Brahman* is known at the empirical level through Its seeming connection with the internal organ or the heart.[80] Although *Brahman* abides in the hearts of all people and Its nature is revealed through all the functions of the mind, it is only those whose intellect is divine or pure that can see It. Śaṅkara makes a distinction between divine or pure intellect or the intellect of the wise men (*deva buddhi, viśuddha buddhi, vidvad buddhi, mahan buddhi* or *viśiṣṭa buddhi*) and the ordinary or the worldly intellect (*sāmānya buddhi, laukika buddhi* or *prākṛta buddhi*).[81] The former is that which, besides its capacity to know

---

[76] *SūB*, I.2.7.

[77] *MuUB*, II.2.9, III.1.7, II.2.2; *TaiUB*, II.6.1.

[78] *Vivekacūḍāmaṇi*, *śl.* 408; *ChāUB*, VIII.1.1, VIII.1.3.

[79] *TaiUB*, II.1.1; *SūB*, II.3.29.

[80] *TaiUB*, II.6.1.

[81] *BṛUB*, II.1, Introduction; *KaUB*, I.3.14, I.2.25; *TaiUB*, I.4.1-2; *KeUB*, I.2; *GKB*, IV.95.

the present, can penetrate into the past and foresee the future.[82] Because of its refined character, it can comprehend those things which are not known through the senses as well as those that are subtle. It is entirely free from all attachments and impurities and is as pure as the Self. In and through such a pure and serene intellect (*buddhi prasāda*) one can see *Brahman*. Whereas the ordinary or impure intellect, because of its involvement in the enjoyment of worldly things and its attachment to the senses and the passions, fails to know the Self, although it is revealed in it. It is finite (*alpa*) and wicked (*kṣudra*). All this does not mean that the divine intellect is something different from the ordinary intellect. They refer to one and the same intellect, that is, human intellect, and the distinction is made only in terms of purity and impurity. Although the Self reveals itself in and through the intellect, it is not the intellect. In reality, the intellect is in no way related to the Self. The Self is the underlying consciousness or that on which the intellect and its functions are based.

Now, that which is revealed in the heart is not the real *Brahman* or *Brahman* in Itself; It is the conditioned *Brahman* or *Īśvara*. By meditating on It and by knowing It one cannot become free from ignorance, the seed of worldly existence.[83] Further, the heart, a mere name and form, is just a symbol of *Brahman* and can only serve the purpose of meditation. And by meditating on *Brahman* that is in the heart, one cannot realize *Brahman* in Itself directly. When the particular name and form of a symbol are negated by knowledge, it no more remains a symbol, but becomes one with *Brahman*.[84] Then there will be no symbols to meditate upon nor will there be any scope for meditation on them. Meditation is based on the idea that the Self

[82] *ChāUB*, VIII.12.5.

[83] *TaiUB*, II.1, Introduction.

[84] *SūB*, IV.1.4.

is a meditator, and *brahmānubhava* is possible only when one realizes that one is not a meditator. Also, there can be no identity between the self which meditates and the symbols that are meditated upon, as both are illusory effects of *Brahman*. Identity is not possible at the level of manifested objects. As gold, all the objects made of gold are one, but as objects having different names and forms, they are not one or identical.[85]

When the intellect is withdrawn from all objects, it shines or remains in itself as pure intelligence, and such an objectless state of the intellect is known as the state of non-duality. It then attains identity with the Self or becomes one with it. Thus to realize *Brahman* as that which is in all beings is to realize it in relation to or as conditioned by the human intellect, whereas *Brahman* in itself is realized when the limitations of the intellect or the heart are transcended.

Independent type of reasoning

As discussed in the first chapter, mere reasoning (*śuṣka tarka*) or reasoning that is not in conformity with the scriptures (*śāstra bahiṣkr̥ta*) is not at all useful in knowing *Brahman* — Śaṅkara is uncompromising in his attitude towards such reasoning and those who rely on it or bad logicians (*kutārkika*). To know *Brahman* is to attain the highest end of life and since *Brahman* cannot be known through reasoning, the highest end of life cannot be achieved through it. Therefore, reasoning should be discarded as ineffective with regard to the highest end of life. But in discarding reasoning as ineffective in matters that lie beyond the empirical realm, its importance within the empirical realm is not at all denied or even questioned by Śaṅkara. As the aim of philosophy, according to him, is to attain immortality or to realize the Self directly, only that which

[85] *SūB*, IV.1.4.

proves to be effective in fulfilling that end should be accepted as finally authoritative.

Reasoning based on Śruti

Śaṅkara distinguishes mere reasoning from reasoning that subserves the scripture. The latter type of reasoning is that which is acceptable or favourable to revelation (*śrutyānugrahīta*). It is not arbitrary or unfettered (*niraṅkuśa*), but follows the lead of the scripture and experience. It is dependent (*ādhārita*) on revelation. According to Śaṅkara, such reasoning alone is helpful in acquiring right knowledge. In other words, reasoning should be taken into consideration, in spiritual matters, only in so far as it does not contradict the scripture. The scriptures themselves allow scope for such reasoning, for they enjoin reflection (*manana*) on the scriptural texts.[86] How such reasoning can help us in acquiring right knowledge is explained by Śaṅkara with the aid of an example. If a man from the country of Gandhāra were to enter a forest and lose his way back home, it would be possible for him to return home if he were properly informed about the path and if he had the ability to judge for himself the information supplied to him.[87] Here the place he wants to reach is known to him already, since it is his own place, but as he has forgotten the way to it, he requires guidance. But if he has no capacity to judge correctly the information given to him, he may be misguided and may not be able to reach his place. Similarly, the Self is known to all, but because of ignorance, its real identity is lost, as it were. Such that to regain one's lost or forgotten identity one must be able to reflect upon the information about it provided by the scriptures and the teacher. On the other hand, if the Self is completely unknown

---

[86] *SūB*, I.1.2; *BṛUB*, II.4.5.

[87] *ChāUB*, VI.14.2; *SūB*, I.1.2.

to one, one has to depend on faith only. But the Self is known to all, though not in its real nature, and as such, besides faith in the guidance of the scriptures, reasoning also proves helpful in knowing it.

Examples of independent-type and Śruti-based reasoning

Some examples of both these types of reasoning will now be presented. Using independent type of reasoning, people try to understand the cause of the universe, which is an observed fact, on the analogy of empirical experience. Basing on the law of causation, which is empirically valid, people try to know the cause of the universe also, for they think that the universe, being an effect, should have a cause. But in the case of the universe, as the cause is completely unknown, there can be no valid inference about the cause of the universe. So whatever people assume to be the cause of the universe is purely a matter of imagination. Thus in this type of reasoning, certain laws and analogies, which are valid within the empirical realm, are extended to the non-empirical realm. When they are so applied, they lose their validity, for then they become unfounded or baseless. Nor is this type of reasoning really an inference, as all the conditions of a valid inference are not fulfilled in it.

Within the empirical sphere causes are also directly observed, but not guessed. When certain things are observed to follow certain other things, and some sort of necessary relationship between them is also observed to exist, then it is possible to establish a cause and effect relationship between them. The conclusion that fire exists where there is smoke is based on actual experience that fire and smoke are related. As such the validity of an inference is not independent of experience; it is based on perception. From this it follows that it is not possible to infer anything about the cause of the universe solely on the basis of what is empirically observed, because the necessary relationship in question cannot be established in the case of the universe. So, the various theories about the cause of the universe propounded by different philosophers cannot be considered as based on valid inference, and they are bound to end in mutual contradiction. Such theories are only a matter of guess work (*utprekṣā*) or imagination (*kalpanā*) and hence they are not universally valid. Thus universally valid knowledge about the cause of the universe cannot be acquired through pure reasoning.

According to Śaṅkara, it is possible to demonstrate the unreality of duality on the basis of reasoning, without depending upon the scriptures.[88] One of his arguments, presented in the form of a syllogism, runs thus: Whatever is perceived is illusory, for dream objects which are perceived are illusory; so, the world is illusory as it is also perceived.[89] But non-duality cannot be demonstrated positively by any inference. However, in his commentary on *Gauḍapāda Kārikā*, Śaṅkara says that it is possible to establish non-duality on the basis of reasoning also.[90] This may seem to contradict his uncompromising attitude towards reasoning with regard to *Brahman*-knowledge. But really there is no such contradiction, because in this context he means by reasoning what he generally favours, that is, the reasoning based on the scriptures and experience. This can be ascertained from his other statements found in the same chapter and elsewhere. Moreover, in all his commentaries on other sacred texts, there can be found no statement treating reason at par with the scriptures, as far as knowing *Brahman* is concerned. Even where he says that reasoning is helpful in knowing *Brahman*, he

---

[88] *GKB*, II.1.

[89] Ibid., II.4.

[90] Ibid., III.1.

immediately asserts that it is the reasoning based on scripture, but not the reasoning of the logicians. In his commentary on *Gauḍapāda Kārikā*, where the above statement is found, we find the following statement also:

> The Self cannot be established by the reasoning of a man who follows the logicians' method of argumentation, as the Self referred to by us is different from the Self established by the logicians.[91]

Again, he says in the same chapter that the false views advanced by the logicians cannot be accepted as true and relied upon.[92] In *Bṛhadāraṇyaka Upaniṣad Bhāṣya*, he advances certain arguments, which are apparently based on natural reason, to prove the existence of *Brahman*, but then he explains that their value is secondary to that of the scriptural statements.[93] Those arguments are not valid independent of the scripture, whereas scriptural statements are intrinsically valid. Therefore, one should not rely solely on those arguments if one wants to become free from ignorance and attain liberation. Śaṅkara says that the rational evidence in favour of *Brahman*'s existence and nature is put forth only to remove certain popular misconceptions about It, such as that *Brahman* does not exist or that its nature is "this" or "that", but not to prove the existence of *Brahman*.[94] The method of negation adopted in Vedānta to communicate the knowledge of *Brahman* may lead to misunderstanding, whereby people may think that *Brahman* is pure void. Therefore, rational evidence is adduced to remove such possible misconceptions about *Brahman* and also to refute untruth, but not to establish anything about *Brahman* positively.

---

[91] *GKB*, III.11, tr. Swami Nikhilananda, p. 155.

[92] Ibid., III.13.

[93] *BṛUB*, III.8.9-10.

[94] Ibid., II.8.9.

Place of reason in Brahmānubhava

The dependent type of reasoning, which Śaṅkara accepts, starts with the presupposition that the scriptural statements are absolutely true. In supersensible matters, like *Brahman*, the authority of the scripture is equivalent to that of perception.[95] The function of this type of reasoning is threefold. First, it supports the scriptural truth by way of interpreting the states of empirical experience, namely waking, dream and deep sleep or it shows how a correct interpretation of these states of experience will confirm the truth of the scriptures. Second, it helps to find out the correct meaning of the important scriptural statements like "That thou art" and "I am *Brahman*". Last, with its aid the Upaniṣadic statements, which are apparently unrelated to each other, can be connected in a coherent way to form a perfect doctrine of non-duality. It also helps in removing the apparent contradictions that may be found in the scriptures. The commentaries of Śaṅkara in which he attempted to connect and interpret the various scriptural statements in a systematic and coherent manner are an outstanding and clear example of this type of reasoning. The following arguments of Śaṅkara may elucidate the "dependent" type of reasoning. The dreaming and waking states of experience exclude each other; therefore the Self is not affected by them. They do not essentially belong to the Self. This may be interpreted to mean: As the dream experience does not accompany the Self during the waking state and as the waking experience is not present during the state of dreams, both these states of experience do not constitute the essential nature of the Self.[96] Besides, as the witness of these states, the Self is different from them and its existence is not dependent on them. On the contrary, if they are to be natural to the Self, it should not be found without them and also one state cannot

---

[95] *SūB*, I.13.28.

[96] Ibid., II.1.6., 9.

sublate the other. This implies that the Self in itself is free from these states of experience. It is beyond what is empirically experienced. Now, if the states of deep sleep and trance (*samādhi*) are taken into consideration and interpreted, the real nature of the Self may become clear.[97] In deep sleep, the Self enters into its own nature of non-duality. It becomes free, as it were, from all the differences and distinctions experienced during waking and dream states and remains in its true nature of pure consciousness. On the basis of the complete absence of self-consciousness and object-consciousness in the states of deep sleep and trance, the real nature of the Self can be known to be undifferentiated consciousness. And because the same empirical self attains the state of non-duality or its own true nature, its fundamental identity with the Self or *Brahman* can also be established. In other words, the same Self which appears as finite, limited and suffering when it is viewed from the standpoints of waking and dream states, is known to be non-dual and pure consciousness on the basis of deep sleep and trance.

Through the same sort of reasoning, Śaṅkara attempts to prove the illusory nature of duality. According to him, the duality is but an imagination of the mind, for its existence is known only when the mind is active. This explains why the duality is experienced during waking and dream states of experience only, but not in deep sleep.[98] In deep sleep, it is not experienced because the mind ceases to be active then. So also, when perfect knowledge of the Self arises duality is not experienced. On the basis of this, it can be established that duality is not ultimately real, and that as it is due to the activity of the mind it disppears along with the mind.[99] This type of reasoning can be extended to prove the existence of *Brahman* and also Its non-dual nature. The illusory

[97] *SūB*, II.1.9.

[98] *GKB*, III.31.

[99] Ibid., III.31, III.18.

nature of empirical experience points out to the existence of something which forms the substratum of it, as no illusion is possible without being based on something which is real.[100] To take the example of rope–snake illusion, the experience of the illusory snake is made possible because of the really existing rope. The reality of rope is the substratum on which the experience of an illusory snake is based. Similarly, *Brahman* is the substratum of the appearance of the world or the world is a superimposition on *Brahman*. However, these conclusions which are arrived at by way of rational interpretation of the observed facts are secondary to scriptural statements. They are supposed to support and strengthen one's conviction and faith in the truth of the scriptures. This is one of the most important functions of "dependent" type of reasoning.[101]

Another important function of it is to bring out the correct meaning of the scriptural statements.[102] The achievement of the highest end of life depends on perfect knowledge, which as the knowledge of an objectively existing reality, does not leave room for variation and contradiction. The knowledge of an objectively existing reality should be objective and universally valid, and such perfect and objective knowledge alone can remove ignorance, the root cause of all suffering. Though scriptural statements are accepted as the source of valid knowledge of *Brahman* by many, there is a diversity of opinion with regard to the real meaning of some of these important statements. Different people interpret their meaning differently, according to their own capacity to understand and reason out. But all those contradictory interpretations of the same sentences cannot be true. Therefore, their real meaning, which should be the same for all, must be ascertained.

---

[100] *GKB*, II.33; *SūB*, II.1.14.

[101] *BṛUB*, III.1, Introduction, IV.5, Introduction; *Upadeśasāhasrī*, XVI.68.

[102] *SūB*, II.1.11; *ChāUB*, VII.15.4; *KeUB*, II.1.

Now, it is reasoning of the dependent type which can assist us in determining the true meaning of the scriptural statements through adequate examination (*parīkṣā*) of them.[103] Thereby the apparent contradictions can also be resolved. This is the proper method of ascertaining the real meaning of the great Upaniṣadic statements like "That thou art" and "I am *Brahman*". When thus employed, reason can save an individual from falling a victim to the wrong interpretations and the consequent absence of liberation.[104] Thus reasoning which is in accordance with the scriptures is essential if *Brahman* is to be realized. In the words of Śaṅkara:

> It is only those who have a firm hold on the scriptrures and reasoning that can accurately determine the meaning of the scriptural passages.[105]

The other important function of this type of reasoning is to mutually relate and harmonize (*samanvaya*) the Upaniṣadic passages, so that the truth which they contain becomes revealed.[106] The various key passages of the Upaniṣads, on which the doctrine of non-duality is founded, are found scattered throughout the Upaniṣads; and there are also apparent mutual contradictions among some of them. Unless the former kind of statements are properly connected and interpreted and their meaning correctly established, they do not serve the higher purpose of man. The latter kind of statements should be discussed, reconciled and their purpose established. "The various passages found scattered in the Upaniṣads should be discussed; for the comprehension of *Brahman* is effected by the ascertainment, consequent on discussion, of the sense of the Vedānta texts."[107] Through this

---

[103] *BṛUB*, III.1, Introduction.

[104] *Upadeśasāhasrī*, XVI.68.

[105] *BṛUB*, IV.5.15.

[106] *SūB*, I.1.2.

[107] Ibid., tr. Thibaut, vol. 1, p. 17.

type of reasoning the doubts of the seeker will be cleared and his faith in the existence of *Brahman* is confirmed. Doubts regarding the validity of the scriptures, existence of *Brahman*, one's identity with It and the possibility of realizing that identity are to be cleared before one gets faith in them. Faith cannot be total and firm when doubts linger in the mind of a believer. According to Śaṅkara, only such knowledge, the certainty of which is determined (*nirdhārita*) by both scriptures and reasoning, is perfect and deserves one's complete faith.[108] "When both scriptural evidence and argument combinedly try to establish the unity of the Self, they can show it as clearly as a *bel* fruit placed on the palm of one's hand."[109] Śankara finds another useful purpose of this reasoning, namely the refutation of the doctrines which oppose or contradict the doctrine of non-duality. To create conviction in the Advaitic interpretation of the scriptures, the various interpretations that oppose it, and also other independent doctrines of Reality are to be refuted, by pointing out the defects inherent in such interpretations and doctrines. In the presence of such interpretations and doctrines, it is not possible to have faith in the validity of Advaita doctrine. They are obstacles in the way to perfect knowledge.

> We expose certain defects inherent in the theories of the logicians, not in the spirit of the logicians, but in order that people desirous of freedom may become devoted to the true import of the Upaniṣads, namely the realization of the Self's non-duality by ignoring those other theories.[110]

Thus while reasoning when it does not take into consideration the scriptural evidence in trying to understand the nature of ultimate reality becomes unfounded, it serves as an auxiliary

---

[108] *GKB*, III.17.

[109] *BṛUB*, III.1, Introduction.

[110] *PrUB*, VI.3, tr. Swami Gambhirananda, vol. II, p. 494.

to the scriptures in generating *Brahman*-knowledge when it recognizes the authority of Śruti in supernatural matters.

Methods of reasoning

Reasoning need not always be in the form of an argument. According to Śaṅkara, a story or a parable (*ākhyāyika*) can also be a form of reasoning.[111] As the truth is highly abstruse and very subtle, it is very difficult to comprehend it if it is presented abstractly through statements that merely convey the bare meaning as logical propositions do. Various methods are therefore adopted in Vedānta to impart instruction about *Brahman*. Presenting truth in the form of a parable or a myth is one such method and is fruitful in promoting easy understanding. The method of dialogue is also useful in promoting understanding of the scriptural truth.[112] This method is employed by Śaṅkara himself in his commentaries. It consists in stating and developing one by one the various possible alternate doctrines to what is the correct one and then systematically refuting them one by one, so that the correct doctrine is established. It may also consist in formulating at length various possible objections to or criticisms of the true doctrine and then systematically refuting them. Another method of reasoning is to discuss a subject thoroughly in an assembly of learned men (*pariṣad*).[113] Śaṅkara says that in trying to understand and solve certain very subtle philosophical problems like the nature of the self and its relation to *Brahman*, deliberation by an assembly of learned scholars is desirable.[114] The outcome of such conferences depends on the qualified persons participating in it. Such learned assemblies may consist of three to ten members. Since men of varied capacities and talents and

---

[111] *BṛUB*, IV.3.2, II.1, Introduction; *SūB*, III.4.24.

[112] *BṛUB*, IV.5, Introduction.

[113] Ibid., IV.3.2.

[114] Ibid.

also well versed in the scriptures and adept in reasoning gather together in such assemblies, it would be easy to determine the correct meaning of the scriptural statements in such assemblies. The assemblies of the learned, organized by King Janaka of old as referred to in the *Bṛhadāraṇyaka Upaniṣad* were of this type. So were Śaṅkara's disputations with different scholars during his peripathetic life.

Śaṅkara also considers the problem of contradiction between reason and *brahmānubhava* and explains that there is no room for any contradiction between them. According to him, contradiction can arise only when the scope and aim of both reasoning and experience are identical; but this is not so. The sphere of reason is determined by its nature and the limitations inherent within it. It operates within the empirical realm only and cannot step into trans-empirical realm. But experience of the sort we are now concerned with is not empirical. Contradiction between reasoning and this experience could arise if both were alternate ways of attaining the supreme truth of non-duality. But as Śaṅkara insists, the truth of non-duality cannot be known through reasoning; it is known by being it or through direct experience of it. Mere reasoning has nothing definite to say about *Brahman* and inference does not operate at all in this case. So, there can be no scope for contradiction between them, just as there is no contradiction between Śruti and perception. They do not talk of the same thing or they are not the sources to know the same reality. Each is valid within its own sphere, and they can contradict each other only when they talk of the same thing in contradicting terms. Śaṅkara asks: "how can the unity of *Brahman* contradict inference of which it is never an object".[115]

[115] *BṛUB*, II.1.20, tr. Swami Madhavananda, p. 317.

6

The Object of Brahmānubhava

WHEN we speak of *brahmānubhava* it may be taken to mean that it is the experience of *Brahman* or in it *Brahman* is experienced as an object, because ordinarily experience is always of an object, either imaginary or real. In this chapter we shall discuss whether *brahmānubhava* has an object and, if so, what is its nature; and if it has an object or if it is the experience of an object, can it still be considered as non-dual?

Has Brahmānubhava an object?

According to Śaṅkara, *brahmānubhava* is an objectless experience. *Brahman* in Itself is never an object (*viṣaya*) of experience.[1] It is the Self of everyone, but not an object that can be experienced as something different from oneself. In the Upaniṣads, *Brahman* is never presented as an object, like Mount Meru, to be attained or experienced. The great Upaniṣadic statements like "That thou art" and "I am *Brahman*", which speak of *Brahman* show that *Brahman* is to be realized as one's own Self, but not as something other than the Self as "this is *Brahman*" or "that is *Brahman*". When the scriptures teach that *Brahman* is to be seen, heard and understood, the purport of such statements, according to Śaṅkara, is not that *Brahman* can be seen, heard or understood, but simply to direct one's

---

[1] *ChāUB*, VIII.6.3, VIII.4.1; *KeUB*, I.4; *KaUB*, II.3.9. In this chapter "object" (*viṣaya*) is used to mean that which is experienced by a subject and not in the sense of a thing (*vastu*).

attention towards one's own Self and away from the external objects, just as the imperative phrases like "look at this" are meant to attract one's attention.[2] Even those statements in which *Brahman* is stated to be "all" or "everything" do not aim at establishing the existence of "all" as something different from the Self. They simply point out that in realizing one's own Self, one attains everything also, as the Self is everything. Thus to attain "all" is not, like a king attaining a kingdom, to attain something which is other than one's own Self, but to realize that the Self is everything or there is nothing different from the Self.[3] As *Brahman* is none other than one's own self in its real nature, *brahmānubhava* does not mean experiencing *Brahman* as an object, but the realization of the real nature of one's own self (*svarūpa pratipatti*). As Śaṅkara says, "abiding in one's own Self (*ātmanyavasthānam*) on the removal of ignorance is the attainment of the highest (*parāprāpti*)".[4]

As it has been pointed out earlier, Self-realization does not mean the Self experiencing *Brahman* as something other than itself or the Self experiencing itself as *Brahman* or the Self becoming an object of experience to itself.[5] As the direct realization of one's own self in its true nature, *brahmānubhava* or Self-realization excludes all such possibilities. In realizing the true nature of one's own self, one does not become an object of experience to oneself. Things become *viṣaya* when

---

[2] *SūB*, III.2.21, I.1.4.

[3] *ChāUB*, VIII.12.1.

[4] *TaiUB*, I.1, Introduction.

[5] The ultimate experience is not the self's experience that it is *Brahman*. If it is the realization of "I" as *Brahman*, it indicates awareness on the part of "I" that it is *Brahman*, as it happens when one realizes "I am so and so". But ultimate experience is just pure consciousness, in which there is neither the awareness of "I", nor of *Brahman*. It is also not the experience of the Self by the Self as "I am I" or "I am what I am". It is not the Self's experience of itself.

they are experienced; whatever can be experienced is an object. According to Śaṅkara, only inert or non-conscious things become objects of experience, for they cannot exist for themselves; whereas the Self is pure consciousness and self-existent. Contrary to this, if the Self or pure consciousness were to become an object of experience, it would require another consciousness to experience it and yet another to experience the latter, and so on unendingly.[6] Moreover, by its very nature, consciousness excludes all possibility of its being experienced as an object, for it is always that which experiences.[7] And also, there is no conscious principle besides the Self to which it may possibly become an object of experience. Besides, as the Self is present everywhere as the self or essence of everything, including the self of the one who wants to experience it, it cannot be experienced as finite things are experienced. There is also no possibility of the Self becoming an object of experience to itself, as its nature is indivisible.

> The Self cannot be attained by the Self, inasmuch as there is no split in its nature and *Brahman* (the ultimate goal) is no other than the Self of the attainer.[8]

Now, that which is commonly known to all as the self or the empirical self of which everyone speaks in such terms as "I know myself" and "I am so and so" is not the real Self which is *Brahman*. It is the Self on which the non-self is superimposed. It is ultimately unreal and has no objective reality. Therefore, to know it is not to know the Self or *Brahman*.

Thus the Self in itself can never become an object of experience. As it is pure consciousness or pure experience, to "experience" it is not to experience it as an object, which is

---

[6] *Upadeśasāhasrī*, part I (prose), 99.

[7] *BṛUB*, II.4.14; *AiUB*, II.1, Introduction.

[8] *TaiUB*, II.5.1, tr. Swami Gambhirananda, vol. I, p. 334.

impossible, but to be it. Although, as pure consciousness, the Self remains the same eternally, because of ignorance it is identified either with the intellect or with the objects experienced thereby. As such, the Self is neither the subject that experiences nor the objects that are experienced. And the Self is realized only when the false notion that it is the subject or the object is given up. In giving up ignorance, the Self is not giving up anything of its own nor gaining anything that it had not, but just becoming self-revealed, as it were. This is figuratively expressed by Śaṅkara as experiencing one's Self.[9] So when it is said in the Upaniṣads that the Self knows itself it does not mean the objectification of the Self (*ātmano viṣayīkaraṇam*), but only means the removal of ignorance; and this is *brahmānubhava*.[10]

The objectlessness of *brahmānubhava* becomes further clear if its unique nature and significance are understood. In the state of duality, there will be objects other than the Self which it can experience, and therefore experience then means the experience of an object by a subject. But when everything is realized as one with the Self and when nothing exists different from the Self, then experience:

> For want of objects (*viṣayābhavāt*) to rest upon becomes

---

[9] *TaiUB*, II.8.5.

[10] *BṛUB*, I.4.10.

The expression is meaningful from the standpoint of duality or empirical experience. It means that the Self is the object of higher realization and it is not experienced by anything other than the Self. It removes the doubt whether something other than the Self is experienced in higher realization and affirms that *Brahman* is not other than the Self. But it does not indicate that the Self is experienced by the Self as an object. See *BṛUB*, I.3.8.

> established in the Self alone (*ātmasamastham*) like the heat of fire (in the absence of fuel). It is birthless, it then attains the state of supreme non-duality.[11]

In *brahmānubhava*, the Self whose nature is pure knowledge, and which is considered to be the object of knowledge (from the empirical standpoint) knows itself by means of unborn knowledge which is the very nature of the Self (*ātmasvarūpa*).[12] Thus in *brahmānubhava*, one does not experience anything other than one's own Self and that too not as an object, but by being it. Such an experience does not relate itself to any object.[13] It is the very nature of the Self. What has been said above clearly shows that *brahmānubhava* and *Brahman* are identical. *Brahmānubhava* is not the experience of *Brahman* nor is *Brahman* experienced as an object in it. While the object of empirical experience and such an experience are essentially different, *brahmānubhava* is not different from *Brahman*. This fact is also attested by those who have realized *Brahman*, according to whom, *Brahman*, which is regarded as the object of higher realization, from the standpoint of non-realization, is not different from such realization or *brahmānubhava*.

> The knowers of *Brahman* say that absolute knowledge (*jñāpti mātram*) which is devoid of all imagination or non-conceptual (*akalpakam*) and is therefore birthless or uncaused is non-different from *Brahman* (*brahman abhinnam*), the knowable; it is identical with *Brahman*, the object of knowledge.[14]

Śaṅkara says that in *brahmānubhava*, the differences of the experiencer (*labdha*), the experienced (*labdhya*) and the experience (*upalabdhi*) are totally absent.

---

[11] *GKB*, III.38, tr. Swami Nikhilananda, p. 199.

[12] *GKB*, III.33.

[13] Ibid., IV.99.

[14] Ibid., III.33.

> Advaita gives the philosophy of the ultimate reality characterized by the identity of the knower, knowledge and the object of knowledge.[15]

The knower or the individual self in its true nature is itself the object of experience, namely the Self, and the nature of it is pure experience. In other words, one experiences one's Self, which is pure experience and that is possible only by being it.

Some Upaniṣadic illustrations

Although *brahmānubhava* is described as unique and non-dual or having no distinction of the experiencer and the experienced, we find in some of the Upaniṣads certain examples illustrating the nature of it in which the distinction of one who attains and the object attained is maintained. These scriptural illustrations may therefore seem to contradict the non-dual nature of *brahmānubhava*. What follows is a discussion of the significance of these illustrations as explained by Śaṅkara. In the *Bṛhadāraṇyaka Upaniṣad*, we find the following illustration.[16] When a lover is fully embraced by his beloved, both desiring each other's company, he is not aware of anything else, either within or without. That is to say, while in the state of union, he is neither conscious of things external to himself as "this is something and that is another", nor does he aware of anything internal as "I am happy or miserable". He is then neither self-conscious nor object-conscious. But one who is not so embraced is aware of external things and of oneself. In like manner, when the individual self is fully embraced by the supreme Self, it does not know anything, either external or internal. In the same Upaniṣad there is another illustration.[17] When a lump of salt, which is a product or modification of sea

---

[15] *GKB*, IV.1, tr. Swami Nikhilananda, p. 214.

[16] *BṛUB*, IV.3.21.

[17] Ibid., II.4.12.

water, is dropped into sea water, its cause, it dissolves and becomes one with sea water. Then no one can trace it in the water or distinguish it from the latter, for they have become one and the same. Likewise, when the individual self enters into its cause, the supreme Self, it becomes one with or indistinguishable from the supreme Self, and loses its separate identity. The following illustration is from the *Praśna Upaniṣad*.[18] When the self attains *Brahman*, its ultimate goal, it loses its individuality and becomes one with *Brahman*, just as the rivers on reaching the sea, their goal, lose their individual identities, consisting of name and form and become one with the sea. In his commentaries on the *Kaṭha* and the *Muṇḍaka Upaniṣad*, Śaṅkara himself says that in attaining *Brahman*, the self, like a blown-out lamp, loses its individuality and becomes one with *Brahman*, just as the space within a pot becomes one with the universal space when the pot is destroyed.[19]

In all these illustrations, which are meant to illustrate the essential nature of *brahmānubhava*, there is the duality of one which attains and the thing attained. Union is the main theme of all these illustrations and union is meaningless without duality. In union two things are related and the oneness which is attained through such union is not the absolute oneness or identity. It is the oneness that results when two things which are different, but alike are united. Between the things united, one is superior to the other and hence one is the goal of the other. Even if the experience resulting from such union is non-dual and undifferentiated, it is produced by the union of two distinct realities. And such union also involves some activity like merging or entering; and anything that can be achieved through effort cannot be permanent and natural. Now, if *brahmānubhava* is to be understood on the basis of these

[18] *PrUB*, VI.5; *MuUB*, III.2.8.

[19] *KaUB*, II.3.14; *MuUB*, III.2.6.

illustrations, the duality of the self and *Brahman* should be admitted. Further, if it is admitted that in *brahmānubhava*, the self is embraced by *Brahman*, like the lover is embraced by the beloved or dissolved into *Brahman*, like salt into water, or entered into *Brahman*, its ultimate goal, like the rivers into the sea, it should also be admitted that *Brahman* is the object of *brahmānubhava* and that the self is somehow distinct from and yet one with *Brahman*. That is to say, the self and *Brahman* are two distinct realities and the self's oneness with *Brahman* is a result of its union with *Brahman*. This means that *Brahman* is the goal of the self or that *Brahman* is the object of higher realization. Then *brahmānubhava* naturally means the experience of *Brahman* by the self. This position contradicts the fundamental doctrine of Advaita, according to which, Reality is one only and there is no second reality besides it. If what exists is one only without a second, any sort of union, whether it is through merging or embracing, is impossible. The experience resulting from such union may be undifferentiated and non-dual, but to produce it there should be two equally real entities, namely the self and *Brahman*. If such is the case, the immutability of *Brahman* should be denied and some sort of change or transformation in Its nature should be acknowledged, for unless there is some change or transformation in *Brahman*'s nature, the self cannot come into existence and the subsequent union between it and *Brahman* cannot take place. Moreover, any experience which is the result of a process cannot be absolute, for whatever is caused is transitory.

All this is unacceptable to Śaṅkara, according to whom, the difference between the self and *Brahman* is only seeming or illusory, but not real. In reality, the self and *Brahman* are not two things. The one and the same reality appears as if it is differentiated into the self and *Brahman* from the standpoint of ignorance. Therefore, the attainment of the Supreme Self means, according to Śaṅkara, the removal of such ignorance which makes one think in terms of duality. It is like removing the darkness to make the rope reveal itself as it is, and not as a snake. If the darkness of ignorance because of which one thinks that one is not *Brahman* is destroyed, one realizes that one is already *Brahman*. This is an objective and eternal fact whether one has realized it or not. Now, if the Upaniṣadic illustrations are rightly understood and correctly interpreted, they do not contradict the fundamental doctrine of Śaṅkara. In the first illustration in which the self is said to be embraced by the Supreme Self, what Śaṅkara means by the Supreme Self is not something different from the individual self which is embraced, if the latter is viewed in its real nature.[20] The individual self is embraced by its own real nature which is the Supreme Self. Hence what is embraced is not different from what embraces. They are not two different realities, but are one and the same. However, as the empirical self thinks of the Supreme Self as something different from itself, before it has realized its real nature, the idea of embracing is meaningful from the standpoint of an empirical self. But what actually happens in *brahmānubhava* is that the Self realizes its real nature by giving up ignorance. In the other illustrations in which the Self is said to merge or enter into *Brahman*, the words "entering" (*praveśa*), "merging" (*āpti*) and "attaining" (*labdha*) are figurative.[21] They only mean that the idea of difference created by ignorance vanishes in realizing one's real nature, and this is figuratively expressed as attaining the Supreme Self or entering into it. Śaṅkara says:

> We hold that it is the definite conclusion of all the Upaniṣads that we are nothing but the Self or *Brahman*, that is always the same, homogeneous, one without a second, unchanging,

---

[20] *BṛUB*, IV.3.21.

[21] Ibid., IV.4.6; *SūB*, IV.3.14; *TaiUB*, II.8.5; *KaUB*, I.3.11; *BGB*, XVIII.55.

> birthless, undecaying, immortal, deathless and free from fear. Therefore, the statement "he is merged in *Brahman*" is but a figurative one (*upacāra*) meaning the cessation of differences created by ignorance as a result of knowledge.[22]

Similarly, in the illustration of a blown-out lamp, the loss of individuality of the self is figurative, for in reality it is not destroyed; it only realizes its real nature by giving up its empirical nature.[23] Only the limiting adjuncts, which are the creation of ignorance, and because of which there seems to be an individual self are discarded, and the Self on which these are superimposed remains unaffected by such removal. The empirical self has no objective existence, as it is only an imaginary entity and, therefore, its destruction can only mean the removal of ignorance. The absence of any sort of duality in *brahmānubhava* is also made clear by Śaṅkara in his commentary on the *Vedānta-Sūtras*. When a doubt is raised whether the distinction of one who conciliates and the Being that is conciliated is not implied in the statement, "the *yogin*s see the unevolved Self free from all plurality at the time of perfect conciliation (*samarādhana*)", Śaṅkara replies that there is no possibility for any such duality, since conciliation just means the realization of the Self's true nature by dispelling ignorance.[24]

Besides, the merger spoken of cannot but be unreal and figurative, for the reason that an unreal and illusory reality, like the individual self, cannot merge itself into *Brahman*, which is absolutely real, in the real sense of the term. It is like saying that an illusory snake is merged into the rope, which is real, when the darkness is removed.[25] Here the simple fact of the disappearance of the illusory things on the removal of

---

[22] *BṛUB*, IV.4.6.

[23] *BGB*, XIII.28; *SūB*, I.3.19, II.3.17, I.4.22.

[24] *SūB*, III.2.24-26.

[25] *ChāUB*, VIII.5.4.

ignorance is figuratively expressed as the merging of the illusory things into the real one. Similarly, all those statements, in which it is said that the senses merge into the mind, and the mind into the Self and ultimately the whole of multiplicity into the ultimate reality are meaningful in the figurative sense only. Moreover, the merger of the Self in *Brahman* or the differentiated universe in *Brahman* is not a natural (*svābhāvika*) merger like the effects merging into their respective causes. For instance, all the things made of clay merge into clay when they are destroyed. The merger of the self in *Brahman*, on the other hand, is a conscious (*buddhipūrvaka*) one and is effected in one's own realization through higher knowledge.[26] The realization through knowledge that everything is in reality *Brahman* only is the conscious merger of everything in *Brahman*. Accordingly, Śaṅkara says:

> That which is consciously effected by the knowers of *Brahman* through their knowledge of *Brahman* is called absolute or perfect dissolution; and it takes place when ignorance is destroyed.[27]

This is figuratively expressed as the ultimate merger of everything in *Brahman*. Again, the fact that liberation is through knowledge only, but not through any change of state or through union (*saṁyoga*) or through going or reaching (*gamana*) also indicates that the merger of the Self in *Brahman* is not literally true.[28] Thus, the problem of duality in *brahmānubhava* arises first, when we try to understand the Upaniṣadic illustrations literally instead of figuratively and, second, when we try to understand the nature of *brahmānubhava* from the standpoint of duality, which is inevitable if we want to have a

---

[26] *BṛUB.*, II.4.11.

[27] Ibid.

[28] *Upadeśasāhasrī*, XVI, *śls*. 39-41.

rational understanding of it. According to Śaṅkara, any comparison must not be taken too literally and extended to all the details of the things compared.[29] Comparison through illustration is made only with reference to a particular aspect in respect of which the two things compared are similar, but not when the things compared are entirely similar or identical. If, on the other hand, there is absolute similarity between any two things compared, then there will be no scope for comparison. It is only when the things compared are similar with regard to a particular aspect, that comparison between them is possible, for comparison is to establish a relation of similarity between two different things, which are similar in one particular aspect, and are otherwise dissimilar. So, in understanding *brahmānubhava* with the help of the Upaniṣadic illustrations, *brahmānubhava* should not be compared in all its aspects with them. The comparison should be limited to that particular aspect only which is similar in both of them. Now, it is the nature of *brahmānubhava* that is sought to be explained with the help of these illustrations and so the comparison should be limited to that only, but should not be extended to other details like how it is attained. Thus, if the purpose of comparison is kept in view, the Upaniṣadic illustrations serve the purpose of elucidating the nature of *brahmānubhava.*

When the higher realization is viewed from the dualistic standpoint, that is, before *Brahman* is actually experienced as one's own Self, it appears as if it is the experience of *Brahman,* because empirically experience means the experience of an object. Before *Brahman* is realized as one's own Self, it is looked upon as something different from one's own Self and, from

---

[29] *SūB,* III.2.20; *Upadeśasāhasrī,* XVIII, *śl.* 86.

The illustrations of a hunter discovering himself to be a prince and a sick person recovering from the sickness, etc. point out how *Brahman* is attained and what such an attainment means.

such a viewpoint, *brahmānubhava* naturally means the experience of *Brahman*. Thus an individual, before realizing *Brahman* directly by being it, thinks of *Brahman* as the object of *brahmānubhava* or *brahmānubhava* as the experience of *Brahman*. He fails to understand the non-dual nature of *brahmānubhava*. Now, what is thus looked upon as an object of experience is different from that which is directly experienced by being it.

Brahman as an object of experience

The difference between *Brahman* in Itself or that which is actually experienced, not as an object of experience, but as experience itself by being It, and *Brahman* that is considered as the object of experience will now be discussed. The latter is pure existence (*sanmātram*), truth (*satyam*), pure knowledge (*jñānam*), infinitude (*anantam*) and pure bliss (*ānandam*).[30] These, according to Śaṅkara, constitute the intrinsic nature (*svarūpa*) of *Brahman*, like heat of fire. They are not the attributes or qualities of *Brahman*, but form the very nature of It. *Brahman* is pure existence (*asthita mātram*). As the ultimate ground of everything its existence cannot be denied.[31] If Its existence is not accepted as the ultimate fact, there results infinite regress, for the chain of causation will have no end if something is not admitted as the final cause. As pure existence the reality of *Brahman* cannot be refuted, since all such refutation presupposes It. It is the basis as well as the ultimate limit of all negation.[32] Absolute negation is not only meaningless, but also not possible. Everything may be denied as non-existing and illusory, but something must be accepted as the ultimate limit of all such negation; otherwise negation becomes meaningless. Negation is possible only when

[30] *TaiUB*, II.1.1; *BṛUB*, III.9.28.7, II.4.12.

[31] *SūB*, II.3.9.

[32] Ibid., III.2.2; *TaiUB*, II.5.1.

something that cannot be negated is considered to exist ultimately. And also, the very process of negation presupposes something whose existence cannot be refuted. *Brahman* is truth. That which is pure existence and pure knowledge cannot be unreal. Śaṅkara says that *Brahman*'s truth is affirmed by speaking of Its existence, because what exists must also be true (*sadaiva satyam*).[33] A thing is absolutely true when its nature is immutable, for the truth of a thing whose nature is ever changing cannot be true absolutely. Hence, to indicate that *Brahman* which is pure existence and pure knowledge is not unreal, it is said that *Brahman* is truth.[34] *Brahman* is pure knowledge or pure awareness (*śuddha caitanya*). It cannot be an insentient matter, for matter is not known to exist for itself. It is known to exist because of consciousness. Whereas *Brahman* is self-existent and self-evident.[35] What is thus absolutely true and pure consciousness cannot be finite and limited in nature. Finiteness involves imperfection and mortality. It is only to eliminate these notions from *Brahman*, it is said that *Brahman* is infinite and unlimited. Infinitude means the non-existence of anything besides *Brahman*. "Infinitude", "great" (*maha*), "unexcelled" (*niratiśaya*) and the "vast" (*bhūma*) are all synonyms.[36] Further, *Brahman*'s infinity also removes the possibility of It being the finite knowledge involving the subject–object duality. In other words, *Brahman* is not the knowledge of something or of someone, but knowledge itself which is infinite. *Brahman* is pure bliss. It is the negation of all suffering and misery.[37] What is infinite is also pure bliss. In what is finite there is no pure bliss, for the finite creates longing

---

[33] *TaiUB*, II.6.1.

[34] Ibid., II.1.1; *ChāUB*, VIII.3.4.

[35] Ibid., II.1.1.

[36] *ChāUB*, VII.23.1.

[37] *GKB*, III.47; *TaiUB*, II.9.1.

in the minds of the people for what is infinite; and all longing is a source of pain and there cannot be perfect bliss in what is the source of pain.[38] The bliss that is *Brahman* is not the bliss that is enjoyed. The bliss that is enjoyed is mortal, limited and transitory. It depends on blissful objects and vanishes along with them. But pure bliss, which is free from the limitations of the enjoyer and the enjoyed, is eternal and perfect.

Out of these, except the words "knowledge" and "truth", the other words like "infinitude" do not define *Brahman* through affirmation. They do so through negation, as for instance, the word "infinitude" defines *Brahman* in so far as it negates finitude.

The *Brahman* thus defined as truth, knowledge, bliss, etc. is not the real *Brahman* or *Brahman* in Itself.[39] The words like "knowledge", "bliss", "truth", *Brahman* and *ātman* which are employed to describe the Absolute fail to comprehend it. These are but the categories of human understanding which are superimposed on it. Śaṅkara says that *Brahman* is said to be truth, knowledge and non-dual only from the standpoint of duality, for of real *Brahman* nothing can be said.[40] In other words, the description of Reality in terms of knowledge, truth, etc., is possible from the standpoint of empirical self only and, hence, its validity and meaningfulness are confined to that standpoint only; and no such definition is possible of *Brahman* in Itself. Moreover, *Brahman* defined as truth, knowledge and bliss is looked upon as the goal of one's life. As the goal of one's life, it presupposes the duality of the individual self and *Brahman*. And as long as *Brahman* is viewed as the goal of one's life, it stands as something different from oneself. Before It is directly

---

[38] *ChāUB*, VII.23.1.

[39] *BṛUB*, II.3.6; *GKB*, IV.61-62; *TaiUB*, II.1.1.

[40] *BṛUB*, II.3.6; *KeUB*, II.1; *ChāUB*, VII.24.1; *BGB*, XIII.12.

realized, something positive should be said about *Brahman*, otherwise no one can ever know what *Brahman* is. If *Brahman* is to be realized, Its nature should be known to the individual in some positive way. If *Brahman* in itself, which is devoid of all attributes and is non-dual, is presented in negative terms as "not this", "not this", it may appear to an individual as if It is nothing. To obviate such possible misconceptions of *Brahman*, and also to provide some positive form of It to the individual self on which it can in the preliminary stages of *Brahman*-realization mediate, the scriptures impose a certain form on *Brahman*.[41] Thus when they say that *Brahman* is truth, knowledge and bliss, the existence of the individual self is presupposed. The above definition of *Brahman* involves another sort of duality, namely the scriptures on the one hand and *Brahman* of which they speak on the other. The *Brahman* which thus admits of duality cannot be the real *Brahman*. According to Śaṅkara, *Brahman* in Itself is not what the scriptures present It to be, for It is beyond the reach of all the sources of knowledge, as they are based on the duality of one who knows and the object known, and the scriptures are not free from such duality. They involve the duality of themselves and *Brahman* of which they teach and also, the duality of themselves and one who receives their teaching. They cannot function unless there is the duality of themselves and the one who receives their teaching or to whom they are intended. Now, anything that is presented to an individual self is looked upon by it as something different from itself, because its separate existence is a presupposition for any such presentation. It is the subject and anything that is presented to it stands as an object. Śaṅkara says that the scriptural statement, "where one sees nothing else, etc.", may mean for an ignorant person the duality of the subject and the object. The word "where" may mean for him, the place or the

[41] *ChāUB*, VIII.1, Introduction.

container and the word "sees" the activity of seeking. Similarly the statement, "It is below, etc.", may mean to an ignorant person that *Brahman* is something different from his Self.[42] Likewise, when *Brahman* is described or defined as existence, knowledge and bliss, it may give rise to the idea that the reality so defined is something beyond the Self. The intention of the scriptures may be to present *Brahman* as non-dual, but when It is presented to an individual, the latter may consider It as an object of his higher realization. Thus any definition of *Brahman*, whether it defines *Brahman* in relation to something or in Itself, in so far as it presupposes a definer, excludes from Itself the definer, and hence It cannot be *Brahman* in Itself which is one without a second. In all definitions there is the duality of the definer and the defined and to know *Brahman* in Itself is to transcend all such duality. For this reason, Śaṅkara says that *Brahman* in Itself is never an object of knowledge, including scriptural knowledge. It is beyond the reach of all scriptural statements.[43] Therefore, what the scriptures present as *Brahman* is not the real *Brahman*. It is *Brahman* in Itself on which some definition or form is superimposed; and *Brahman* in Itself cannot be defined or presented in any way or form. What the scriptures present is only an approximation of It. *Brahman* in Itself cannot be presented as this or that thing, for there is nothing other than It to which It can be presented so. What is directly experienced in or as *brahmānubhava* is neither an object nor a subject. It is that which is beyond all relations and differences. It is a mass (*ghana*) of pure consciousness and the word *ghana* is

[42] *ChāUB*, VII.25.1.

[43] *SūB*, IV.1.16; *TaiUB*, II.1.1; *BṛUB*, IV.4.20.

Scriptures merely indicate or point out the existence of *Brahman* and direct our attention towards It. On the other hand, whatever is said in positive terms is said about the conditioned form of *Brahman*. About *Brahman* in Itself scriptures adopt the method of negation or silence.

used to exclude from the nature of *Brahman* everything that is alien to it (*jātyantara*). It is like a lump of pure gold in which there is nothing that is not gold.[44]

Brahman is defined as truth, knowledge, etc. to meet the demands of intellect.[45] It is the intellect which tries to comprehend *Brahman* as if It is an object, and in doing so, it imposes some form on It. It is logic which requires that what exists absolutely must also be real and that such a reality cannot be insentient, finite and mortal. All this is due to the active functioning of the intellect which tries to determine the nature of everything. In its attempt to explain what is empirically experienced, it conceives some principle as the ultimate basis of all that is empirically experienced, and for it *Brahman* is such a basis. For this reason, it is said that *Brahman* in Itself cannot be conceived, and hence defined; and what, on the contrary, is conceived and defined is not the real *Brahman*.[46] It is beyond the reach of the mind and also of the scripture, or to put it differently, it is not possible to have any type of objective knowledge, whether perceptual or conceptual or scriptural, of *Brahman*. About It nothing can be affirmed. Another reason why the defined *Brahman* cannot be the real *Brahman* is the former's incompleteness (*asamasta*). *Brahman* is variously understood, for example, as Indra, *Īśvara*, vital force and mind, and meditated upon by various people, depending upon their capacity to understand and the purity of their minds.[47]

In the absence of correct understanding of *Brahman*'s nature, one superimposes one's own understanding of It on real *Brahman*, which is the substratum of all superimposition and thinks that what one has understood as *Brahman* is the real

---

44 *BṛUB*, II.4.12.

45 *GKB*, IV.61-62.

46 *SūB*, III.2.22; *MāUB*, I.7.

47 *GKB*, II.20-28.

Brahman. The highest of such conceptions is that *Brahman* is existence, knowledge, bliss, etc. The defect with these conceptions is that they are not all-inclusive and complete. For instance, when the ultimate reality is conceived as something, some other thing will be excluded from it. Thus whenever any particular thing is asserted about *Brahman*, it may mean the exclusion of other things from It, and as a result *Brahman*'s nature becomes limited (*alpam*). And what is not all-inclusive or what is finite cannot be absolute and ultimate. Such that, even the highest definition of *Brahman* as "truth", "knowledge" and "bliss", though seems to define the intrinsic nature of *Brahman*, is incomplete, as it, by presupposing the individual self to which the definition is meant, excludes the individual self from itself. Accordingly, Śaṅkara explains that the meaning of the word *Brahman* excludes from itself the individual self which is finite and mortal, and *Brahman*, which is the basis of all that is manifested, is excluded from the meaning of the word "self".[48] They thus exclude each other and between them there is a polarity and duality. Until *Brahman* is realized as one's Self, that is, by being It, this polarity or duality subsists and *Brahman* is looked upon by the individual self as something "other" (*anya*) than Itself. An ignorant person thinks that he is different from the highest (*parasmād anya*) and that *Brahman* is different from himself (*anyat brahman*).[49] And as long as Reality is considered to be the "other", it is incomplete, because from it is excluded the one who considers it to be so. To transcend such duality is to realize *Brahman* in Itself, and it is possible by being It only. This is the real significance of the word "non-duality". "It is One because there is no second. It is ignorance that creates a second entity and in reality, there is no second entity different from the Self to be seen or heard."[50] "The Self is the total negation

---

[48] *ChāUB*, V.11.1.

[49] *KaUB*, II.1.10; *TaiUB*, II.7.1.; *BṛUB*, IV.4.19.

[50] *BṛUB*, IV.3.32.

of the phenomena of duality and therefore it is non-dual."[51] The same has been lucidly explained by Śaṅkara in his commentary on *Bṛhadāraṇyaka Upaniṣad*.[52] People wrongly understand the Self as vital force, mind, etc., depending upon the different functions the Self seems to perform in relation to the superimposed limiting adjuncts. It is known as vital force, when it is viewed in relation to the functions of living, as mind in relation to the mental functions, and so on. But this type of understanding of the Self is partial, but not perfect and complete. It is not an understanding of the Self in its real (*vastu*) nature. The Self in its real nature is all-inclusive. It is a whole (*krustna*) in which all these particular functions are included, but as people do not know it as such, they do not know it correctly and completely. Thus, according to Śaṅkara, "when one sees another, hears another, knows another there is limitedness, mortality and unreality".[53]

And so long as one thinks that *Brahman* is something other than one's own Self, one cannot really know *Brahman*. It is known only when one realizes that It is not different from one's Self. Till then what one knows as *Brahman* is not *Brahman*.

> The (Upaniṣadic) statement, that *Brahman* is different from the known and the unknown, having amounted to *Brahman* being denied as an object to be acquired or rejected, the desire of the disciple to know *Brahman* (objectively) comes to an end, for *Brahman* is non-different from the Self. For nothing other than one's own Self can possibly be different from the known and the unknown.[54]

---

[51] *GKB*, II.35, tr. Swami Nikhilananda, p. 130.

[52] *BṛUB*, I.4.7.

[53] *GKB*, III.2, tr. Swami Nikhilananda, p. 138, see also *ChāUB*, VII.24.1.

[54] *KeUB*, I.4, tr. Swami Gambhirananda, vol. I, p. 50.

> *Brahman* in Itself is that in which "one sees nothing else, hears nothing else, understands nothing else and that is what is much (*bhūma*)".[55]

While the conception of *Brahman* as existence, knowledge and bliss is the highest, to think of It as *Īśvara* is a lower way of thinking. When *Brahman* is viewed in relation to the universe and the individual selves, It appears as *Īśvara*. But, as the creation and the individual selves are ultimately unreal, *Brahman*'s creatorship and Lordship are also illusory. On the contrary, if they are to form its essential nature, creation cannot be unreal and the individual self can never attain identity with *Brahman*. Then they are to be considered as co-eternal with *Brahman*. Thus any definition of *Brahman* is not valid from the standpoint of *Brahman* in Itself.

Since any positive definition of *Brahman* is not all-inclusive and free from duality, there can be no positive definition of *Brahman* in Itself. Hence the only and appropriate way of describing such a non-dual reality is to describe it negatively.[56] The method of negative description may seem to reduce *Brahman* to mere nothingness if one fails to appreciate the real significance of negation. According to Śaṅkara, negation is a method and it is adopted to communicate the knowledge of *Brahman* as It is in Itself. Its purpose is to point out ultimately that the inward self is *Brahman* and that *Brahman* is all. The sense in which the negative particles of "not this", "not this" (*neti, neti*) are used is all-inclusive, so that the negation includes everything that is superimposed on *Brahman*.[57] If each particular thing superimposed on *Brahman* is negated individually, a doubt may arise whether some other thing is *Brahman* or not. To obviate any such possibility, the negation includes

---

[55] *SūB*, I.3.8, tr. Thibaut, vol. I, p. 162; see also *ChāUB*, VII.24.1.

[56] *BṛUB*, II.3.6; *SūB*, III.2.22.

[57] *BṛUB*, II.3.6.

everything that can possibly be superimposed on *Brahman*. Thus when every possible conception of *Brahman* is negated, it gives rise to the understanding that whatever can be known or thought of is not *Brahman*; and thereby one's desire to know *Brahman* objectively becomes extinguished and one's attention will be turned towards the inner self which, as the basis of all negation, can never be negated.[58] The intellect then becomes prepared and also fit to know the self in its real nature. To understand this fully, we have to understand the significance of the method of superimposition (*adhyāropa*) and negation (*apavāda*) or attribution and denial. Explaining this method, Śaṅkara says:

> In all the Upaniṣads first identity is broached, then by means of illustrations and reasons the universe is shown to be a modification or part or the like of the Supreme Self, and the conclusion again brings out the identity.[59]

Explaining this point further, Śaṅkara says that in the beginning all this was *Brahman* only, but owing to ignorance, It was differentiated into many by way of superimposing different names and forms on It, and so, all that was superimposed upon *Brahman* should be negated to establish Its identity. In other words, the Upaniṣads start with the assertion that "in the beginning this was *Brahman* only, one without a second", then they explain how the universe of differences has come into existence out of It, and finally by negating all the differences, consisting of name and form, from *Brahman* they conclusively establish the absolute identity of *Brahman*.[60]

---

[58] *BṛUB*, II.3.6; *KeUB*, I.4.

[59] *BṛUB*, II.1.20, tr. Swami Madhavananda, p. 302.

[60] *BṛUB*, II.1.20.

Brahman as "experience or as realized"

When one, under the influence of ignorance, identifies *Brahman* with any particular name and form, one fails to comprehend its all-inclusive nature. One fails to realize that *Brahman* is really everything. The scriptures, therefore, negate all the names and forms that can possibly be superimposed on *Brahman*, to point out the all-inclusive nature of *Brahman* or to show that *Brahman* is everything. To attribute a particular name and form to *Brahman* is like restricting the sovereignty of a king to a particular village when, in fact, he is the king of the whole country.[61] Thus, though *Brahman* is everything, It is not any particular thing. To identify an all-inclusive reality with any particular thing is to limit its all-inclusive nature. Such that, as long as a thing is seen in its particular name and form (*viśeṣākāra*), it is not *Brahman*, though as free from them it is one with *Brahman*. For instance, a pot is not identical with the clay, or a wave with the sea, so long as they are seen in their particular names and forms, that is, as a pot or a wave, but when their particular names and forms are negated, they cannot be different from clay and sea. Moreover, the differentiation of *Brahman* into name and form is not real. It is due to ignorance, and so when ignorance is destroyed all the differences cease to exist. Śaṅkara says that while things are unreal, in so far as they are seen in their particular names and forms, they are real in themselves, that is, when they are seen in the form of pure Being (*sanmātra rūpa*).[62] In the *Bṛhdarāṇyaka Upaniṣad Bhāṣya*, Śaṅkara says that as long as one, viewing the Self as performing different functions like seeing, hearing and thinking, which are due to the superimposition on it of various limiting adjuncts, thinks of the Self as seer, hearer, thinker, etc. one does not know the Self. To know the Self as thinker

[61] *ChāUB*, VI.16.3.

[62] *ChāUB*, VIII.5.4.

or hearer or seer is to know it incompletely, for in identifying the Self with thinker, people exclude from the Self the other functional names like hearer and seer. Whereas the Self is everything or in it all these functions are included. So, to know the Self truly is to know it as it is in itself, but not through any particular function it appears to perform.[63]

Now, the purpose of superimposition and negation is to communicate the knowledge of *Brahman*.[64] While the purpose of superimposition is to help one in understanding *Brahman*, the purpose of negation is to make one know what *Brahman* in Itself is. Thus *Brahman* is conceived as having a form (*mūrta*) or some positive form is superimposed on *Brahman* to serve the practical purpose of meditation, and what is thus superimposed on *Brahman* is latter negated, so that *Brahman* in Itself is comprehended.

Difference between Brahman as an object of experience and Brahman as "experience"

On the basis of the above discussion, it can be said that the main point of difference between *Brahman* that is treated as an object of higher realization and *Brahman* that is actually realized as one's own Self is the latter's non-dual nature and completeness. When *Brahman* is looked upon as an object of higher realization or as the goal of one's life, It implies the duality of the self and *Brahman*. Whereas when It is directly experienced by being It, such duality is transcended and the self and *Brahman* are realized to be one and the same. In other words, for an ignorant person *Brahman* is the goal, and for the wise man It is no other than his own true self. To the

---

[63] *BṛUB*, I.4.7.

[64] *SūB*, III.2.14, I.1.12; *BṛUB*, II.3.1; *ChāUB*, VIII.1, Introduction; *TaiUB*, I.5.1, Introduction.

person who has realized *Brahman* by being It, it is everything, but not a formless something over and above what is empirically experienced. Whereas for an ignorant person, *Brahman* is something different from his self and also different from the world. This idea is very finely presented by Śaṅkara in the following passages.

> The wise man endowed with perfect enlightenment sees through the eyes of perfect knowledge the entire universe in his Self and realizes everything as the Self and nothing else.[65]

> The whole universe which, at first is regarded as an illusion and hence unreal is, on the dawn of perfect knowledge, realized to be everlasting non-dual Self.[66]

It is impossible to have an objective knowledge of *Brahman* in Itself. While It is looked upon as an object and sought as the goal of one's life, before It is actually experienced, is found out to be one's own Self when It is experienced. It is not possible to know *Brahman* in Itself from the standpoint of duality and when it is transcended in realizing It, there will be left no scope either for an experiencing principle or for the objectification of *Brahman*. Such an experience is objectless, complete and all-inclusive. This is possible only when the Self's empirical nature or individuality is lost in experiencing its true nature. As such nothing positive can be said about *Brahman* in Itself; and whatever is said of It in positive terms is valid only from the standpoint of ignorance or from the standpoint of an empirical self. Therefore, all that has been said in positive terms or through affirmation cannot be true of *Brahman* which is experienced as one's own Self. Now, the problems such as, whether *brahmānubhava* has an object or not, and if it has an

---

[65] *Ātmabodha, śl.* 47.

[66] *Dakṣiṇāmūrty Aṣṭakam, śl.* 1.

object how can it be non-dual, and if it has no object how can it be considered as *brahmānubhava* arise only when the absolute experience is sought to be understood and explained from the standpoint of empirical experience. Whereas, from the standpoint of *brahmānubhava* there are no such problems. When *brahmānubhava* is spoken of as the knowledge or experience of *Brahman*, it is not the true knowledge of *Brahman* which is not different from *Brahman*. True knowledge of *Brahman* is free from the duality of *Brahman* and the knowledge of it. Any knowledge of *Brahman* is only an indirect knowledge of It. *Brahmānubhava* which is nothing but *Brahman* Itself is the direct and immediate knowledge of It, by being It, and in it there is no distinction of *Brahman* and the experience of *Brahman*. *Brahmānubhava* is *Brahman* Itself.

7

The Validity of Brahmānubhava

THE validity of *brahmānubhava* presupposes the validity of scriptural knowledge, for *brahmānubhava* is not possible independent of scriptural knowledge. Although scriptural knowledge is not the cause of *brahmānubhava*, still it is indispensable for the attainment of the latter. In so far as it causes the destruction of ignorance, which is tantamount to the realization of *Brahman*, it is considered to be the cause of *brahmānubhava*. It is through the scriptures one comes to know the real nature of *Brahman* and one's identity with It. As such, without determining the validity of scriptural knowledge, the validity of *brahmānubhava* cannot be decided. We shall discuss in the first part of this chapter, the validity of scriptural knowledge.

The validity of scriptural knowledge

According to Śaṅkara, scriptures (Upaniṣads), the main source of *Brahman*-knowledge, in their primary (*mukhya*) sense signify knowledge (*vidyā*) of a knowable entity (*vedya vastu*) rather than the mere books called the Upaniṣads or the words assembled in them.[1] The word "Upaniṣad" derives its meaning from its capacity to lead to truth, those who, having been thoroughly dissatisfied with the things seen and unseen, seek liberation from ignorance, the source of bondage and suffering, by destroying it.[2] It makes one attain the supreme

[1] *KaUB*, Introduction; *TaiUB*, Introduction; *MuUB*, I.1.5; *BṛUB*, II.1.20.

[2] *KaUB*, Introduction; *TaiUB*, Introduction.

Brahman (*param brahma gamayati*). The Upaniṣads are competent to accomplish all this, for in them the highest truth that can lead us to the attainment of the highest end of life (*parama śreya*) is embodied. Whereas, the Upaniṣads as mere books are not capable of fulfilling all these, for the obvious reason that mere mastery of the Upaniṣadic texts, without acquiring the perfect knowledge which they communicate, does not result in the destruction of ignorance and the realization of the Self. While those who have simply mastered Upaniṣadic texts, but have failed to acquire perfect knowledge of the Self are seen to suffer from ignorance and its consequences, those who have acquired perfect knowledge of the Self, which is the real essence of the Upaniṣads, are not seen to suffer from ignorance and its consequences. However, scriptural knowledge cannot be separated from the scriptural sentences which convey it, though they can be grasped as distinct intellectually. As the words and ideas, though they are distinct, are inseparably related, the Upaniṣadic sentences and the knowledge of *Brahman*, which they communicate, are inseparably related. For this reason, the books (Upaniṣads) in which the perfect knowledge is embodied are also called Upaniṣad(s) in a secondary sense, just as it is said that *ghee* is life. Though *ghee* is not life in the primary sense of the word, it can be said to be so in a secondary sense as it sustains life. The word "Upaniṣad" means the knowledge of a knowable entity and the books are called Upaniṣad(s) by virtue of their association with such knowledge.[3] Thus the word "Upaniṣad" primarily means *Brahman*-knowledge (*brahmavidyā upaniṣad*), whereas the books are called Upaniṣad(s) by virtue of their containing such knowledge.

---

[3] *KaUB*, Introduction.

Analyses of scriptural sentences on Self-Brahman identity

The knowledge which the great Upaniṣadic sentences like "That thou art", "I am *Brahman*" and "All this is *Brahman*" communicate is not either figurative (*upacāra*) or secondary (*gauṇa*). Nor is this knowledge mental (*mānasika*) or purely subjective, just as the knowledge based on scriptural sentences enjoining meditation is mental. Nevertheless, as the form and structure of the scriptural sentences, "That thou art" and "I am *Brahman*" are similar to that of the sentences like Bhadrasena is myself and "you are a lion", a doubt may arise whether the meaning and validity of the former set of sentences are not similar to that of the latter set of sentences. Seeing the similarity of form and structure between the two sets of sentences, people may consider that the Upaniṣadic sentences, like the other sentences, are not meant to communicate any objective knowledge, but are meant to express a state of mind. Therefore, they may consider that the meaning and the validity of the scriptural sentences like the meaning and validity of other sentences are only psychological and figurative, but not objective and real. But, according to Śaṅkara, the significance and validity of the scriptural sentences are not the same as that of the other sentences, though there is a similarity of form and structure between them. Śaṅkara analyses and contrasts these two sets of sentences in order to demonstrate the essential difference between them and also to establish the objective validity of scriptural knowledge.

As the scriptural sentence "I am *Brahman*" seeks to establish the identity of the Self with *Brahman*, the sentence "Bhadrasena" is my self may also appear to establish identity between "Bhadrasena" and "myself". But the sentence "Bhadrasena" is myself expresses in a figurative way one's feeling of love and gratefulness towards Bhadrasena.[4] In fact,

[4] *ChāUB*, VI.2.4; *SūB*, I.1.7.

Bhadrasena is altogether a different person from the one who speaks that "Bhadrasena is myself", and therefore, there is no objective identity between them. The identity between "Bhadrasena" and myself is possible only in feeling and hence the validity of the sentence is only psychological and figurative. In its direct sense, this sentence has no meaning as the persons identified are two distinct individuals different from each other in many respects. As such it does not convey any objective fact. It only conveys a state of mind which is purely subjective. Thus the sentence has no objective validity. The meaning and validity of the scriptural sentence "That thou art" may appear to be similar to that of the sentence "you are a lion". But in the sentence "you are a lion" a particular individual is identified with the lion, by virtue of his possessing great courage as a lion does.[5] In fact, the man and the lion are two different beings existing independently of each other and possessing contradictory natures, except for the similar quality of courage. Therefore this sentence also, in its direct or primary sense, is meaningless as there is no total and objective identity between a lion and a man. As the identity which the sentence tries to establish is based on the similarity of a particular quality, but not on an objective fact, it is secondary (*gauṇa*). In like manner, the sentence "air is indeed the absorber; breath is indeed the absorber" also tries to establish identity between air and breath based on the similarity of a special function of absorbing found in both of them.[6] Hence, in this case also the identity is not objective, but only figurative. Thus in all these sentences, identity is sought to be established on the basis of a feeling, or a particular quality or function which is commonly shared by the things identified. As such, if at all there is any identity between them, it is only partial and that too in a figura-

---

[5] *SūB*, I.1.4; *ChāUB*, VI.16.3.

[6] *SūB*, I.1.4.

tive sense, but not objective and total. For this reason, all these sentences are not meaningful in their primary or direct sense, for then they are contradicted by observed facts. Observation never confirms the identity between a man and a lion. As, according to Śaṅkara, empirical experience, got through the various sources of knowledge, holds supreme authority as far as the empirical world is concerned, anything that contradicts it at that level cannot be valid. And as the scope of the sentences like "you are a lion" is empirical, their validity should also be determined in terms of empirical experience. Moreover, in all these sentences the fact of the duality of the things identified is recognized. They never try to deny the duality, but only try to assert the relation of identity between two different things, in so far as they resemble each other with regard to a particular quality or function. In all such cases of identity, one is well aware of the process of identification and never thinks that there is any real or objective identity between the things identified. The identification is deliberate and imaginary, and hence its validity is figurative. It is meaningful for those who can appreciate the figurative sense of the sentences. On the other hand, if people fail to apprehend the well-established difference between the objects figuratively identified and mistake them to be really identical, then their knowledge is simply erroneous (*bhrānti*).[7]

As stated earlier, the knowledge of Self-*Brahman* identity is not mental or based on the scriptural statements enjoining meditation. To make this clear, we shall now consider some of the scriptural statements which speak of an identity that is to be achieved mentally through imagination and meditation. The statement, "the mind is indeed infinite and infinite are the Viśvedevas; and through this meditation the aspirant wins

[7] *SūB*, I.1.4.

infinitude" speaks of such identity.[8] It says that there is a similarity of infinitude between the mind and the Viśvedevas, for the mind is infinite in its modifications and the Viśvedevas are infinite in number. So, if one meditates on the mind, after identifying it with the Viśvedevas in imagination, one attains the infinite world. In this case, one deliberately identifies the mind with the Viśvedevas, so that one can transcend one's finitude. One tries to transcend one's finitude by identifying oneself with an infinite object through an imaginative meditation on an infinite object.[9] As the infinitude so attained is based on the imaginary identification with an infinite object, it is purely subjective.

In the sentences "one should meditate upon the mind as *Brahman*" and "one should meditate upon the sun as *Brahman*", there is a conscious attribution of the idea of *Brahman* to the sun or the mind for the purpose of meditation, just as a devotee consciously imposes the idea of Viṣṇu on a stone image to serve the practical purpose of devotion.[10] In imposing the idea of Viṣṇu on an image, the devotee is clearly aware of the fact that Viṣṇu is not the stone image. The stone image is only a symbol (*pratīka*) and is meant to serve the purpose of achieving concentration of the mind. Similarly, the person who meditates on the mind or the sun as *Brahman* is definitely aware of the fact that *Brahman* is neither the mind nor the sun. He knows that the idea of *Brahman* is superimposed on the mind or the sun for the purpose of *Brahman* realization.[11] Scriptures also do not say that the sun and the mind are *Brahman*. They only enjoin meditation on them as *Brahman* "for one who clearly

---

[8] *BṛUB*, III.1.9.

[9] Anandagiri and Ratnaprabha on *SūB*, I.1.4.

[10] *ChāUB*, III.18.1, III.19.1.

[11] *SūB*, I.1.4; *BṛUB*, I.3.1.

knows that those things are different from *Brahman*. It is like meditation on the image, etc. as Viṣṇu".[12] As against this, if a person mistakes a stump for a man out of ignorance, it is not a conscious, but an erroneous act, whereas meditation on the mind or the sun as *Brahman* is not due to any such error, but is deliberate or conscious.[13] Moreover, the presence of the word "as" in the sentences "mind or sun as *Brahman*" precludes the possibility of identifying the mind or the sun with *Brahman*. It clearly indicates that they are not really identical with *Brahman*, but are to be viewed as *Brahman* for the purpose of meditation. Besides, the mind and the sun possess certain qualities while *Brahman* is devoid of them, and therefore there cannot be any real identity between them.[14] Meditation is purely subjective, for it is based entirely on the activity of the mind (*citta vyāpāra*). As such an individual is free to choose this or that object for meditation. He is also free to accept or reject identification of *Brahman* with this or that object, and also to meditate in one's own way.[15] Such identification of *Brahman* with this or that object can neither claim objective validity, nor can it demand universal acceptance, as it depends purely on one's choice. As such it should be accepted on faith in the scriptures.

We shall now discuss the nature of the Upaniṣadic sentences, "That thou art" and "I am *Brahman*" to determine their validity. These are not relational in their nature, that is, they do not try to establish any sort of relation between the things presented in them, as there are no two things in reality to be related. These sentences, according to Śaṅkara, are also not meaningful and valid in their direct sense, for "That" and

---

[12] *BṛUB*, I.3.1, tr. Swami Madhavananda, p. 46.

[13] *SūB*, I.1.4.

[14] *ChāUB*, VI.16.3.

[15] *SūB*, I.1.4.

"thou" or "*Brahman*" and "I" in their primary sense are two different realities possessing contradictory characteristics. There is a polarity between them. As "thou" or "I" the Self is not identical with "That" or "*Brahman*". Therefore, these sentences are significant and valid only in what they indirectly indicate.[16] They show That the notions of "That" and "thou" "I" and "*Brahman*", which are apparently presented in them, are only appearances, and as appearances they point out to a reality which is their basis. While that reality indicated by "That" and "thou" cannot be expressed, and is absolutely real and undifferentiated, the entities "That" and "thou" are ultimately unreal and are only its appearances. Now, the aim of these sentences is to reveal that non-dual reality by way of removing the apparent duality of "That" and "thou" or "I" and "*Brahman*" caused by ignorance. Thus when Śaṅkara speaks of identity, he means by that the absolute oneness (*ekatva*) of Reality. The oneness of Reality is an objective fact, but not something that is to be achieved. It is to be discovered or realized. Identity, according to Śaṅkara, is not a word of relation, expressing a relation between two different and yet identical entities. So, when he speaks of identity between the Self and *Brahman*, he means that the Self and *Brahman* are only names or appearances of one and the same reality. On the contrary, if the duality of the Self and *Brahman* is accepted as ultimately real, and the relation of identity between them is sought to be established on the basis of some similarity found between them, there will be some scope then for considering Self-*Brahman* identity as either figurative or mental. If there is a real duality of the self and *Brahman*, one can think of identifying the self with *Brahman* either through attribution of the idea of *Brahman* to the self, or through imagination that the self is *Brahman*. But when there is oneness it is not possible to imagine any sort of relation in it.

---

[16] See Chapter 2.

The knowledge which the scriptural sentences like "That thou art" communicate is objective (*vastu*) as contrasted with the knowledge which the scriptural sentences enjoining meditation like "the sun is to be meditated upon as *Brahman*" and other figurative expressions like "you are a lion" convey.

> Objective knowledge is the result of the different means of (right) knowledge, and those have for their objects existing things; knowledge can therefore not be either made or not made or modified, but depends entirely on existing things (*vastu tantram*) and not either on Vedic statements or on the mind of man.[17]

Therefore, the origination as well as the validity of such knowledge depends on the object, but not on a person's choice or will. For instance, the knowledge of a pot does not depend on what people think of it, but on its nature. Perfect knowledge, according to Śaṅkara, is that which is universally valid and acceptable to all.[18] It does not vary from person to person or from, place to place, but remains unalterably the same for all people and for all times. It cannot either be accepted or rejected arbitrarily. It cannot also be modified or interpreted according to personal choice. *Brahman* is an objective (*vastu*) reality, and as the self of all, Its existence can neither be doubted nor denied. In nobody's case the Self's existence is adventitious. As its reality is objective, the knowledge of it does not depend on the free choice of anyone. As Śaṅkara puts it:

> The knowledge of *Brahman* does not depend on the active energy of man, but is analogous to the knowledge of those things which are the objects of perception, inference, and so on, and thus depends on the objects of knowledge only.[19]

---

[17] *SūB*, I.1.4., I.1.2.

[18] Ibid., II.1.11.

[19] Ibid., I.1.4, tr. Thibaut, vol. I, p. 31.

In this connection, it should be noted that although *Brahman*-knowledge is objective, it is mental in a sense, as all knowledge is both objective and mental.[20] An object should be reflected in the mind if it is to be known. Even the self-luminous objects like the sun require a conscious principle if they are to be known. In this sense all knowledge is mental and *Brahman*-knowledge is no exception to this, for *Brahman*, prior to Its being realized by being It, is reflected in the mind as if It is an object, and is known as a modification of the mind (*vr̥tti-jñāna*). At the same time, such *vr̥tti-jñāna* should not be confused with the knowledge which is entirely based on the mind.

Brahman-knowledge is not the creation of the scriptures also, for they cannot promote knowledge in the absence of objectively existing things, nor do they interpret the knowledge obtained through other means of knowledge.[21] They express things as they are. Scriptural knowledge is perfect, because it is, firmly based on an objectively existing reality, that is, *Brahman*.[22] Interpretation is a subjective way of looking at things, or it is mental articulation of facts on the part of someone, and so varies from person to person and cannot have any objective validity, though it is based on facts. As the job of the scriptures is to present things as they are (*vastu pratipādanam*), the scriptural sentences like "That thou art" convey an objective truth which cannot be known through other sources of knowledge like sense perception. In doing so, the scriptures do not present Reality as if it is an object different from the knower, but merely direct one's attention gently to one's own self and pronounce that the self in its true nature is *Brahman*.

---

[20] *ChāUB*, Introduction; *SūB*, I.1.4.

[21] *PrUB*, VI.2; *SūB*, III.2.21, I.1.4.

[22] *SūB*, II.1.11.

Scripture as a source of valid knowledge

What was said above is based on a presupposition that the scripture is a source of valid knowledge. But how are we to know that? According to Śaṅkara, scriptural knowledge is intrinsically valid; the scriptures are self-authoritative with regard to what they say.[23] He says that the capacity of the scriptures to make one realize *Brahman* is also known through the scriptures.[24] *Brahman*-knowledge, which the scriptures communicate, is got through a continuous tradition (*pāramparyakrameṇa samprāpta*); and handed down by the great seers (*parama ṛṣi*) beginning from Brahmā, who have directly seen (*sākṣāt dṛṣṭavanto*) or realized (*avagata vanto*) *Brahman*.[25] The sacred texts reveal the nature of the Self as seen by seers like Triśaṅku and Vāmadeva, through the eyes of a seer (*ārṣa darśana*).[26] In another context, describing the state of one who has realized *Brahman*, Śaṅkara observes that the realized person is not impelled by anything, not even by the scriptural sentences, for they emanate (*uthāna*) from his own wisdom (*svavijñāna*).[27]

Truth is giving utterance to one's own experience (*ātmānubhava*) of things as heard or seen with a view to communicating it to others.[28] Moreover, as the knowledge of the Self is identical with the Self, it is uncaused and eternal. The scriptures, therefore, cannot either cause it or present it as it is in itself. What they communicate is not pure Self-knowledge or as it is in itself, but as it is conditioned or determined (*pariśchinnam*) by the limiting adjuncts called mental states

---

[23] *SūB*, II.1.1; *BṛUB*, II.4.10, II.3.6.

[24] *BṛUB*, II.1.20.

[25] *MuUB*, III.2.11.

[26] *TaiUB*, I.10.1.

[27] *AiUB*, Introduction.

[28] *BGB*, X.4.

(*manovṛtti*).[29] Thus, as forming the very nature of the Self, the knowledge of the Self reveals itself, like a man's breath, spontaneously without any effort on the part of anyone. As the knowledge of an eternal object, it cannot either be created or interpreted by any man or by the scriptures. It is co-eternal with the Self. It is, therefore, unborn, eternal and objective. For these reasons, Śaṅkara compares the validity of scriptural knowledge with that of perceptual knowledge.[30] As the latter's authority is supreme within the empirical realm, the former's authority is supreme in trans-empirical matters.

However, some people may doubt the validity of scriptural knowledge and demand direct proof of its validity. But the validity or non-validity of scriptural knowledge cannot be determined either by any of the natural means of knowledge or by reason. As it has been made clear in the first chapter, *Brahman* cannot be known through the natural means of knowledge and reasoning. Sense perception is competent to know only the illusory effects of *Brahman*, but they do not form the essential nature of It.[31] Reasoning can only suggest or point out, in a probable manner, the possibility of Its existence as the ground of everything that is manifested.[32] Even if it is assumed that it is possible to establish, with certainty, the existence of *Brahman* on the basis of reason, it is not possible to know anything about Its nature through reasoning. Thus when all the means of knowledge and reasoning are not competent to know *Brahman*, they cannot also be employed to determine the validity or non-validity of *Brahman*-knowledge. The validity of that, which cannot be known through a particular source of knowledge, cannot be

[29] *TaiUB*, II.3.1.

[30] *SūB*, I.3.8.

[31] Ibid., II.1.27, I.1.2.

[32] *KaUB*, II.3.12-13.

determined by that source of knowledge. Nor can they contradict scriptural knowledge, for each source of knowledge is effective and valid within its own sphere, and also because what is known through a particular source of knowledge cannot be known through other sources.[33] Though what one sense organ perceives differs from what is perceived by the other sense organs, the former is neither disproved nor contradicted by the latter. For instance, there is no contradiction between what is perceived by the eyes and what is perceived by the ears, though each is different from the other. As the truth of the scriptures transcends the empirical sphere, to judge its validity by empirical standards will be as meaningless and undesirable as to judge the validity of perceptual knowledge in terms of the scriptures. Similarly, the worldly reason or common sense (*laukika buddhi*), which is utilitarian or is meant to serve the practical needs of man, cannot be the judge of the validity of scriptural knowledge which is not meant to serve the worldly needs of man.[34] It is only those who have overcome their pride of learning and attained perfect purity of heart, and have implicit faith in the scriptures, and are desirous of attaining liberation that can know the validity of the scriptures as clearly and definitely as we know of the object of perception.[35]

How to determine scriptural validity

Although scriptural knowledge is intrinsically valid, its validity can be determined in two ways and thereby we can also know whether the scriptures are really a source of valid knowledge or not. One of them is to find out whether the scriptural knowledge has the capacity to produce certain results which

---

[33] *BṛUB*, II.1.20.

[34] *TaiUB*, II.6.1.

[35] *BṛUB*, I.4.6.

can be directly observed. The second is to find out whether the object of scriptural knowledge can be directly experienced if one wants to experience it for oneself. According to Śaṅkara, while any knowledge is valid when it can bring forth certain palpable results, that knowledge which fails to produce such results is invalid. He says:

> A means of knowledge is or is not really a means of knowlededge according as it leads or does not lead to valid knowledge.[36]

And,

> the test of the authority or otherwise of a scriptural passage is not whether it states a fact or an action, but its capacity to produce certain and fruitful experience (*niścita phala vijñāna*).[37]

According to this criterion, the Upaniṣadic sentences like "That thou art" convey valid knowledge, because the knowledge to which they give rise is effective in destroying ignorance and its effects like grief, delusion and fear.[38] In the *Bṛhadāraṇyaka Upaniṣad Bhāṣya*, answering a possible objection that may be raised against the validity of scriptural knowledge on the ground that it does not produce palpable results, Śaṅkara retorts:

> Do you not see the result of knowledge in the removal of the evils like ignorance, grief, delusion and fear which are the root of worldly existence? Or, do you not hear those hundreds of Upaniṣadic texts such as "Then what delusion and what grief can there be for one who sees unity", "I am but a knower of *mantras*, not of the Self, so I am tormented with grief; and you sir, must take me beyond the reach of it.[39]

---

[36] *BṛUB*, II.1.20, tr. Swami Madhavananda, p. 309.

[37] Ibid., I.4.7, tr. Swami Madhavananda, p. 134.

[38] Ibid., I.4.7, II.1.20.

[39] Ibid., I.4.7, tr. Swami Madhavananda, p. 134.

The fact that the scriptural knowledge removes the basic ignorance and its consequences is also confirmed by the actual experiences of the sages. The fact that certain other sentences, which are similar in form and structure to scriptural sentences, do not produce any palpable results is not a valid argument against the validity of scriptural sentences which are seen to produce such results. Despite all this evidence, if one is persistent in denying the validity of scriptural knowledge without giving any valid reason then no reason can be adduced to prove the validity of scriptural knowledge. That is to say, if one refuses to see the validity of scriptural knowledge, as if on faith, nothing can be done to convince him.[40]

The ultimate validity of scriptural knowledge lies in its capacity to culminate in self-evident experience. The scriptural knowledge speaks of one's identity with *Brahman*, and if one can realize that directly, the validity of scriptural knowledge becomes established. Though scriptural knowledge is intrinsically valid, its validity is not self-evident to an individual. Scriptural knowledge is indirect and mediate to an individual. That is to say, before it is directly experienced, *Brahman* is known indirectly or mediately through the scripture and therefore it is not self-evident to an individual. To become self-evident and certain to an individual, *Brahman* which is known mediately through the scriptures must be directly experienced by him. Then only he can be sure of the validity of scriptural knowledge. According to Śaṅkara, the fact that the scriptural knowledge is capable of producing self-evident experience is attested by the actual experiences of the sages like Vāmadeva and Triśaṅku,[41] and all those who are qualified to receive *Brahman*-knowledge can also attain such experience.[42] Thus the ultimate validity of scriptural

[40] *BṛUB*, II.1.20.

[41] *ChāUB*, VIII.12.6; *BṛUB*, IV.4.9; *TaiUB*, I.10.1.

[42] *ChāUB*, VIII.12.6; *BṛUB*, IV.4.9.

knowledge, which is indirect (*parokṣa*), lies in its capacity to produce direct experience (*aparokṣānubhūti*). In short, its validity lies in *brahmānubhava*. However, after attaining *brahmānubhava*, one's interest in the validity of scriptural knowledge ceases, for then there remains nothing different from *Brahman* or the Self. Then all the differences cease to exist and the scriptures become no scriptures (*aveda*) or cease to be of no use or value.[43]

Validity of Brahmānubhava

Now, let us come to the validity of *brahmānubhava*. In the *Chāndogya Upaniṣad Bhāṣya*, after establishing the identity of the Self with *Brahman*, anticipating a possible objection that such an identity, like the one indicated in the sentence "Bhadrasena is myself", may be figurative, Śaṅkara explains that it is not so, but "objectively true, for Self-*Brahman* identity realization results in liberation".[44] A further objection is then raised whether liberation itself is not figurative, just as the remark "I have reached the village" which a person figuratively makes when he is about to reach the village of his destination for the purpose of quickening his march. According to Śaṅkara, this objection would be valid if the scriptures were to declare that to attain liberation something other than the Self should be known or attained. If liberation is consequent to the experience of something other than the Self, then there may be some possibility for considering such an experience as either figurative or imaginary. Whereas, the scriptures are unanimous in affirming that to attain liberation is to realize one's own Self, that the Self is the ultimate reality and that there is nothing besides the Self. Contrary to this, if the

---

43 *SūB*, IV.1.3; *BṛUB*, V.1.1.

44 *ChāUB*, VI.2.4.

scriptures are to maintain the duality of the Self and *Brahman*, one's identity with *Brahman* may be due to one's imagination and hence it may be figurative. But that is not the case.

Brahmānubhava is not due to the cultivation of the notion (*buddhimātra*) that "I am *Brahman*", nor is it a delusion (*bhrama*) produced because of imagined identity.[45] If an individual aspiring to become *Brahman* becomes *Brahman* simply by imagining himself to be *Brahman*, then there would be no necessity at all for understanding the scriptures and following any spiritual discipline to attain *brahmānubhava*. Then it can be attained by mere imagination or simply by forming the idea of identity in the mind once. Further, if the identity of the Self with *Brahman* is something that can be brought about mentally, but not an objective fact, scriptural prescription of certain means to attain it would be meaningless, for what is can only be known or attained.[46] It is contradictory to speak of means to attain that which is purely mental or imaginary. Moreover, actual observation shows that by merely forming the idea of identity ignorance is not destroyed.

One may imagine oneself to be *Brahman*, but thereby one is not liberated from ignorance. Therefore, *brahmānubhava* is not something that can be cultivated, nor does it depend on the attainment of something which is not already attained. As pure consciousness, it is always attained. Śaṅkara says that "release is not something which is to be brought about, but something whose nature is permanently established".[47] As such the scriptural statements of identity like "That thou art" and "I am *Brahman*" are not meant for cultivating the idea of identity, but to realize the identity, which is an objective fact.[48]

---

[45] *ChāUB*, VI.16.3; *SūB*, II.1.14.

[46] Ibid., VI.16.3.

[47] *SūB*, III.4.52, tr. Thibaut, vol. II, p. 330.

[48] Ibid., III.3.17, II.1.14.

There could be another doubt regarding the validity of *brahmānubhava*. It is based on the scriptural assertion that *Brahman* is realized through intense meditation on the scriptural sentences like "I am *Brahman*". Recognizing the varied capacities of the mind, Śaṅkara says that it is possible for the mind to objectify an imaginary thing or to visualize that which is not there through constant and pointed meditation.[49] A person can achieve a sort of imaginary identification with any object through intense and uninterrupted meditation on it.

> A person by meditating upon a thing with great assiduity and firm conviction that he is that thing, becomes that thing. This may be understood from the illustration of the wasp and insect (*bhramarakīṭavat*).[50]

A particular type of insect, it is believed, becomes transformed into a wasp, as a result of the latter's intense and constant thinking to that effect. Likewise, it may be argued that one may become *Brahman* by a constant meditation on the scriptural sentences like "I am *Brahman*". One may adduce also in support of his argument to the fact that scriptures themselves enjoin meditation on the sentences of identity to attain *brahmānubhava*. Śaṅkara also admits such possibility, for he says:

> By the thought of an object (*bhāva vṛttya*) the mind verily becomes identified with the object. By concentrating on the idea of void (*śūnya*), it becomes mere void, but on the other hand, it attains perfection or completeness (*pūrṇatvam*) by meditating on the idea of *Brahman*.[51]

As such, how can it be denied that the realization of one's identity with *Brahman* is not due to an intense meditation on the idea of Self-*Brahman* identity as suggested by the

---

[49] *SūB*, I.3.13.

[50] *Aparokṣānubhūti*, *śl*. 140; see also *Vivekacūḍāmaṇi*, *śl*. 359.

[51] *Aparokṣānubhūti*, *śl*. 129.

scriptures? If it is not the case, it may be argued, why the realization of *Brahman* is not immediately attained on hearing the scriptural sentence "That thou art" without requiring any meditation upon it?

Meditation on the great scriptural sentences is necessary for the realization of *Brahman*, but this does not mean that *brahmānubhava* is caused by such meditation. Śaṅkara emphatically denies that *brahmānubhava* is an effect of any process. It is not the result of human or divine endeavour. No doubt, in meditating on the statements like "I am *Brahman*", *Brahman* may seem to have become an object of meditation, but this is inevitable so long as the polarity between the Self and *Brahman*, created by ignorance, is not transcended. As long as this polarity subsists, one thinks of experiencing *Brahman* as an object and therefore meditates on *Brahman*. But as there is no duality between the Self and *Brahman* in reality, the objectification of *Brahman* is simply due to ignorance, and with the destruction of it such objectification of *Brahman* also comes to an end, and *Brahman* is realized as one's own Self. "In this way there arises in the pure-minded a state of *Brahman* awareness (*vṛttijñāna*) which afterwards becomes *Brahman* Itself."[52] Thus the function of meditation in *Brahman* realization is mainly nagative, that is, to dispel ignorance and the duality caused by it. Meditation on the scriptural sentences of identity serves the purpose of liberating one from the false consciousness that one is an individual self, mortal, limited, etc. When this false identity is destroyed, the true identity of the Self, which is pure consciousness, becomes spontaneously revealed without any further endeavour. Śaṅkara says:

> All mental activities have for their end intuition (*darśana*), for hearing and so on, when repeated, terminate in intuition and thus subserve a seen purpose, just as the action of

[52] *Aparokṣānubhūti, śl.* 137.

beating, etc. results in freeing the rice grains from their husks.[53]

Śaṅkara also says that in the case of those people, whose minds are already pure and who are full of faith, *Brahman* is experienced if the Upaniṣadic sentences are heard but once; and this shows that *brahmānubhava* is not caused by meditation. Repetition and meditation are necessary for those who cannot understand the purport of the scriptural sentences by hearing them once and who are not spiritually mature to realize what they have understood, but are still desirous of attaining *brahmānubhava*.[54] Thus while repetition serves the purpose of clearing the mind of its doubts and misconceptions, meditation helps in ripening the knowledge, so that the scriptural knowledge culminates in the direct experience of *Brahman*.

Determining the validity of Brahmānubhava

Brahmānubhava is objective. Scriptures, as means of valid knowledge, provide information about an objectively existing reality, that is, *Brahman*, and *brahmānubhava* is the inward and direct realization of it (*vijñāna*). Further, as the direct realization of one's own Self in its real nature, *Brahmānubhava* cannot be in any way figurative or mental, for in no one's case the Self is adventitious, to be either accepted or rejected at one's will. It is not the experience of someone or of some object, so that it may be possible for us to judge it as either subjective or objective. As pure knowledge, it transcends the subject–object duality of empirical experience. Nevertheless, its reality is undeniable, for it forms the basis of all empirical knowledge. The validity of *brahmānubhava* does not depend on anything else. It is self-valid. As it is essentially non-dual,

---

[53] *SūB*, IV.1.1, tr. Thibaut, vol. II, p. 332.

[54] Ibid., IV.1.2.

it excludes the possibility of there being another knower or knowledge which can determine its validity. According to Śaṅkara, *brahmānubhava*, like the experience of pain and pleasure, is purely inward.[55] It is like the experience of satisfaction which one gets after eating food.[56] "The fruit of *Brahman*-knowledge is purely inward (*ātmasākṣikam*) and supremely unique (*anuttamam*)."[57] It gives rise to a firm conviction that one's life is fulfilled (*kṛtārtha*). And as the direct experience of one's own Self, it requires no other witness than the testimony of one's own experience (*ātmapratyaya sākṣī*), and as pure consciousness, it is in need of no other knowledge to validate it, just as the light of the sun requires no other light to illumine it. According to Śaṅkara, "bondage, liberation, satisfaction, anxiety, recovery from illness, hunger and such other states of experience are known to those who have them", and their validity is not a problem for them.[58] To the person who has experienced them they are as certain and real as the objects of perception. They are self-valid. The inwardness of an experience is not a sufficient reason to invalidate it. The distinction between inward and outward makes no real difference to a person's experience.[59] Nor can they be used as criteria to judge the validity of an experience. The experience of pain and pleasure is inward, whereas the perception of a pot, etc. is outward or outward directed, but both are objective to the one who experiences them, and therefore their validity is equal to him. As the objects like pot are experienced as existing outside the mind, they are called external from the standpoint of the mind; while the experience of pain and

---

[55] *BṛUB*, IV.4.8; *BGB*, IX.2; *Vivekacūḍāmaṇi*, *śl*. 475.

[56] *BṛUB*, IV.4.8.

[57] Ibid.

[58] *Vivekacūḍāmaṇi*, *śl*. 475.

[59] *ChāUB*, VIII.5.4.

pleasure is considered inward from the standpoint of those objects and the senses. The mind is an internal organ and compared to it, the senses and their objects are external or outward. Therefore, the distinction between internal and external or inward or outward, need not be taken as constituting the validity of an experience. What is outward need not be more valid than what is inward. What is inwardly experienced by one cannot be observed by others, but that is no reason to deny its objectivity. Its validity is beyond doubt to the person concerned and for him its validity is independent of other factors.

Sense perception and reasoning cannot determine the validity of *brahmānubhava*. The Self is the basis and witness of both perception and reasoning.[60] It is because of the Self that the senses and the intellect appear to be conscious and are able to apprehend their respective objects. Therefore, pure consciousness (*brahmānubhava*) does not stand in need of sense perception and reasoning for its validity.[61] As knowledge in itself, it is the essence of all the means of knowledge or it is their basis, and therefore it cannot either be validated or contradicted by those which can function only when they are based on it. According to Śaṅkara, any experience is intrinsically valid and remains so until it is contradicted or sublated by another experience. Nothing is impossible when it can be experienced and so, to dismiss an experience because it is not common to all is unjustifiable, for the question of impossibility of what is directly experienced does not arise.[62] Śaṅkara says that it is not possible for any one to doubt or

---

[60] *BGB*, III.42; *SūB*, II.3.7.

[61] Pure consciousness, which is self-evident, is the basis of all the means of knowledge and, therefore, it does not stand in need of these to prove its validity.

[62] *BṛUB*, I.4.10; *SūB*, II.2.29.

deny the validity of what is self-evident to oneself, or what is one's own direct experience, and to accept what contradicts it.[63] Thus while the validity of an experience is not a problem for one who has it, though it is a problem for those who do not have it, they have no right or basis either to deny its possibility or to doubt its validity. "How can one man contest the fact of another possessing the knowledge of *Brahman* vouched for by his heart's conviction?"[64]

While *brahmānubhava* is intrinsically valid and absolutely self-evident and certain to the person who has attained it, to those who do not have it, its validity is known through some of the characteristics that accompany it.[65] That one has experience of *Brahman* may be inferred by others from those marks which follow *brahmānubhava*. "Those are the marks which serve the purpose of others; and for the person concerned, the experience is self-valid."[66] Before explaining those characteristic marks of *brahmānubhava* in terms of which its validity can be known, we have to consider two other sources of its validity, namely the Upaniṣads and the teacher. The Upaniṣads and the teacher, who are the sources of *Brahman*-knowledge, can also testify the validity of *brahmānubhava*. The Upaniṣads repeatedly assert that the individual self in its real nature is absolutely identical with *Brahman* and that this can be directly experienced by all. The Upaniṣadic statements, "he understood what he said" and "when one understands the True then alone one does declare the True; and without understanding the True one does not declare it" point out to the fact that the Upaniṣadic knowledge is based on actual

---

[63] *SūB*, II.2.29.

[64] Ibid., IV.1.15, tr. Thibaut, vol. II, p. 358.

[65] *GKB*, IV.92; *BGB*, XIV.22.

[66] *BGB*, XIV.22; see also, *BṛUB*, IV.4.8; *Vivekacūḍāmaṇi*, *śl*. 475.

experience.[67] Further it is the promise of the scriptures that the Self is liberated in knowing its true nature, as we find it in the *Chāndogya Upaniṣad* (VIII.11.3) where, after explaining the nature of the Self, the teacher introduces the topic of the liberated Self to confirm the truth of what was said earlier about the Self in the words "him being free from the body neither pleasure nor pain touches", and concludes by saying "by his own nature he manifests himself, and that is the highest Self".[68] This scriptural instruction about the Self freed from ignorance implies the possibility of experiencing the Self in its true nature which is identical with *Brahman*. What is said by the Upaniṣads is attested by the experiences of the sages and teachers.[69]

Now, an essential characteristic that invariably follows Self-realization is the complete absence of ignorance, the root-cause of all suffering and bondage.[70] And along with ignorance, the tendencies and impressions born of it are also destroyed; and this is a mark by which others can know whether one has *brahmānubhava* or not. Before the realization of *Brahman*, one sees differences due to the presence of ignorance and thinks in terms of "I" and "mine". Also one identifies oneself with the body, mind and the senses, and consequently thinks of oneself as mortal, finite and miserable. Because of such wrong identity, one distinguishes oneself from others and is afraid of them. In short, he suffers in all mortal ways. But with the removal of ignorace, the basic source of all differences, one sees everything as identical with the Self or sees the Self as everything, and loses one's spearate identity and becomes free from the "I"-sense. When once the state of non-duality is

---

[67] *ChāUB*, VII.17.1.

[68] *SūB*, IV.4.2.

[69] *TaiUB*, I.10.1; *BṛUB*, I.4.10.

[70] *SūB*, II.1.14; *MāUB*, II.1.10; *BṛUB*, II.1.20.

attained, there is no return from it into ignorance or the state of duality. Śaṅkara says that, as a matter of fact, everyone becomes one with *Brahman* in deep sleep and at the time of death and ultimate dissolution of the world — everything is *Brahman* whether one is aware of it or not — but an ignorant person or one who has not realized that fact, takes his birth again and again and suffers in all possible ways. The following examples given by Śaṅkara may illustrate this point. In a trial by ordeal, while a guiltless person is saved from being burnt by a heated axe when he touches it, one who is guilty of committing a sin is burnt.[71] A man who has attachment for his wealth grieves over the loss of it, but when he has no attachment he does not grieve.[72] Similarly, a man who is ignorant of the fact that everything, including himself, is *Brahman* in reality suffers, while the one who has realized that does not suffer. The significance of *brahmānubhava* does not consist in the removal of ignorance only; for it is a state of positive bliss and absolute freedom. One attains immortality thereby. As it is not the *nirvāṇa* of the Buddhists, it is not complete passing away. It is passing away from ignorance and remaining in one's own Self. The supreme end of life, according to Śaṅkara, is not the *nirvāṇa* of Buddhists.[73] He says that if a thorn sticks into a person's body, the removal of the pain caused by it is the result he would seek. But in removing the pain, by removing the thorn, if he passes away, the removal of pain would be meaningless, as there would be none to get the relief.[74] Likewise, if one's existence is totally extinguished in attaining *nirvāṇa* and if there remains none to enjoy or to be benefited by that, talking of it as the highest human end

[71] *ChāUB*, VI.16.3; see also VI.16.1-2.

[72] *SūB*, I.1.4.

[73] *BṛUB*, IV.3.7.

[74] Ibid.

becomes meaningless. As against this, *brahmānubhava* is a state of positive bliss which is the very nature of the Self. In *brahmānubhava*, the Self remains as Self; only the misunderstanding about it vanishes.

Another principle by which the validity of *brahmānubhava* can be determined is the principle of non-contradiction (*abādhitattva*).[75] Empirical experience is denied ultimate validity because its validity is limited to the empirical means of knowledge and also because it is found to be unreal and illusory on the emergence of *brahmānubhava*. Self-realization sublates one's empirical existence and when it is sublated the empirical experience based on it also becomes sublated. But there is no higher experience than *brahmānubhava* by which it can be sublated. And when once it is attained, it is never lost and hence there is no possibility of another experience. Consciousness is present in both *brahmānubhava* and empirical experience, but in empirical experience, it appears as if it is conditioned by various factors, whereas in *brahmānubhava*, it reveals itself as it is or in its unconditioned nature, that is, as pure consciousness. Conditioned experience as conditioned experience is not everlasting, for it vanishes along with the conditions which give rise to it, but pure consciousness of which it is a conditioned state, is not destroyed thereby, though it may appear to be so. For instance, the consciousness of a pot is lost if the latter is destroyed, but consciousness as such remains unaltered. *Brahmānubhava* is that unconditioned consciousness and therefore, it cannot either be sublated or contradicted, as it presupposes anything that may possibly sublate or contradict it.

Śaṅkara refers to another characteristic feature of *brahmānubhava* which not only helps in determining its validity,

---

[75] *SūB*, II.1.14; *AiUB*, Introduction.

but also distinguishes it from other similar experiences. It is the all-inclusive nature and completeness of *brahmānubhava*. To realize the Self is to realize everything as the Self, or in other words, through Self-realization everything is realized, as there is nothing that is not the Self. Such realization of everything as the Self (*sarvātmabhāva*) is the main significance of *brahmānubhava*.[76] This is not possible if the realization of the Self is not the highest realization, and if the Self is not the ultimate reality, the basis as well as the essence of everything. *Brahman* is an all-inclusive reality for there is nothing besides It. It is the self of all and to experience such reality is to see It everywhere or to see everything as *Brahman*. It is not limited to any particular state of experience or to any particular place or object. This universality of realization is a unique characteristic of *brahmānubhava* in which there is no scope for exclusion, hatred, opposition and attachment. Nothing is different from *Brahman* or the Self and even those who oppose non-duality, says Śaṅkara, are indeed one with it or the Self.[77] Some may, out of their ignorance, oppose *brahmānubhava*, but the man of Self-realization finds no scope for retaliation, for he realizes them to be one with his Self. If at all pure knowledge is opposed to anything, it is opposed to ignorance which causes duality and generates attachment and hatred.

---

[76] *MuUB*, II.1.10; see also Chapter 2.

[77] *GKB*, III.17-18 .

8

Empirical Experience and Brahmānubhava

Śaṅkara makes a broad distinction between empirical experience (*vyavahāra* or *laukika*) and trans-empirical experience (*pāralaukika* or *lokātīta*) or *brahmānubhava*. While the latter, which is very rarely attained by people, is non-dualistic, unconditioned and uncaused, the former, which is common to all, is dualistic, conditioned and caused. We have already discussed *brahmānubhava* in all its aspects and we shall now discuss the nature and validity of empirical experience. This may help us in understanding *brahmānubhava* in relation to empirical experience.

Nature and validity of empirical experience

Empirical experience includes the whole of human experience involving subject–object duality. It may be of the apparently manifested universe of differences or that of the Lord (*Īśvara*), its creator, and is attained through all the possible means of knowledge, including the scripture.[1] According to Śaṅkara,

---

[1] (a) Śaṅkara uses the word *Īśvara* to mean both the conditioned and the unconditioned Reality. He is the non-dualistic Lord (*advaiteśvera*) or the unconditioned Reality (*SūB*, IV.1.3). But, in general, the word *Īśvara* is used to represent the Lord of Creation. When we try to give a form to the formless *Brahman*, It becomes conditioned or appears as *Īśvara* (*BṛUB*, II.3.1). Śaṅkara says, "when the Self has the limiting adjunct of the power (*śakti*) of *māyā* (manifesting through) eternal and unlimited knowledge (*nitya niratiśaya jñāna*), it is called the internal ruler (*antaryāmin*) and *Īśvara*" (*BṛUB*, III.8.12). He creates the universe →

anything that can be known is limited, mortal and is the source of bondage and suffering.[2] Whatever that can be known or thought of is not *Brahman*, and except the fourth state of experience (*turīya*) or *brahmānubhava*, every other experience is based on ignorance and hence empirical.[3] In other words, all experience that is based on the duality of the experiencer and the experienced or the creator and the created is empirical. Thus empirical experience comprises the experience gained during the three states of waking, dream and deep sleep.

→ and, as the Lord of Creation, He exists in relation to His creation. As such in the absence of creation or when it is realized to be unreal, it is not possible to think of its creator also. The idea of *Īśvara* can thus be conceived only in relation to creation. He is the Ruler (*īsitru*) and everything else is ruled (*īsita*) by Him. Such dualistic experience is possible only in the empirical sphere of ignorance, for all duality is the creation of ignorance (*dvaitamavidyākṛtam*). Thus, according to Śaṅkara, the conditioned *Brahman* is the subject matter of ignorance and hence empirical. In this sense, *Īśvara* is also a mortal (*ārārtama*) (*BṛUB*, III.7.23). In this chapter, *Īśvara* is used always to mean the conditioned reality or the Creator of the Universe.

(b) Scriptural knowledge is also empirical, for it also presupposes the existence of a knower to whom it is intended. "The meditation taught in the Vedānta-texts, whose aim is the realization of the Self as represented by the Upaniṣads, is possible only if the Self is the agent." (*SūB*, II.3.39). Only when there is such an agent, scriptures find their scope. Therefore, they also, like other means of knowledge, can operate within the realm of duality of the knower and the known. But scripture is superior to other means of knowledge in so far as it reveals the highest reality by removing ignorance. But ultimately scriptural knowledge is also unreal. Beyond the empirical realm of ignorance it also does not find its validity and scope. Thus scriptural knowledge, like perception, falls within the empirical sphere (*BṛUB*, V.1.1; *TaiUB*, II.8.5; *GKB*, IV.73).

[2] *KeUB*, I.4: *yadviditam tadalpyam atyanta dukhātmikam cheti heyam.*

[3] *SūB*, III.2.22; *BṛUB*, IV.5.15.

Waking experience, which is common to all human beings, is dualistic and is characterized by the subject–object relationship. It is gained through the various cognitive instruments such as the senses and the mind, and includes all our activity, whether secular or sacred, done during the waking state. Among the ten sense organs (*indriyas*) — the five organs of knowledge (*buddhi*) and the five organs of action (*karma*) — the five organs of knowledge are the primary sources of knowledge of the manifested world. They are the doors of perception and without their activity no experience is possible.[4] By illumining (*dyotana*) their respective objects, the senses bring them to our view and in their turn the objects stimulate (*dīpana*) their corresponding sense organs, so that the process of perception is initiated.[5] For instance, when sound, the object of hearing, stimulates the ear, its sense organ, the process of hearing takes place. These sense organs, according to Śaṅkara, are so constituted that each of them can perceive or act only on a particular sense object. Each sense organ can determine the nature of a particular sense-object only, as for instance, the ear can determine the nature of sound only, the eye that of form and colour only, the nose that of smell only, and so on. Thus the activity of sense organs is limited to their respective sense-objects, and any sense organ cannot act on any sense-object, for the reason that the sense organs and their corresponding sense-objects belong to the same category (*samāna jātīya*) or are made up of the same substance.[6] The sense organs are the modes (*viśeṣa*) or modifications (*saṁsthānantara*) of their corresponding sense-objects, just as light is but a mode of colour.[7] As a mode of colour, light helps

[4] *BGB*, XIV.11.

[5] *IUB*, IV; *BṛUB*, IV.3.5.

[6] *BṛUB*, II.4.11; *SūB*, II.3.18.

[7] *BṛUB*, II.4.11.

in revealing the colours. Similarly, the eye which is also a modification (*rūpātmaka*) of colour is also the instrument through which the colours are perceived.[8]

The human body is the abode (*adhiṣṭhāna*) of the sense organs, for without it they cannot exist. The senses, like the horses of a chariot, drive the body towards the sense-objects.[9] But, as they are by nature inert, neither the body nor the senses can experience things independently. On the contrary, if it is supposed that the body is the experiencer, the absence of experience in a dead body cannot be explained, and if the same is supposed of the sense organs, knowledge, memory and desire cannot be explained. Just as the perceptual experience of different persons cannot be connected or as what one has seen cannot be recollected by another, so also, if the senses are to be independent experiencers, we cannot explain memory, knowledge and desire in the same person, for want of any principle common to and higher than all the senses, which can co-ordinate the different sensations and store them in the form of impressions for future, to make memory and knowledge possible.[10] In the absence of such a principle, what is perceived through the eyes stands unrelated to what is perceived through the ears; and without being related, the sensations cannot produce any knowledge. Further, dream experience would not be possible if the senses are the real experiencers, for during the dream state they do not function. Moreover, the absence of the experience of objects in deep sleep and at the time when the mind is not attentive cannot be explained on this basis, for during those periods of time there is no experience of objects, though the senses and their objects are in direct contact.

[8] *BṛUB*, III.9.20.

[9] *KaUB*, I.3.4.

[10] *KeUB*, I.6; *BṛUB*, I.4.7; *ChāUB*, II.7.1.

Over and above the senses, the internal organ (*antaḥkaraṇa*) is the other important organ which helps us in experiencing objects. It is also known as mind (*manas*), intellect or reason (*buddhi*), understanding (*vijñāna*) and thought (*citta*).[11] Although all these words are used by Śaṅkara at various places as synonyms for the internal organ, they are more appropriately used to indicate the different specific functions of the internal organ. The one internal organ performs various functions, depending upon which it is known differently as the mind, intellect, etc.[12] It is also a sense organ, but internally situated. In its capacities it is more subtle and comprehensive than all the other senses.[13] It is a subtle body (*sukṣma śarīra*) formed of pure matter (*śuddha sattva*) or fine elements (*bhūtasūkṣma*).[14] Its position is in between the senses and the Self. The existence of it must be admitted, otherwise the fact of perception cannot be explained. It is an observed fact that at times, even during the waking state, one does not experience objects although one's senses are in direct contact with them. It is because one is inattentive at such times, that is to say, one's mind is not focused on the things with which one's senses are in direct contact. In the words of Śaṅkara:

> Something other than the senses, namely, the mind or internal organ, in the absence of which the senses fail to perceive the objects, though they are in direct contact with them and are capable of perceiving them, and in the presence of which they are able to do so, should exist.[15]

---

[11] *SūB*, II.3.32; *Vivekacūḍāmaṇi*, *śl.* 93.

[12] *BṛUB*, I.4.7; *Vivekacūḍāmaṇi*, *śl.* 94.

[13] *SūB*, II.4.17; *BGB*, XIII.5; *AiUB*, III.1.2.

[14] *KaUB*, I.3.10; *ChāUB*, VI.5.1; *BṛUB*, II.1.9; *SūB*, I.2.12.

[15] *BṛUB*, I.5.3, tr. Swami Madhavananda, p. 214.

It thus connects the senses with their respective objects. Further, if the internal organ does not mediate between the senses and the Self, there would be either continuous perception or continuous non-perception. If the senses, objects and the Self are sufficient for perception to take place, it should be continuous whenever they are in contact. Or there should be no perception at any time even if all these three are in contact. But actual experience does not confirm either of the two, for in deep sleep there is no perception even though all these three factors are in contact, for the obvious reason that the mind is not functioning then.[16] It is only when the mind is in attention that perception occurs. This is another reason why the internal organ, through whose attention and non-attention perception and non-perception take place, should be accepted. This cannot be explained meaningfully either in terms of the Self or in terms of the senses, for it is not possible to conceive any breach in the nature of the Self, or occasional failure in the capacity of the senses to perceive, so that the gaps in our perceptual experience may be attributed to either of them.

There can be no disruption in the nature of the Self, for it is eternal and immutable, and normally the senses do not fail to perceive unless they are disabled. Another argument which Śaṅkara adduces for the existence of internal organ is that when one is touched from behind by an unseen person, one is able to judge the nature of that sensation, that is, whether it is caused by the touch of a knee or a hand, and this capacity does not belong to the senses. It is a function of the mind.[17] Again, man's capacity to have knowledge of the past and to anticipate the future proves the existence of the mind, for the sense activity by its nature is limited to the present only, because the sense organs can operate only when the objects are present before them. Thus on the basis of our actual

[16] *SūB*, II.3.32.

[17] *BṛUB*, I.5.3.

experience, the existence of the mind, whose scope is more extensive than the senses, which is more comprehensive in its capacities and which is common to all the senses, must of necessity be admitted.

In the process of perception, the mind or rather a particular function of the internal organ, holds a higher position than the senses. Being common to all the senses, it makes them act on their respective objects, or it is only when the mind is active that the senses can operate on their respective objects. It controls the senses, just as the reins control the horses of a chariot.[18] It is the chief of all the senses and they follow it, just as the members of a family follow their chief.[19] As it is common to all the senses, it can comprehend all the objects perceived by them, whereas any particular sense organ can apprehend only its corresponding sense-object. Being commom to all the senses, the mind co-ordinates the different sensations, so that knowledge is attained. It is also known as the receptacle (*nidhāna*), because the objects apprehended by all the senses are stored in it in the form of impressions, and it is because of this capacity of the mind one is able to remember, recollect and imagine.[20] Higher than the mind is reason (*buddhi*), another function of the internal organ. It can discriminate between what is real and what is unreal, between good and evil, and so on. It also determines or decides (*adhyavasāna*) the nature of things and conveys them to the Self. It is more subtle and comprehensive in nature and guides the body, mind and the senses, just as the driver of a chariot holds the reins and guides the chariot.[21] All the activities of man, whether bodily or mental, are directed by it. The distinction between reason

[18] *KaUB*, I.3.3.

[19] *BṛUB*, I.4.17.

[20] *ChāUB*, II.7.1.

[21] *KaUB*, I.3.3.

and mind is not a real one, but is made to facilitate understanding of the process of perception. They are different functional names of one and the same internal organ. The internal organ, in its varied capacities, assists the self in experiencing the manifested world of differences. It is the seat of all psychic activities like thinking, feeling and willing. But the internal organ is also not the real experiencer. Formed of fine matter, it is non-sentient and hence cannot experience. Besides, it is always an object of experience, and so can never be the subject which experiences. While the gross body, which is the seat of the senses and the mind, is the abode of empirical experience (*bhogāyatana*), the subtle body consisting of the mind and its functions is the instrument of experience (*bhogasādhana*).[22] As the chariot, horses and the charioteer are meant to serve the purpose of the master of the chariot, the gross and subtle bodies are meant to serve the purpose of the Self. They depend on each other and work together to fulfil the purpose of the individual self. The individual self, which is the real experiencer, is the master of the body (*adhyakṣa*) and through the instrumentation of the body, mind and the senses, it experiences the world of differences.

Through its identification with the internal organ, the Self appears to experience things other than itself. Because of its proximity to the Self and its transparent character and subtlety, the internal organ is able to reflect in itself the nature of the Self or the nature of the Self is superimposed on it.[23] It thus becomes an image of the Self and appears as if it is the source of consciousness, though by nature it is inert. The other sense organs and the body, which are also inert by nature, are consciously illumined by the internal organ. That is to say, they are able to function because they are inspired (*preraṇā*)

---

[22] *Ātmabodha, śl*s. 12-13.

[23] *BṛUB*, IV.3.7.

by the internal organ. The sense organs participate in the nature of the internal organ and by virtue of such participation, they are able to perceive. Thus through the inspiration of the internal organ, which is figuratively expressed as the internal organ becoming the senses, the eye which by itself cannot see things sees, the ear hears, the nose smells and so on. Through similar participation, the mind, a functional aspect of the internal organ, is able to perform its functions like doubting, and the heart or intellect, another functional aspect of internal organ, is able to discriminate and determine.[24]

Thus, because of its capacity to act on all the objects, both perceptual and intellectual, the internal organ is able to assist the knower in knowing everything. And the Self seems to experience things, though in reality it does not, as there is nothing besides it, by following (*anuvidhāna*), as it were, the internal organ, just as the moon reflected in water appears to possess the qualities of the water such as shaking.[25] Therefore, the waking experience is that which the individual self experiences through the senses and the internal organ, during the waking state, and the Self is known to be awake in so far as it seems to experience things through its identification with the internal organ. All that is thus experienced during the waking state is not the imagination of the mind, or the objects experienced during the waking state are not the creation of the mind. They exist outside the mind and independent of it. As far as the empirical experience is concerned, the objectivity of sense experience is not questioned by Śaṅkara. Not only in refuting the Buddhist doctrine of subjective-idealism, but in general, Śaṅkara accepts the objective existence of the things experienced. In the empirical context, he accepts the theory of those who maintain that our experience is caused by externally

---

[24] *AiUB*, III.1.2.

[25] *BṛUB*, II.1.19, IV.3.7.

existing objects. At that level, the objects of perception as well as the subject that perceives them are equally real. On the other hand, to deny objective existence to things experienced at the empirical level is contrary to "common and altogether rational opinion".[26] The very fact that everyone perceives the objects as existing outside of one's mind, says Śaṅkara, proves their independent existence.[27] Moreover, the independent existence of objects perceived is proved by all the means of right knowledge. Therefore, to deny them independent existence while actually experiencing them to be so would be like denying the fact of eating and being satisfied while actually eating and experiencing satisfaction.[28]

It is simply baseless to deny what is actually experienced unless something that contradicts it is experienced. No one has the right to deny or contradict that which is actually experienced; and the question of impossibility of what is actually experienced does not arise.[29]

> Nobody when perceiving a post or a wall is conscious of the perception only, but all men are conscious of posts, walls and the like as objects of their perception.[30]

Even those, like the followers of Vijñānavāda, who contest the objective existence of things experienced, and according to whom, the objects experienced are nothing but the ideas of the mind, however, admit that the ideas of objects somehow appear to be as existing outside of the mind; and this, according to Śaṅkara, would not be possible if the objects of experience do not really exist outside of the mind.[31] Further, it is not possible

---

[26] *SūB*, II.2.28.

[27] Ibid.

[28] Ibid.

[29] *BṛUB*, I.4.10.

[30] *SūB*, II.2.28, tr. Thibaut, vol. 7, p. 421.

[31] *SūB*, II.2.28.

to explain, on the basis of Vijñānavāda, the variety and multiplicity found in our experience, that is, different colours, sounds and tastes, etc. They cannot be attributed to the internal organ, for it remains the same throughout empirical experience. If, on the other hand, the internal organ or the subjective factor in experience were to undergo change every moment, then rememberance would not be possible. We are able to remember things because the internal aspect of our experience is not changing along with the objects experienced. So, the variety in our experience must be due to variety in objects experienced.[32] To say that what we experience are only ideas of the mind, but not objectively existing objects is not valid for the further reason that the ideas cannot arise in the absence of objects.

Ideas are caused by the objects, for the former are the mental counterparts of the latter. Moreover, the fact that everyone is able to distinguish ideas from objects shows that the ideas are different from the objects.[33] The very nature of perceptual experience provides the reason for the existence of objects. If sense-perception is an activity of our senses, we should also admit the existence of objects, for without them the activity of the senses is not possible. To assert that the senses perceive and at the same time to deny the existence of objects, which they perceive, is to deny the basis of sense-perception.[34] Thus empirically, experience means the experience of something and of someone. Except in deep sleep and in the fourth state (*turīya*), consciousness becomes revealed simultaneously along with the objects which it reveals. Empirical experience is either object-consciousness or self-consciousness, implying thereby that if there is no object-consciousness there can be no consciousness of the subject also.

---

[32] *SūB*, II.2.30.

[33] Ibid., II.2.28.

[34] Ibid., I.1.3, II.2.28.

Thus at the empirical level, pure consciousness or objectless conciousness is not possible. The subject and the object are interdependent and reveal each other. According to Śaṅkara, even self-consciousness is not without an object, since the notion of "I" (*aham*) or what one thinks of oneself is the object of self-consciousness.[35] Thus the analysis of empirical experience shows that both subject and object are equally real. According to Śaṅkara, whether what we experience has an objective validity or not is not a problem to be discussed, but something which is to be settled by direct experience, for "the possibility or impossibility of things is to be determined only on the grounds of the operation or non-operation of the means of right knowledge".[36] What is possible and what is not possible are not dependent upon what we think of them.

> Possible is whatever is apprehended by perception or some other means of knowledge, impossible is what is not so apprehended.[37]

Therefore, there can be no meaning in trying to dispute or deny the truth of what is directly evident to oneself, and as all are conscious of the objectivity of things experienced, there is no point in disputing their validity.

Now, waking experience is not limited to sense experience only; it includes the knowledge obtained through the scriptures and inferential reasoning. As the scope of the mind and the intellect is more comprehensive than that of the senses, with their help man can know things which cannot be known through the senses. For instance, one can know things of the past and anticipate the future with the aid of mind.[38] It can operate even

---

[35] *SūB*, I.1.4, II.3.40.

[36] Ibid., II.2.28, tr. Thibaut, vol. I, p. 421.

[37] Ibid.

[38] *ChāUB*, VIII.12.5; *SūB*, II.4.6.

when the senses are not functioning.[39] And the intellect has various capacities like thinking, discriminating and reasoning. "Intellect stands for pondering (*manana*), reasoning (*tarka*) and paying attention to the objects received through the senses."[40] Because of it, one can understand the significance of things experienced and also can ascertain the purpose underlying them. It is the principle in terms of which the whole of sense experience can be interpreted and integrated. It can go beyond the range of sense perception, and try to understand what is not directly seen on the basis of what is directly seen. In trying to do so, it is guided by certain principles like causation.

The principle of causation refers to our understanding everything in terms of a cause. This faith in causation (*hetuphalāveśa*) makes man constantly formulate theories of creation. There are thus many theories of creation speculatively arrived at by those who could reflect on the origin and the process of creation (*sṛṣṭi cintaka*). In Śaṅkara's philosophy also we find an explanation of the universe in terms of an ultimate cause, but it is mainly based on the authority of the scriptures, though he admits that through reasoning also such an explanation can be formulated.[41] The explanation of the world in terms of an ultimate cause or principle is inevitable if we wish to understand the nature of the manifested universe. The manifested world of differences is an effect, because it did not exist in its manifested state of name and form before it was created and is also proved to be unreal when the ultimate reality is realized. It has a beginning and so will come to an end.[42] It has come into existence in time; and what is manifested

[39] *ChāUB*, II.7.1.

[40] *ChāUB*, VII.18.1.

[41] *SūB*, I.1.3., II.1.37.

[42] According to Śaṅkara, the universe is beginningless, as ignorance, its cause is beginningless. What he calls the universe includes its →

in time is but an effect. Since it is an effect and subject to change (*vikāra*), it cannot be regarded as self-existent and eternal. It does not remain the same for even a moment, but undergoes constant change.[43] Moreover, as the nature of the world can be determined and known, it is finite and limited. It appears and disappears, exsits and ceases to exist. According to Śaṅkara, the world is based on or projected by the knowledge and actions of man which are unregenerated or are not in accordance with the scriptures, and is characterized by means and ends, actions and their results and is held together by the stream of actions and impressions (*vāsanā*) of innumerable human beings.[44] It is, therefore, transient, impure and sapless (*asāra*) and, like a plantain trunk, worthless and, like a flowing river or a burning lamp, constantly changing. He compares it to foam, a mirage, a dream and an illusion.[45]

The universe may appear to be self-existent and ultimately real for those who are ignorant and non-discriminative, but it is finite, limited, imperfect and impermanent for those who can reflect on it and can think beyond sense-experience. It has no self-existence. It exists because something other than it is existing as its cause. The fact that the universe is not self-sufficient makes one think of its cause, just as the existence of a tree makes one think of its cause. According to Śaṅkara, *Īśvara* or the conditioned *Brahman* is the final cause of the universe. He not only creates the universe, but also sustains and finally absorbs it into Himself. The universe is created out of matter (*prakṛti*) and spirit (*puruṣa*) or *kṣetra* and *kṣetrajña*,

→unmanifested state also. But the differentiated universe of name and form has a beginning, that is, when the undifferentiated becomes differentiated into name and form (*BṛUB*, I.4.7; *SūB*, II.1.36).

[43] *BGB*, XV.1.

[44] *BṛUB*, I.5.2.

[45] Ibid.

which form his twofold nature.[46] Matter is known as his lower or impure nature and the spirit as his superior or pure nature.[47]

As the Lord is eternal, it is but necessary that His nature should be co-eternal with Him.[48] His Lordship consists in His possession of twofold nature by which He creates, sustains and dissolves the world. His lower nature or matter evolves itself into the physical world or all that can be known or experienced represents His lower nature or *kṣetra*.[49] His superior nature is that which enters into the physical world and sustains it. As the conscious principle, it is in all living beings. As experiencer or knower, it is the basis of all experience and as agent, of all action. In a man, His lower nature is represented by the body which includes the senses and the mind, and His superior nature is represented by the self. "*Puruṣa, jīva, kṣetrajña* and *bhoktā* are all synonymous terms."[50] In short, what experiences is the *puruṣa* and all that is experienced is the *prakṛti*. For this reason, Śaṅkara says that *prakṛti* and *puruṣa* constitute the womb of all creation. They evolve into the physical and spiritual aspects of the universe and the Lord unites (*saṁyoga*) these two, and this act gives rise to the origination of all beings.[51] The act of creation does not bind *Īśvara* at all. He remains detached from it, just as the ether (*ākāśa*) supports the all-expansive wind without having any attachment to it. *Īśvara* is not the source of inequality and evil found in the world. In creating men, the Lord is not

---

[46] *BGB*, XIII.19, VII.6, XIV.3.

[47] Ibid., VII.5-6.

[48] Ibid., XIII.9.

The Lord's eternity is relative. He is eternal only from the empirical standpoint. He is not absolutely eternal since He is ultimately unreal.

[49] *BGB*, XIII.2.

[50] Ibid., XIII.20.

[51] Ibid., XIV.3.

impelled by anything of His own, but is guided solely by the merit and demerit of them. He only judges the actions of men in apportioning the fruits of their actions. His role in this regard is similar to that of rain in bringing forth and nourishing the various plants. So the rain is not in any way responsible for the differences among the plants; they are completely due to the differences inherent within their seeds.[52] In like manner, *Īśvara* is only the common cause of all creation and the individual differences in respect of happiness and suffering are due to good and bad deeds done by men.

> The activity of the Lord is a mere sport and follows the law of His own nature with no purpose.[53]

Like the process of inhalation and exhalation, the creation proceeds from the Lord's nature spontaneously without any reference to His purpose. It may be possible to detect, in the case of man, some subtle motive for his sportful action, but even that is absent from the Lord who is perfect and has no unfulfilled wishes. He, as mere witness, presides over the entire universe. At the level of human beings, He is the witness consciousness (*sākṣī*) which is a mere spectator untainted by all that is witnessed. Although it witnesses all the activities of the individual self, as it is not involved in them, it is neither influenced nor bound by them. *Īśvara* is the inner principle (*antaryāmin*) in all living beings and the nature of all elements.[54] He is the humanity in all men or that by which a man is regarded as a human being. In Him, as humanity, all men are fastened or woven together (*prota*).[55] He is thus the Self of everyone and the essence of everything. All beings exist because of Him and through Him, for He is the Self or essence

[52] *SūB*, II.1.34.

[53] Ibid., II.1.33.

[54] *AiUB*, III.1.3; *MāUB*, VI.

[55] *BGB*, VII.8.

of them all, and anything that is devoid of Self or essence cannot exist. Therefore, that into which the Lord has not entered as the Self or essence would be selfless and void.[56]

There is no other cause for the existence of the universe except the Lord. He is the material out of which the entire universe is shaped as well as the intelligence which shapes the universe. By virtue of His twofold nature, *Īśvara* is the material basis of creation as well as the creative principle which is responsible for the orderly evolution of the matter. While His lower nature forms the material basis of the universe, His higher nature helps matter in evolving itself into the universe. He is thus the creator and the created or the designer and the designed. The scriptural statement, "through the knowledge of the one everything is known", according to Śaṅkara, means that *Īśvara* is the material cause of the world, for the knowledge of everything is possible only through the knowledge of the material cause, as the effects in their substance are non-different from their material cause.[57] As the objects of clay are known when their material cause, the clay, is known, all things can be known if their material cause is known. Moreover, that from which something springs up and into which it returns cannot be anything other than the meterial cause, because the effects cannot be reabsorbed into anything other than their material cause.[58] As into the Lord the universe will be dissolved in the end, He must be its material cause. Generally, the operative cause will be external to or different from the material cause. But, according to Śaṅkara, there can be no principle besides the Lord which can form the operative cause of the universe. There is nothing besides *Īśvara* to which He can look for help or guidance in creating the universe. If there

---

[56] *BGB*, X.39, IX.4.

[57] *SūB*, I.4.23.

[58] Ibid., I.4.25.

were to be something different from *Īśvara*, which acts as an operative cause, then it would not be possible to know everything by knowing *Īśvara*. Besides, the scriptural statement that the Lord thought of becoming many, before creating the world, proves reflection on the part of *Īśvara* and His being the operative cause of the world besides His being the material cause of it.[59] Another Śruti statement "That (*Brahman* or *Īśvara*) created Itself by Itself", represents the Lord as the object of action as well as the agent of action.[60] Thus the Lord's twofold nature is sufficient to explain the world and its creation.

Let us now consider another type of empirical experience, namely dream experience. Although the senses do not function, the mind is active during the dream state, and the Self by identifying itself with the mind seems to experience the objects created by the mind.[61] Many objects are experienced during the dream state, but they are not objectively real. They are purely mental or the creation of the mind. The impressions or images left by the objects experienced during the waking state become the objects of dream experience. Although the dream experience is purely mental or subjective, it is dualistic. The extra-mental objects of waking experience are here replaced by the objects created by the mind. While the objects of waking experience are gross and exist independent of the mind, the objects of dream experience are subtle and have no existence independent of the mind. Nevertheless, the duality of the experiencer and the experienced is also the characteristic of dream experience.

Although there is no such duality in deep sleep, it is not completely free from it. The factors of duality exist in their

---

[59] *SūB*, I.4.24.

[60] Ibid., I.4.26; *TaiUB*, II.7.1.

[61] *PrUB*, IV.5; *BṛUB*, IV.3.9.

potential or unmanifested condition in deep sleep. As such there is no object-consciousness in deep sleep. However, it is the causal state of both waking and dream states of experience. The causal state of the world is analogous to the state of deep sleep.[62] Before it is manifested, the entire universe of names and forms exists in its unmanifested condition in its causal state which is the nature of the Lord. Thus, in all empirical experience, the individual self is the active agent and the experiencer. As the subject in experience, it abides unchangingly throughout the empirical experience. It is the "I" (*aham*) in all empirical experience and everything else, including *Īśvara*, stands opposed to it either as an object of enjoyment or as an object of devotion. While the world is an object of enjoyment to the individual self, *Īśvara* the Creator and the Ruler (*prabhu*) of the world is the supreme object of devotion. He is the Ruler and the self is the ruled.

So far, we have discussed the nature of empirical experience and have not touched the problem of its validity. According to Śaṅkara, it is not possible to judge the validity or otherwise of an experience from the standpoint of that experience, for every experience, whether of illusory or of real objects, is real and valid in so far as it is viewed and judged from the standpoint of that particular experience.[63] Nothing in itself is illusory or unreal so long as it is experienced. An experience can be judged only from the standpoint of another, and in judging so, the former may be found illusory or unreal. Such that, it is not possible to criticize the validity of empirical experience from the standpoint of itself. It is only when the non-dualistic experience or *brahmānubhava* is attained that empirical experience or the experience based on the differences comes to be known as unreal or illusory,

---

[62] *MāUB*, V.

[63] *ChāUB*, VIII.5.4.

and prior to that there is no basis for doubting the validity of empirical experience. Before *Brahman* is realized, there is not the slightest reason to doubt the validity of empirical experience. It is the supreme authority as far as the empirical world is concerned. Therefore, empirical experience is not unreal or illusory for those who have not transcended it. It is the whole of reality for them.

Although dream experience is accepted by all as a definite experience, nobody accepts it as valid as waking experience. The validity of waking experience is considered to be greater than that of dream experience, and the objects of dream experience are considered to be unreal when compared with the objects of waking experience. Certain conditions like space, time and causation, which are fulfilled during the waking state, are not only fulfilled during the dream state, but are also contradicted during that state.[64] First, though there is not enough place in the body of a dreaming person to accommodate the dream objects like chariots, one experiences them during a dream. The argument that the Self goes out of the body during a dream to experience such objects cannot be correct, for a person, who has dreamt that he had been to another country and did not return from there, will find himself in his own place after that dream is over. Second, dream experience is in conflict with the concept of time. One who is asleep at night may dream that it is day or may spend several years within the short duration of the dream. Last, the law of causation does not operate during the dream state, for there is sense experience though the senses that cause it do not function. Further, dream experience is sublated by waking experience and the dream objects are realized to be unreal when one passes from that into the waking state. A particular

---

[64] *SūB*, III.2.3; *GKB*, II.1.2.

dream experience may even be contradicted by another gained during the same dream, as for instance, the same thing which at first was experienced as a chariot may later be experienced as a man. But the realization that the world of dreams is unreal is not possible while one is actually dreaming. Dream experience in itself is not unreal; it is so only from the standpoint of the waking experience. Likewise, from the standpoint of a dream experience the waking experience may be considered as unreal.[65] Thus each state of experience is vaild in itself, or from its own standpoint; and no particular state of experience is valid beyond itself.

The world of waking experience may seem to be ultimately real, before one comes to know it to be an effect or a dependent reality. It may appear to be self-existent and self-sufficient. But when the existence of the Lord, its cause, is known, its reality becomes contingent. But, as the effect is different from its cause only in name and form, the universe is not different from *Īśvara*, its cause, except for the difference of name and form.[66] The relation between the Lord and His creation is comparable to the one that exists between the ocean and its various modifications like foam and waves.[67] When they are viewed from the standpoint of modifications, the foam and the wave are real and are different from their cause, the sea, but from the standpoint of their substance, the sea water, they are not different from it except for the difference of name and form. Likewise, from the standpoint of itself, the world of names and forms is real and is different from *Īśvara*, its cause, whereas from the standpoint of *Īśvara*, it is nothing but *Īśvara* differentiated into name and form. Thus when viewed in relation to its cause, the world is not unreal like a dream; only

---

[65] *ChāUB*, VIII.5.4.

[66] *SūB*, I.1.25, II.1.14, I.4.14, II.3.6.

[67] *AiUB*, I.1.1, I.1.2; *SūB*, II.1.14.

its status is reduced to that of an effect or a contingent reality. Therefore, the world cannot exist without its cause, just as a pot cannot exist without clay.

However, from the standpoint of *brahmānubhava,* the world and its creator are not real. Śaṅkara says that the comparison of the relation that exists between *Īśvara* and the world with that which exists between the ocean and its modifications rests on a false assumption that the world of names and forms is real.[68] When *Brahman* is realized, the world ceases to have any reality and the above analogy loses its significance. Then the experience based on the differences like the knower and the known, ruler and the ruled, and the creator and the created will have no objective validity, for all these distinctions are ultimately based on ignorance.

> Just as dreams appear to be true as long as one does not wake up, so the identification of oneself with the body, etc. and the validity of sense-perception and the like in the waking state continue as long as there is no Self-knowledge.[69]

The ultimate unreality of empirical experience becomes clear if its basis is understood. Empirical experience, according to Śaṅkara, is based on the superimposition of the nature of the intellect on the Self. In reality, neither the Self nor the intellect can independently experience things, for the Self is pure consciousness, non-dual and devoid of all activity, and the intellect, being constituted of matter, is insentient. But because of the latter's purity, illuminative character and proximity to the Self, people fail to discriminate between the nature of the intellect and the nature of the Self and superimpose the one on the other. Due to this superimposition, the Self appears to

---

68 *SūB*, II.1.14.

69 *Upadeśasāhasrī*, XI.5., tr. Swami Jagadananda, p. 117.

be the individual self (*jīva*) and seems to experience things other than itself. In other words, because of its identification with the intellect or by its following the intellect, the Self seems to perceive, think, reflect, feel, will, doubt, discriminate, reason out, etc. The empirical self in its turn superimposes such distinctions as the ruler and the ruled, imagined by it on differenceless *Brahman*. In other words, it imagines all types of differences in *Brahman* and empirical experience is based on such superimposed differences. Now, non-discrimination and superimposition are not possible in the absence of duality. They require two things. They naturally imply the existence of the Self and something other than it or non-self (*anātma*) which is superimposed on it, or vice versa. Otherwise, there is no scope for non-discrimination and consequent superimposition. Therefore, the nature of the non-self is to be inquired into. According to Śaṅkara the non-self is the creation of *māyā* (illusion) or it is *māyā* itself.[70]

Māyā is the creative force (*śakti*) of the Lord by which He creates the world. It is the unmanifested state of the universe. It is name and form which are the two limiting adjuncts of the Lord, and are also the sources of variety and multiplicity.[71] It is also identified with sense-knowledge (*indriya prajñā*) and the mind.[72] In a nutshell, it is the basis of everything except the Self. As will be shown later, the existence of *māyā* is simply due to ignorance (*avidyā*) or wrong knowledge. Like an illusory snake, it has no objective existence, and whatever reality it possesses it owes to ignorance. The fact that one has experienced an illusory snake for a certain time is no valid reason to assume its objective existence. The existence of *māyā* is wrongly imagined in *Brahman*. If, on the other hand, *māyā*

---

70 *BṛUB*, II.4.14; *TaiUB*, II.6.1; *Aparokṣānubhūti, śl.* 69.

71 *SūB*, II.1.14; *BṛUB*, III.8.12.

72 *GKB*, III.24; *Vivekacūḍāmaṇi, śl.* 169 and 180.

has positive existence, there can be no end to the world process and to the bondage of the Self. *Māyā*, which is the source of all differences and the seed of all sufferings, cannot also belong to *Brahman* whose essential nature is undifferentiated pure consciousness. If both *Brahman* and *māyā* are to be true and belong to the same order of reality, the man who finds satisfaction in the phenomenal world cannot be considered as ignorant. Also, empirical experience would in no way and at no time become unreal and could never be sublated.[73]

At various places, Śaṅkara identifies *māyā* with *avidyā* and treats the two words as synonyms.[74] They are not two different things in any sense. As *māyā* is characterized by both existence and non-existence, so is *avidyā*. *Avidyā* is also regarded as the basis of name and form, and both *māyā* and *avidyā* are ultimately undefinable. However, Śaṅkara refers to *māyā*, mostly, when the process of creation is to be explained, as for instance, *Īśvara* creates the world out of His twofold nature which is *māyā*. But the ultimate explanation of everything empirical, including *Īśvara*, lies in *avidyā* or false knowledge (*mithyājñāna*). Thus the existence of the universe and its explanation in terms of the twofold nature of *Īśvara* are ultimately based on ignorance or are valid from the standpoint of ignorance. This becomes clear by the following statements of Śaṅkara in which he maintains that ignorance is the ultimate cause (*nidāna*) of everything. He says that the existence of a conditioned *Brahman*, that is, *Īśvara*, who creates, sustains and finally dissolves the universe with the help of *māyā* is based on ignorance. It is nothing but an imagination of the individual self.

> Name and form are the presentations of ignorance which in turn form the limiting adjuncts of the Lord.[75]

---

[73] *SūB*, II.1.14.

[74] Ibid., I.3.19; *ĪUB*, XII.

[75] *SūB*, II.1.14, II.2.2.

> The Lord's being a Lord, His omniscience, His omnipotence, etc. depend on the limitation due to the adjuncts whose essence is ignorance.[76]
>
> Name and form have ignorance as their basis.[77]

Thus the basis of all empirical experience is ignorance because of which the empirical self wrongly imagines the existence of the empirical reality and then formulates various theories to explain it. The word imagination (*kalpanā*) is mostly used by Śaṅkara to explain the world process. He says that the name and form, which constitute the non-self, are the imaginary creation of ignorance (*avidyā kalpita* or *avidyā kṛta nāmarūpa*). The essence of name and form is ignorance (*avidyātmaka*). They are the presentations of ignorance.[78] He even says that *māyā* as such is caused by *avidyā* (*avidyā kṛta māyā*).[79] This can be further confirmed by analysing the nature of *avidyā* or *ajñāna*. According to Śaṅkara, *avidyā* has the two capacities of veiling (*āvaraṇa*) and projecting (*vikṣepa*). Because of its veiling power, *avidyā* veils, as it were, the true nature of the Self and this gives rise to various misconceptions of it. In the absence of perfect knowledge of the Self, people project various wrong notions on it. In this context, if we consider the following statement of Śaṅkara that "it is extremely difficult to conquer the projecting power of *avidyā* unless its veiling power is perfectly rooted out",[80] it becomes evident that the projection of the universe, etc. on *Brahman* can be stopped only by stopping the veiling power of *avidyā*. Veiling means the absence of the perfect knowledge of the Self. This absence of the

---

76 *SūB*, II.1.14, tr. Thibaut, vol. I, p. 329.

77 Ibid., II.1.14, III.2.6.

78 Ibid., II.1.14.

79 *GKB*, I.6.

80 *Vivekacūḍāmaṇi*, *śl.* 344, tr. Swami Madhavananda, p. 152.

perfect knowledge of the Self is the source of the imagination of differences. In other words, the world of differences is imagined in or projected upon *Brahman* by the individual self out of ignorance concerning Its true nature. Accordingly, Śaṅkara says that the veiling power is the primary cause (*nidāna*) of the Self's empirical existence and it initiates the action of the projecting power.[81] Thus ignorance or the absence of perfect knowledge of the Self is basically responsible for the entire creation. It is the sole basis of empirical experience. In the words of Śaṅkara:

> This entire apparent world, in which good and evil actions are done, etc. is a mere illusion, owing to the non-discrimination of (the Self's) limiting adjuncts, namely body and so on, which spring from name and form the presentations of ignorance, and does, in reality, not exist at all.[82]
>
> This universe in its manifested and unmanifested forms, consisting of gross and subtle things and the impressions produced by them, is an object of ignorance (*avidyā viṣaya*) and is superimposed by it on the Self.[83]
>
> It is ignorance which imagines (*parikalpita*) the non-self; strictly speaking, there is nothing but the Self.[84]

So also, the empirical nature of the Self (*saṁsāritva*) and the creatorship (*sṛṣṭṛtva*) of *Brahman* are due to ignorance.[85] The absolute oneness of *Brahman* leaves no room for the differences of the ruler and the ruled, and the creator and the created. They are the creations of ignorance, and pertain to the empirical sphere.

---

[81] *Vivekacūḍāmaṇi, śl.* 113.

[82] *SūB*, II.1.22, tr. Thibaut, vol. I, p. 345.

[83] *BṛUB*, I.1, Introduction.

[84] Ibid., II.4.14, tr. Swami Madhavananda, p. 375.

[85] *SūB*, II.1.22, II.1.14.

Ignorance is in no way related to the Self or *Brahman*, nor does it belong to the individual self.[86] As the source of wrong knowledge, it can only belong to the organs of knowledge, but not to the Self, just as an eye disease belongs to the eye only, but not to the person who sees.[87] In *Vivekacūḍāmaṇi*, Śaṅkara says that there is no ignorance outside the mind.

> Man's empirical existence or transmigration (*saṁśruti*) is due to the evil of superimposition, and the bondage of superimposition is imagined by the mind.[88]

> Those who have realized the highest declare the mind as *avidyā* (*mano avidyā*).[89]

On the contrary, if *avidyā* were to form a part and parcel of the Self, its destruction would be not possible with the dawn of perfect knowledge of the Self, whereas it is completely destroyed when the Self is realized. According to Śaṅkara, any further enquiry into the cause and origination of ignorance does not serve any useful purpose of the individual. As far as empirical experience is concerned, its existence is a natural fact (*svābhāvika*) and it does not seem to have a beginning. It is something adventitious, so its destruction can be effected. Therefore, the fact of its presence should be realized, so that one can strive to get rid of it. By realizing its presence and by understanding its nature one can become free from it. Whereas, no independent purpose is served by understanding its origin.[90] Similarly, by trying to know the process of world creation and its cause, one is neither saved nor is one's supreme end of life accomplished.

---

[86] *BGB*, XIII.2; *BṛUB*, IV.3.20; *TaiUB*, II.8.5.

[87] *BGB*, XIII.2.

[88] *Vivekacūḍāmaṇi*, *śl.* 179.

[89] Ibid., *śl.* 190.

[90] *BGB*, III.2.

While the realization of one's identity with *Brahman* results in absolute freedom, no such result is obtained by understanding how *Brahman* has become the universe.[91] As the main purpose of Vedānta is not to explain the universe and its origin, it pays little or no attention to the theories of creation, as they cannot help one in becoming free from ignorance. Accordingly, Śaṅkara says that the Vedānta texts mention about the origin, etc. of the world only to strengthen or confirm one's belief that *Brahman* is a homogeneous reality and that It is the Self of all, but not to make one understand the nature of the world and the process of its creation.[92] The observation of the world, which is but an illusory effect of *Brahman*, makes a reflective person to think of *Brahman*, its cause, just as the observation of a pot made of clay forces on one who is reflective the idea of clay as the cause of the pot.[93]

The Vedāntic theory of creation is meant to help an individual realize his identity with *Brahman*. To make everyone realize that the Self is fearless and one with *Brahman*, the ideas of creation, maintenance and dissolution of the universe are imagined in or superimposed on *Brahman* by the scripture. Illustrating this with an example, Śaṅkara says that in order to teach the nature of numbers, one may draw some figures or lines (digits) and name them as "one", "two", "three", etc., but in doing so one never thinks that the real numbers are those figures. Likewise, in teaching the alphabet, one may take the help of paper, ink, figures, etc., but no one thinks thereby that these things are the letters. They are employed as means to explain the nature of the letters of an alphabet.

---

[91] *SūB*, II.1.14.

[92] Ibid., I.4.14.

[93] *Aparokṣānubhūti*, *śl.* 67.

Similar is the case with the theories of creation.[94] Through such theories and various other means, the knowledge of *Brahman* is sought to be communicated. Contrary to this, if such doctrines of creation are taken to be really valid, instead of as passing means to the realization of the highest, man becomes deluded.

> Those, who fail to understand that the means have only one purpose, namely the realization of the end, make a mistake by thinking that what are suggested as the means have the same reality as the end.[95]

Thus out of ignorance people attribute objective reality to all that is superimposed and fail to understand its unreality.

Since one's entire empirical experience is based on ignorance, it comes to an end when one is freed from ignorance. Though ignorance seems to have no beginning (from the empirical standpoint), it has an end, and with it everything that is based on it will also come to an end. Thus if the real nature of the Self, which is one with *Brahman*, is realized, the reality of the empirical self is done away with, and along with it, the whole of empirical reality, which is based on it, stands annulled.

> If the doctrine of the independent existence of the individual self has to be set aside, then the opinion of the entire phenomenal world — which is based on the individual self — having an independent existence is likewise to be set aside.[96]

However, an illusory experience is not possible in the absence of a substratum, for no illusion is possible without a substratum

---

[94] *BṛUB*, IV.4.25.

[95] *GKB*, III.26, tr. Swami Nikhilananda, p. 181.

[96] *SūB*, II.1.14, tr, Thibaut, vol. I, p. 322.

(*adhiṣṭhāna*). "By no one the illusion of the rope–snake or mirage, etc. is ever perceived without a substratum."[97] In the examples of illusion like shell–silver, rope–snake and sand–water (mirage) given by Śaṅkara to illustrate the nature of empirical experience, the illusory experience of silver, snake and water is based on the objective reality of shell, rope and sand, respectively. Shell, rope and sand form the basis of our illusory perception of silver, snake and water. Similarly, empirical experience, which is also illusory, must be based on something, which is ultimately real and objectively existing. It is the experience of that reality as it appears. Ignorance which means wrong cognition (*viparīta darśana*) or false understanding (*anṛtabuddhi*) or the absence of perfect knowledge distorts the true nature of a thing and makes it appear in a different way (*anyathā jñāna*). Because of its presence, things are not seen in their real nature. Thus if we admit our empirical experience, the experience of a snake in a rope, as wrong, we should also admit the existence of something of which empirical experience is the wrong experience. In the absence of such a substratum, experience as such, whether right or wrong, is not possible. When we perceive something as some other thing, the former is the basis for the experience of the latter, and in its absence, the experience of the latter will not be possible. *Brahman* in Itself is the substratum on which the whole of empirical experience is based. It is That which appears as the universe, etc. to the deluded or it is the substratum on which the whole of empirical reality is superimposed. Now, the problem is to determine the nature of the relationship, if any, that exists between *brahmānubhava* and empirical experience. Before we do so, we should note their fundamental differences.

---

[97] *GKB*, I.6, tr. Swami Nikhilananda, p. 38.

Empirical experience and Brahmānubhava

Empirical experience is a caused experience. It is due to the activity of the mind, for it is not present when the mind stops functioning, as in deep sleep or in the fourth state. It is based on the differences created by ignorance and is not possible without them. There is no objective reality corresponding to it. Hence, its validity is limited to the sphere of ignorance. It is not permanent, since it is sublated by *brahmānubhava*. As the experience of a reality, which has no objective existence, empirical experience is ultimately untrue and has no objective validity. Thus empirical experience is relative, conditioned, imperfect and impermanent. On the contrary, *brahmānubhava* is uncaused. It is not a result either of the activity of the senses or of the mind. It is experience pure and simple. It is completely free from ignorance. It is absolutely true, unconditioned and eternal. It cannot be sublated by any experience, for it is the highest realization and the basis of every experience. As the two experiences differ so widely and fundamentally, there can be no real relation of any sort between them. The only thing that is common to both of them is that they are experiences. Even as experiences they fundamentally differ. While one is pure experience or experience in itself, the other is the experience of an object by a subject. One is transient and unreal, while the other is absolutely real and eternal. However, Śaṅkara has discussed various relations that might exist between them and has disproved them.

It cannot be one of identity. The empirical experience of differences can in no way be identical with *brahmānubhava* which is absolute and undifferentiated. The experience of an appearance is something different from the experience of its substratum, although the object is the same in both the experiences. The experience of an illusory snake and the experience of its basis, the rope, are in no way identical although the object of both the experiences is the same. While the experience of differences is the source of suffering, *brahmānubhava* is pure bliss. While one experience binds man, the other frees him. If they are to be identical, there can be no meaning in striving to attain *brahmānubhava*, for empirical experience is attained by all without any effort.[98] If both are identical, *brahmānubhava* need not be considered as limited to the fourth state only, and the other three states of empirical experience need not be looked upon as unreal and unworthy. But this is not so, as the empirical experience is actually sublated or found out to be unreal, the moment *brahmānubhava* is attained. Although, as a matter of fact, *Brahman* is the object of experience in both the experiences, the fact of ignorance, which causes empirical experience, makes it differ from *brahmānubhava*. Thus while one is the experience of *Brahman* from the standpoint of ignorance or as conditioned by ignorance, the other is the experience of *Brahman* as it is in Itself or it is *Brahman* Itself.

It also cannot be the "one–many" relation. This type of relation is meaningful and valid within the empirical sphere of ignorance, and beyond that it has no validity. The "many" cease to exist when the "one" is realized and the "one" is not realized as long as the "many" is experienced. While the experience of the "one" is absolutely true and objectively valid, the experience of the "many" is ultimately untrue and has on objective validity. Therefore, it is not possible to conceive any relationship between an illusory experience of the "many" and an absolute experience of the "one". It is also not possible to conceive between them a relation of the type that exists between the reflected and the reflection. To think of such a relation is to accept the existence of a medium in which *Brahman* can reflect Itself. But the existence of anything besides *Brahman*,

[98] *SūB*, II.1.26, II.1.27.

which may act as a medium of reflection, cannot be thought of.[99] It cannot be the relation of transformation, that is, the relation that exists between milk and curd, as *Brahman*'s nature is absolutely immutable (*kūṭastha*). Nor can it be the relation that exists between the conditioned and the unconditioned, for there does not exist anything different from the Self which can condition or limit it. The conditioning of the Self is only apparent, but not real, as in itself the Self is eternally free. Finally, it is not the relation of cause and effect. Śaṅkara never accepts causation in *Brahman*, as causation cannot take place without producing some change in the cause. Moreover, if the universe is really an effect of *Brahman*, it should be as real as its cause and also must be co-eternal with *Brahman*. Then it cannot be sublated at any time.

Thus from the standpoint of *brahmānubhava*, there can be no relationship between it and the empirical experience, simply because there does not exist anything besides *Brahman*. Some sort of relationship would have been possible if somehow the empirical reality exists besides *Brahman*. *Brahman* which is the object of both empirical experience and *brahmānubhava* is in no way responsible for the difference between them. It is caused by ignorance and therefore, the only type of relationship that is conceivable between them is the one that exists between ignorance and knowledge, and even this is meaningful and valid from the standpoint of empirical experience only. It is the relation that exists between the experience of an appearance and the experience of reality on which the appearance is based. That is to say, the difference between empirical experience and *brahmānubhava* is not due to any difference in the object experienced, but solely due to the presence and absence of ignorance.

---

[99] *SūB*, III.2.19.

While empirical experience marks the presence of ignorance, *brahmānubhava* is completely free from it. *Brahman* in Itself is one only without a second and It is absolutely immutable; nevertheless, It is experienced as empirical reality because of ignorance. In other words, the same Reality, that is, *Brahman* in Itself is experienced as the empirical reality due to the presence of ignorance and when it is removed, It is experienced in Its real nature or *brahmānubhava* is attained. As such, there is no change in the nature of *Brahman* corresponding to our wrong experience of It; and the empirical experience is a wrong experience of *Brahman* caused by ignorance. In the words of Śaṅkara:

> The evolution of name and form is the appearance of *Brahman* as many, and in no other way can one justify either the evolution of *Brahman* into many or Its finitude.[100]

As the same object, for example the rope, is differently experienced because of ignorance as a snake, the same *Brahman* is experienced differently by different people because of the influence of ignorance.

Śaṅkara unequivocally asserts that the same reality, which is experienced as the differentiated universe because of ignorance, is realized to be *Brahman* when ignorance is destroyed.

> Whatever a deluded person sees in his ignorance is nothing but *Brahman* only.[101]

> The universe is an unbroken series of perceptions of *Brahman*, hence it is in all respects nothing but *Brahman*. One has to see this with the eye of illumination and a serene mind under all circumstances.[102]

---

[100] *TaiUB*, II.6.1.

[101] *Vivekacūḍāmaṇi*, *śl.* 236.

[102] Ibid., *śl.* 521, tr. Swami Madhavananda, p. 226.

In *Brahman* realization the idea of the universe is negated and the pure identity of *Brahman* is experienced. The same reality, which was experienced as the universe prior to the removal of ignorance, will be experienced as *Brahman* when ignorance is removed. Thus there are no two different realities corresponding to the two experiences in question; they are only two different experiences of one and the same reality. While one of them is wrong experience or empirical experience, the other is right experience or *brahmānubhava*; and to attain the latter the former should be completely given up. The following statement of Śaṅkara expresses this clearly.

> Although one and the same Self is hidden in all beings, movable as well as immovable, owing to the gradual rise of excellence of minds which form the limiting conditions (of the Self), scripture declares that the Self, although eternally unchanging and uniform, reveals itself in a graduated series of beings, and so appears in forms of various dignity and power.[103]

When the two experiences are in no way positively related, as one is illusory and the other is absolutely real, there can be no scope for contradiction between them.

> There is no contradiction between the two views. We do not maintain the existence of things different from *Brahman* in the state when the highest truth has been definitely known, as the Śrutis say, "one only without a second" and "without interior or exterior". Nor do we deny the validity, for the ignorant, of actions with their factors and results while the relative world of name and form exists. Therefore, scriptural (*śāstrīya*) or empirical (*laukika*) outlook depends entirely on knowledge or ignorance. Hence there is no apprehension of a contradiction between them.[104]

---

[103] *SūB*, I.1.11, tr. Thibaut, vol. I, p. 63.

[104] *BṛUB*, III.5.1, tr. Swami Madhavananda, pp. 478-79.

Contradiction is possible only if Advaita accepts that both difference and unity form the nature of *Brahman*. They cannot be experienced in the same reality at the same time, just as heat and cold can never be experienced as forming the nature of the same object. But when Śaṅkara admits empirical experience based on differences, he accepts it as experience only. He does not admit any objectivity to it. It is illusory. It is valid only as an experience and in reality refers to *Brahman*. Therefore, it cannot contradict the pure experience of identity. The following examples given by Śaṅkara may clarify this. One can experience two moons because of an eye disease, but this experience of two moons does not in any way contradict the real experience of the moon being one. One can see water in the sand (mirage), but that water cannot really wet the sand. The sun reflected in the water may appear to be cool and shimmering, but this does not contradict the real nature of the sun. A magician may appear as different persons, but these do not interfere with the unity of his person. Likewise, the multiplicity experienced during the empirical state of experience does not contradict the undifferentiated nature of *Brahman* revealed in the fourth state.[105]

> By that element of plurality which is the fiction of ignorance, which is characterized by name and form, which is evolved as well as non-evolved, which is not to be defined either as the existing or the non-existing, *Brahman* becomes the basis of this entire apparent world with its changes, and so on, while in Its true and real nature, It at the same time remains unchanged, lifted above the phenomenal universe. And as the distinction of names and forms, the fiction of ignorance, originates entirely from speech only, it does not militate against the fact of *Brahman* being without parts.[106]

---

[105] *SūB*, II.1.28.

[106] Ibid., II.1.27, tr. Thibaut, vol. I, p. 352.

The problem of contradiction between them is only apparent but not real. It arises when people wrongly attribute objectivity to empirical experience which, in reality, it does not possess. Or again when the standpoints of ignorance and knowledge are confused and when both empirical experience and *brahmānubhava* are taken to be equally real and valid, which is never the case, there arises the problem of contradiction between them. What appears as real and valid from the standpoint of ignorance has no reality and validity from the standpoint of *brahmānubhava*, and *brahmānubhava* cannot be fully and perfectly understood from the standpoint of ignorance. As long as the illusory nature of empirical experience is not realized, and the world of differences is not transcended, one cannot understand the absolute oneness of *Brahman*. According to Śaṅkara, any inference about their contradiction cannot be more valid than the actual realization which does not find any such contradiction.[107]

[107] *BṛUB*, II.1.20.

9

Comparisons and Conclusions

In this chapter, we shall briefly compare what Śaṅkara said about *brahmānubhava* with what was said about mystic experience by two of the most authoritative exponents of Christian and Islamic mysticisms, namely St. John of the Cross and Jalālu'd-Dīn Rūmī. The main purpose of this comparison is to make Śaṅkara's position further clear and at the same time to understand it from two different mystical perspectives. Thus while the previous chapters attempt to elucidate Śaṅkara's position from within Vedāntic tradition, this chapter tries to do so from without, but still keeping ourselves within two great religious traditions. The first part of this chapter is a brief exposition of the teachings of St. John of the Cross and Rumi concerning mystic experience.

St. John of the Cross

According to him:

> God dwells and is present in every soul, even in that of the greatest sinner in the world.[1]

God is the centre of the soul and every soul is substantially and naturally united with Him. This union is never broken; it is eternal, for without it the soul ceases to exist. God preserves the being of the soul through such union. However, it is not

---

[1] *The Complete Works of St. John of the Cross*: in three volumes, tr. ed. E. Allison Peers, London: Burns Gates and Washbourne, 1957, vol. I, book II, ch. V, p. 75.

the supernatural union of the soul with God in love, which according to St. John of the Cross, is the ultimate consummation of spiritual life.

In supernatural union, the soul and God become one in spirit and love, although they are really different, just as when the light of a candle is united with that of the sun, what shines is not the candle, but the sun which has absorbed in itself the light of the candle.[2] Now, Divine union consists in the total transformation of the soul in the nature of God, so that there exists nothing in the soul that is contrary to the nature of God.

> When there is union of love, that it is true to say that the Beloved lives in the lover and the lover in the Beloved, and such manner of likeness does love make in the transformation of the two that are in love that it may be said that each is the other and that both are one.[3]

Thus in the state of Divine union, "each lives in the other, and the one is the other, and both are one through the transformation of love".[4]

To attain such union "is to have a soul most like to God in purity, having in itself no admixture of imperfection".[5] The soul should abandon from itself all that is unlike and repugnant to God and "remain as spotless and as void as possible, as if nothing has ever passed through her".[6] Because two natures, which are opposed to each other, cannot co-exist in one person,

---

[2] *The Complete Works of St. John of the Cross*, vol. II, stanza XXII, p. 293.

[3] Ibid., stanza XI, p. 65.

[4] Ibid.

[5] Ibid., vol. I, book II, ch. V, p. 77.

[6] Quoted by Jacques De Marquette, *Introduction to Comparative Mysticism*, Bombay: Bharatiya Vidya Bhavan, 1965, p. 154.

and as the natures of the soul and God, like light and darkness, are opposed to each other.

> The soul (should) be stripped of all things created, and of its own actions and abilities — namely of its understanding, perception and feeling — so that, when all that is unlike God and unconformed to Him is cast out, the soul may receive the likeness of God.[7]

In thus emptying itself of everything that is not in conformity with the nature of God, the soul attains perfect purity, which is essential if God is to communicate Himself with the soul supernaturally in love. "The soul cannot come to this union without great purity."[8] The transformation of the soul is to the extent of its perfection, and if the soul is perfectly pure, its transformation in the nature of God will be perfect. When the soul is perfectly pure, God works in the soul and the soul is illumined by and gets transformed into the nature of God by that work or grace of God. God then communicates to it His Being in such a manner that the soul appears to be God Himself or will come to possess all that God Himself has. This is "participant transformation" of the soul in God in which the soul is totally transformed in God's nature and assumes His attributes. It is also known as the "union of likeness", because through it the soul will attain the likeness of God and everything of the soul will be filled with or transformed into God's nature, as for instance, the will of the soul will be transformed into the will of God, its understanding into His, its delight into His, and so on. The following illustration given by St. John of the Cross may help us in understanding the nature of Divine union clearly.[9] When a ray of light passes through a glass window, the latter will be illumined and

---

[7] *Complete Works*, vol. I, book II, ch. V, p. 76.

[8] Ibid., ch. XXIV, p. 455.

[9] Ibid., ch. V, p. 77.

transformed into the nature of ray. However, if the glass is not perfectly pure, the ray may fail to illumine it perfectly. It is only when the glass is perfectly pure that ray will be able to illumine and transform it perfectly, in such a manner the distinction between the ray and the glass may seem to disappear.

In being transformed into the nature of God, the soul does not lose its individuality or selfhood. Its being is neither merged into the Being of God, nor is it annihilated. Only those things which it has acquired through sin are dissolved. Thus what is annihilated is its "unruly nature" or "the old man". In other words, the soul ceases to live in itself, but lives in God or God lives in it. The soul lives, but it is God that really lives in it. "We live, yet not we, for God liveth in us."[10] It regains its original purity or likeness to God which it has lost because of sin. As already pointed out, the faculties of the soul are not destroyed, but instead of serving the purpose of the soul, they now serve the purpose of God. For instance, the will of the soul is not destroyed, but becomes one with the will of God and serves His purpose, not as a slave, but as a free being. Thus in becoming united with God, the soul's knowledge and attributes are overwhelmed by the wisdom and attributes of God, just as when two lights are united, one smaller and another greater, what then shines and gives light is the greater one though the former does not cease to exist. If we consider the illustration of glass window in this context, the disappearance of the distinction between the window and the ray of light is only due to the confusion caused by the total transformation of the former into the nature of light, while in reality the existence of the window is neither destroyed nor does it cease to have its own nature which is different from that of the ray.

---

[10] *Complete Works*, vol. II, stanza, XI, p. 66.

Nevertheless, because of the soul's attainment of perfect purity and likeness to God, the distinction between it and God may seem to disappear, though in reality the soul is distinct from God and retains its individuality. St. John of the Cross says that in the state of divine union, the soul:

> Is like the crystal that is clear and pure; the more degrees of light it receives, the greater concentration of light there is in it, and this enlightenment continues to such a degree that at last it attains a point at which the light is centred in it with such copiousness that it comes to appear to be wholly light and cannot be distinguished from the light, for it is enlightened to the greatest possible extent and thus appears to be light itself.[11]

Thus while God is God by nature, the soul becomes like God by virtue of its transformation in His nature.

Jalālu'd-Dīn Rūmī

The ultimate goal of spiritual life, according to Rūmī, is re-union of the soul with God. God is perfect unity in which all the souls live as units without suffering the loss of their individual essence. Like lamps, the souls are many, and God, like light, is one and their essence. In its essence, the soul is one with God and in realizing its essence, it is united with God or regains its lost unity with God.

> O Thou Whose soul is free from "we" and "I", O Thou Who are the essence of the spirit in men and women, when men and women become one, Thou art that one; when the units are wiped out, Lo, Thou art that Unity.[12]

---

[11] *Complete Works*, vol. III, stanza, I, p. 23.

[12] *Rumi: Poet and Mystic, Selections from his Writings*, tr. Reynold A. Nicholson, London: George Allen and Unwin, 1956, p. 33.

Through so many examples Rūmī tells us that the essence of every soul is God and that without Him the souls would be like shadows. He is like sea and we are like foam and waves, His manifestations. He is to the soul what the human soul is to the human body, and because of Him only the soul is able to do everything.

> Thou art as the soul, we are as hand and foot; soul instructs hand and foot to hold and take.[13]

> Foamed the sea, and at every foam-fleck something took figure and something was bodied forth. Every foam-fleck of body, which received a sign from that sea melted straightway and turned to spirit in this Ocean.[14]

Before one realizes Divine unity — the underlying essence of everything — one thinks of oneself as something different from God and sees the world as different from oneself and also from God. But in realizing the unity of God, one sees the same love, the same spirit and the same essence enlivening all that is. Thus to see God in everything, as the essence of everything, is to realize His unity.

> The Beloved is all in all, the lover only veils Him. The Beloved is all that lives, the lover a dead thing.[15]

> I, All in All becoming, now clear see God in All.[16]

> When these "we" and "ye" shall all become One Soul, then they will be lost and absorbed in the Beloved.[17]

---

[13] *Wisdom of the East: The Persian Mystics (Jalaluddin Rumi)*, tr. F. Handland Davis, London: John Murray, Albemarle Street, 1912, p. 88.

[14] Ibid., p. 54.

[15] Ibid., p. 69.

[16] Ibid., p. 66.

[17] Ibid., p. 93.

The soul's union with God is timeless and eternal. It existed even before the phenomenal world of forms and multiplicity has come into existence. This oneness of the soul with God is similar to the oneness of spirit which two friends experience in love though they are bodily different.[18] In another example, he says that when a burning candle is brought into the presence of the sun, the essence of the former, which is identical with that of the latter, is united with that of the latter or becomes one with it.[19] The purpose of all these examples is to show that the soul's existence is in and through God, and that when the soul realizes its soul or essence, that is, God, it is united with God.

The soul regains this union when it becomes completely free from its natural attributes which constitute its individuality. When its individuality is annihilated (*fanā*) in the presence of God, the soul realizes its essential unity with God and abides in Him (*baqa'*). The soul's individuality will then be lost, and in its essence it will be absorbed in the unity of God. Rūmī says:

> The spiritual way ruins the body and having ruined it, restores it to prosperity: Ruined the house for the sake of the golden treasure and with that same treasure builds it better than before.[20]

While the attributes that constitute its individuality are annihilated in Divine union, its essence remains unannihilated. The soul loses only its individuality in regaining its unity with God, but not its essence which can never be destroyed. The flame of a candle loses its individuality in the presence of the sun, for it then gives no light as its light has become one with

---

[18] *Rumi: Poet and Mystic,* p. 134.

[19] Ibid., p. 180.

[20] Ibid., p. 52.

that of the sun, but in its essence it exists, for if some cotton is placed on it the cotton will be burnt.[21] This, according to Rūmī, is the real significance of the mystic utterance "I am God" (*ana'l haqq*). He explains that a mystic who realizes that he is God does not think of his individuality as against the Unity of God. He denies his individuality or selfhood and asserts the sole existence of God, for in reality God alone exists in the sense that He is all, as the essence of everything, and there exists nothing besides Him. Contrary to this, one who thinks that "I am the slave of God" asserts oneself or one's individuality besides God and that is not a sign of spiritual perfection. To realize oneself as nothing in the presence of God and to realize that God is everything is extreme humility and highest spiritual perfection. One's individuality should be completely annihilated, so that one becomes as dust to bear the marks of God's feet on it.[22] Nevertheless, as dust bearing the imprint of God the soul continues to exist. Then it will not be conscious of its existence and, like a fly plunged into honey, loses all its initiative and movement. Its existence then becomes lawful or justified, since it beholds the nature of God in itself and in all that it does. About this, Nicholson says:

> As the raindrop absorbed in the ocean is not annihilated, but ceases to exist individually, so the disembodied soul becomes indistinguishable from the universal Deity.[23]

To quote Arberry, another scholar on Sufism:

> By passing away from self the mystic does not cease to exist, in the true sense of existence, as an individual; rather his individuality, which is an inalienable gift from God, is

---

[21] *Rumi: Poet and Mystic*, p. 180.

[22] Ibid., p. 178.

[23] *The Mystics of Islam*, R.A. Nicholson, London: Routledge and Kegan Paul, 1963, p. 167.

> perfected, transmuted and eternalized through God and in God.[24]

However, Rūmī says that because the mystic provides spiritual food to all those who have faith in him, he may be called by the name of God figuratively, just as we call a basket full of apples an apple tree without any impropriety.[25] According to Rūmī, every soul in fact enjoys such Divine union in deep sleep in which it becomes free from all the differences like "I" and "you", whereas a mystic enjoys such a blissful state of unity even while he is awake.

> Our spirits are set free every night from this cage, they are done with audience and talk and tale. At night prisoners forget their prison, at night governors forget their power. There is no sorrow, no thought of gain or loss, no idea of this or that person.[26]

Comparisons

We shall now present together and compare what the three mystics said about God, soul, their relation, the realization of which is the supreme end of life and the way to it. In doing so the precept of Śaṅkara that the purpose of a comparison is not to undermine the doctrines of others, but to understand one's own doctrine better and realize the truth will be followed.[27] This, according to him, is more important than refuting rival doctrines.

The Concept of God

The Supreme Reality, which is *Brahman* according to Śaṅkara, and God according to St. John of the Cross and Rūmī, is

---

[24] *Sufism*, A.J. Arberry, London: George Allen and Unwin, 1956, p. 58.

[25] *Rumi: Poet and Mystic*, p. 185.

[26] Ibid., p. 49.

[27] *BṛUB*, III.2.13, IV.4.15; *PrUB*, VI.3; *SūB*, II.2.1.

beyond the range of human understanding. All of them maintain that He cannot be known through the natural means of knowledge, but can be known indirectly through the scriptures, and directly through mystic experience.

Brahman is unknowable and undescribable. Nothing can be affirmed of It in positive terms; and whatever that can be known and described in positive terms is not *Brahman*. The only way to describe It is to negate every possible conception of It or all that is superimposed on It, so that one may come to know Him indirectly as the substratum on which everything is superimposed. Similarly there can be no objective knowledge of It, for being the basis of all the means of knowledge, including the scripture, it is beyond their comprehension. Śaṅkara says that those who think that they know *Brahman* do not really know It, for it is impossible, and that It is known to those who have realized the impossibility of Its being known as an object.[28] This shows that *Brahman* is beyond the comprehension of human understanding, and that It can be known only when human understanding is completely withdrawn from its attempt to know *Brahman*. But this does not mean that it is impossible to know *Brahman* in any way, for It is known directly by being It; and that is the only way of knowing what *Brahman* in Itself is. In accepting the scripture as the only source of *Brahman*-knowledge, Śaṅkara never thinks that *Brahman* is an object of scriptural knowledge, or the scripture can present *Brahman* in positive terms as if It is there as an object. The only purpose which it serves, according to him, is to dispel ignorance, because of which the self-evident reality of *Brahman* is veiled, as it were. With the removal of ignorance, *Brahman*, which is by nature self-revealed, becomes revealed, as it were. All this clearly shows that *Brahman* is known not through any effort on the part of man, but because of Its very nature. Effort is required

---

[28] *KeUB*, II.3.

only to discover that fact which is seemingly veiled by ignorance. It is known when man, realizing the utter incapacity of his understanding to reach *Brahman*, withdraws it or makes it completely passive. Thus, in a sense *brahmānubhava* is given or received, for it is there already, and man has only to discover it. It is not in any sense got by human effort.

According to St. John of the Cross also, God is known to man not because of the latter's active understanding, but solely because of God's grace. It is given. Man's knowledge of God is purely an act of grace on the part of God. The reason for this is that there is no essential resemblance between the soul and God.

> Neither the creatures, nor intellectual perceptions, natural or supernatural, can bring us to God, there being no proportion between them. Created things cannot serve as a ladder; they are only a hindrance and a snare.[29]

God transcends human understanding and is therefore incomprehensible and inaccessible to it. Not realizing this, if we try to know Him with the aid of our understanding we will be withdrawing ourselves from Him, instead of approaching him. It is only when the active understanding of the soul is stilled or made completely passive that God reveals Himself to the soul "in a most hidden and secret manner, without her knowing how".[30] It is "understanding yet understanding not" meaning thereby that the knowledge of God is given to man by God Himself, but not acquired by man as a result of his active understanding. To our senses and understanding God is complete darkness. He reveals to the soul all that He is in the state of Divine union.

---

[29] Quoted by W.R. Inge, *Christian Mysticism*, London: Methuen & Co., 1925, pp. 226-27.

[30] *The Complete Works*, vol. II, stanza XXXVIII, p. 172.

Before one feels the presence of God directly in the state of Divine union, God is known mediately through faith in the revelation. Faith alone is the "proximate and proportionate" means to know God, and also the means whereby the soul is united with God.[31] But what faith communicates to us is God as covered by the silver of faith. While faith in scriptural statements is comparable to silver, the truth that is embodied in those statements is comparable to gold. Thus faith, like silver, is less valuable when compared to the gold of direct experience. Faith is only a means to the vision of God.

> The same substance which now we believe, clothed and covered with the silver of faith, we shall behold and enjoy in the life to come, fully revealed and with the gold of the faith laid bare.[32]

Now, coming to Rūmī we find that according to him also, human understanding, which is a gift of God or His creation, cannot fathom the nature of God, its creator. Human understanding is essentially relative, that is to say, it can know things through their opposites, as for example, the nature of light is made known to us by its contrary, darkness. But as there is nothing besides God with which He can be contrasted and compared, our understanding fails to comprehend Him.[33] He says:

> The story admits of being told up to this point. But what follows is hidden, and inexpressible in words. If you should speak and try a hundred ways to express it, it is useless; the mystery becomes no clearer.[34]

Since God eludes our understanding, what different religions speak of Him can only be partial and imperfect. Illustrating

---

[31] *The Complete Works*, vol. I, book II, ch. IX, p. 93

[32] Ibid., vol. II, stanza XI, p. 64.

[33] *Rumi: Poet and Mystic*, p. 118.

[34] Quoted by Nicholson, *The Mystics of Islam*, p. 148.

his point, Rūmī tells us the famous parable of the seven blind men and the elephant. Some blind men wanted to know the nature of an elephant. As they could not see it with their eyes, they tried to know it by feeling it. So, each one of them touched its various limbs and thought of it differently as a waterpipe, a fan, a pillar and so on.[35] Similar is our knowledge of God, partial and incomplete. Different people understand God differently, depending upon their capacity to understand; but none can in terms of one's natural understanding comprehend God fully and perfectly.

God cannot be known through tradition also, for the knowledge obtained through tradition has no finality and certainty, and hence cannot bring about real spiritual perfection. Comparing such knowledge with hearing, he says that hearing can only transform some of the qualities and attributes of the hearer, but cannot bring about that total transformation of the soul which the immediate and direct vision of God can alone accomplish.

> In hearing, there is transformation of qualities; in seeing, a transformation of essence. If your knowledge of fire has been ascertained from words alone, seek to be cooked by fire! There is no intuitive certainty until you burn; if you desire that certainty, sit down in the fire![36]

Thus becoming it is necessary to know the real nature of a thing. Thus, according to all the three mystics we are comparing, the highest reality or God cannot be known truly without directly experiencing Him. Our understanding and faith can take us to a certain point beyond which they are useless.

---

[35] *Tales from Masnavi,* A.J. Arberry, London: George Allen and Unwin, 1961, p. 208.

[36] *Rumi: Poet and Mystic,* p. 99.

While *Brahman* in Itself is not the creator, God is the creator of the universe. *Brahman* is not the creator, as there is no creation in reality. What we see as creation is only an illusory reality imagined to exist because of ignorance. *Brahman* is undifferentiated and homogeneous. It is non-dual; and therefore nothing exists besides It. Things like the individual self, *Īśvara* and the universe, being the appearances of *Brahman*, are ultimately unreal and have no objective existence.

According to St. John of the Cross, God is the creator of the world and the individual souls. He is therefore different from the world and the individual souls. He is the Lord of the souls and hence an object of their devotion and ultimate union.

Rumi's position is different from that of both Śaṅkara and St. John of the Cross. The universe and the individual souls are not illusory, as in the doctrine of Śaṅkara, and at the same time they have no existence apart from God. Their individual existence, according to Rūmī, is only phenomenal, and when the unity of God is realized their individual identities are lost in the unity of God, and they cease to exist independent of God. God is the only reality that really exists and everything else exists in and through Him. Creation, which exists as an idea in the knowledge of God, manifests itself into the phenomenal world, and along with it the soul descends into it from the state of Divine union. And when the soul ascends to or regains its original union with God, the manifested world of forms reaches its perfection, that is, it is not looked upon as having any existence independent of God. As the essence of the soul is not annihilated in the state of Divine union, God is not an undifferentiated and homogeneous reality like *Brahman* without any internal differences. He is One containing within Himself all or in Whom everything exists in its essence. He is Unity. Whereas *Brahman* is pure identity. It is One without a second and is devoid of internal differences. God, according to

Rūmī, is like ocean, and the souls, like foam and waves, are His manifestations. But the essence of foam and wave is the sea and without it they cannot exist. As long as they are seen apart from their source, they appear to be different from it and also seem to possess individuality, but when they are dissolved into their source they become one with it and lose their individuality. However, their essence is not destroyed.

While Rūmī's concept of God is in many respects comparable to the concept of *Īśvara* in Śaṅkara's philosophy for the following reasons, no such comparison is possible between the concept of *Īśvara* and the concept of God, according to St. John of the Cross. According to Śaṅkara, creation is the manifestation of what is potentially there in the twofold nature of *Īśvara*. The world of name and form is a manifested state of matter and spirit which constitute *Īśvara*'s nature. While all that is spiritual in the world represents the spiritual aspect of His nature, all that is physical in the world is an expression of the material aspect of His nature. Since He is the creator of everything, He is the Lord of the individual selves, and hence a supreme object of their devotion. The whole creation is like body and soul to the Lord, and as forming His nature, it is essentially one with Him, except for the difference of name and form. At this level, the individual selves and the universe are as real as their creator. Therefore, to realize *Īśvara*, which however is not the highest spiritual realization, is to see Him in and through His creation. He is the essence of everything and the inner self of all. Thus *Īśvara* is a unity in so far as every manifested thing is an expression of His nature. Before things are actually manifested or differentiated into name and form, they exist in Him as His nature. Thus *Īśvara* is not pure identity, but unity. The individual self is not identical with its creator. It is distinct from Him, nevertheless, it is one with Him in its essence.

But the reality of *Īśvara* is valid only from the standpoint of empirical experience which is based on ignorance. He is not ultimately real and absolute for two reasons. First, He is the absolute reality as viewed in relation to the phenomenal world or on which the illusory notions, like the creator, are superimposed. Therefore, the reality of *Īśvara* is relative to human understanding. He is the highest reality as conditioned by the various notions superimposed on it. When the superimposed notions are to be negated to realize the nature of *Brahman* as It is in Itself, It no longer appears as *Īśvara*. Second, as the individual selves and the universe exist besides Him, His reality is not complete and all-inclusive.

As far as human understanding is concerned, the ultimate reality is *Īśvara*, the ultimate cause of the world and the architect of human destiny. In trying to comprehend the nature of ultimate reality, the human mind, consciously or unconsciously, imposes its own categories on it. Therefore, the meaningfulness and validity of such a concept, though seem to be absolute from the standpoint of an individual self, may not be so from the standpoint of Absolute. Any conception of Reality has to presuppose the existence of the individual self. Now, if the human mind is to be granted the capacity to conceive Reality, then there can be no valid reason to reject any conception of Reality, as every conception of Reality is meaningful and valid for those who conceive it. If at all any conception of Reality is to be rejected as not truly portraying the nature of Reality, then all the conceptions of it, in so far as they are conceptions, are to be rejected. The nature of ultimate reality cannot be pinned down to any particular concept. However, the rejection of all the concepts of Reality does not in any way amount to the denial of Reality as such, but only shows, on the one hand, the inadequacy of the human mind, however pure and perfect it may be, to comprehend the nature of ultimate reality as it is in itself, and on the other, the reality as the ultimate ground of all such conceptions. In this context, if we try to understand the Christian concept of personal God and also the concept of God, according to Rūmī, it becomes clear that those concepts of God cannot be meaningful and valid absolutely. Though they admit that God in Himself cannot be really known, for He is unapprochable to human beings, yet they stick to a particular concept of God and believe it to be absolute and exclusively true. If the concept of a personal God is meaningful and also valid from the standpoint of a believer or a worshipper, in that case there can be many such conceptions of God satisfying different types of believers or worshippers. Then there can be no valid argument to consider any one concept among many as the only valid concept. One may point out here that if every concept of Reality is somehow conditioned and relative, it is something which cannot be avoided, for as long as we are active and try to understand Reality, we can know it as it is known to us, but not as what it is in itself. But it makes all the difference. If people were to realize this then they would not cling to any particular doctrine of God, but realizing the relative nature of all the concepts of God, they would try to transcend them. To transcend them is to transcend one's individuality, the source of all such conceptions or superimposition. Such that, so long as one is not able to transcend the sphere of superimposition or one's individuality, which is shaped and influenced by various factors like tradition, one may not be able to know Reality as it is in itself. When one's individuality is transcended, there can be no knowing of Reality in the ordinary sense of the word "knowing".

This may take us to the problem of revelation. It may be

contended, and rightly so, that the God of Christianity is not at all a concept, but a revealed truth, that too revealed by God Himself, and attested by the experiences of the mystics. Whatever may be the content of revelation, in so far as it is meant for man, man interprets it while trying to understand it. Thus human understanding is active not only in conceiving God independently, but also in understanding the meaning of revelation. In so far as there is scope for human understanding in making out the truth of revelation, the possibility of the human mind imposing its own pecularities on the revealed truth is present. This may be the reason for the emergence of various sects, according to different interpretations of one and the same revelation, either in Christianity or in Hinduism or in any other religion. Thus the knowledge of God, whether it is based on reason or on revelation is bound to be anthropomorphic; and one who has realized this has no other way than to deny absolute truth and validity to all conceptions of God and to accept truth as that which transcends all conceptions. This need not land one in scepticism, for the existence of Reality reveals itself as the substratum of all such conceptions. The argument that the concept of a personal God fulfils the highest spiritual aspirations of man may be true, but such a concept may not meet the demands of truth. If truth and truth alone can ultimately satisfy man, but not the fulfilment of some of the deeper urges of his soul, then man cannot rest contended with the anthropomorphic views of God. The realization of the absolute truth fulfils the highest end of life, and for that reason anything that can fulfil the human life cannot be the absolute truth.

This is precisely the standpoint of Śaṅkara. He could reject much of what the scriptures present as irrelevant to know the truth, and whatever he accepted as having truth-value he tried to transcend latter in realizing the truth directly. Everything, including the scripture, is only a pointer to truth, for everything is ultimately based on it. So, *Brahman* cannot be conceived of or whatever that can be conceived by the human mind is not *Brahman*; and liberation is the highest end of man, because it is the realization of highest truth. Thus not for the sake of liberation *Brahman* is to be realized, but in realizing *Brahman* one is naturally liberated from ignorance. Thus perfect knowledge of Reality is the aim of philosophical enquiry. Accordingly, Śaṅkara says that while *jñānī* (seeker of truth) seeks liberation, a man who has realized the truth is absolutely detached or has no such purpose.[37] Though the scriptures enjoy absolute validity before the reality is directly realized, they are to be transcended if it is to be realized as it is in itself. Even in helping one to realize the truth, their function is not to depict or present what *Brahman* is, which cannot be done, but only to guide a seeker of truth by way of pointing out the nature of Reality indirectly. Thus as long as one is not able to experience the truth free from all superimpositions, which is possible only by being it, the concepts of *Īśvara* and *mokṣa* are perfectly valid and form the goal of one's life. Thus, seeing the ultimate uselessness of both reason and revelation, Śaṅkara tried to transcend them both in realizing the truth free from all superimpositions, whether imposed by the human mind or by the scriptures. Whereas, it is doubtful whether St. John of the Cross and Rūmī, according to whom also revelation is a means of realizing the highest, could transcend the scriptural conception of God.

Concept of the self

While the Self is not a created thing, according to Śaṅkara and Rūmī, it is created by God in His likeness, according to St. John of the Cross. According to Śaṅkara, what everyone knows

[37] *jñānī mokṣabhilāṣī ca tattvajñe nābhimānita*, taken from a minor work of Śaṅkara.

as the self (*jīva*) is not the real Self (*ātman*). While the Self, which is not different from *Brahman*, is absolutely real, there is no individual self in reality. The empirical self, which is the experiencer and the agent, has no validity beyond empirical experience. Since it is known only in relation to the objects experienced, when the empirical experience ceases, the reality of the individual self comes to an end. There is no objective reality corresponding to it, whereas the Self of which the former is a distorted or wrong view, is objectively real. The empirical self is nothing but the Self in its empirical predicament. Pure Self is not different from *Brahman*, though it appears to be so when it is identified with the non-self. Of this real Self there can be no objective understanding, for as pure consciousness, it is the basis of all understanding. It is known only by being it. It has no bondage and so its liberation is meaningless.

The soul, according to St. John of the Cross, being created by God, has no resemblance to God, and the difference between it and God is infinite.

> There is no essential resemblance or connection between them (creatures) and God — on the contrary, the distance between their being and His Divine Being is infinite.[38]

The soul has a nature of its own and it is not annihilated even after the soul is united with God. Although there is a gulf of difference between the soul and God, yet in so far as the former is created in the latter's image, which the soul has lost because of sin, to the extent it regains it, it becomes united with God.

The soul is not a created being, according to Rūmī, for he says that "a sūfī has no God, he is not created".[39] The soul exists eternally in the unity of God or its union with God is

---

[38] *The Complete Works,* vol. I, book II, ch. VIII, p. 89.

[39] Quoted by Roma Chaudhuri, *Sufism and Vedānta*, part II, p. 132.

beginningless. It existed even before the creation of the world, that is, before the soul has descended into the world of forms.

> The *pīrs* are they whose spirits were in the Sea of Divine Munificence before this world existed. They lived before the creation of the body, they harvested the wheat before it was sown.[40]

According to him, there is an essential unity among all the individual souls, for they have emanated from the same Divine Spirit. The one and the same Divine Soul appears as many, because of its association with different bodies, just as the light of the sun becomes differentiated because of its reflection in different mediums.

> The sun of the souls has been split up in the windows of the bodies. Differences are found out in the animal soul, the human soul is only one. God has said "He sprinkled His light upon them" and Divine light cannot be broken up.[41]
>
> Their bodies are numerous, but their soul is one.[42]

Although the soul is the light of God and is eternally united with God in its essence, it is not identical with God as it is not one in kind with God.

> I am not a congener of the king — far be it from Him! — but I have a light from His radiance.[43]
>
> My genus is not the genus of my king.[44]

---

[40] *Rumi: Poet and Mystic*, p. 86.

[41] Quoted by Roma Chaudhuri, *Sufism and Vedānta*, part II, p. 132.

[42] *Rumi: Poet and Mystic*, p. 51.

[43] Ibid., p. 178.

[44] Ibid.

The Relation between the soul and the highest reality

As, according to Śaṅkara, the Self is not different from *Brahman,* the question of their relationship does not arise, for any relationship is possible only between two different things. As the Self is absolutely the same as *Brahman* — the difference between them is due to ignorance — *brahmānubhava,* the highest spiritual realization, is not different from Self-realization in which the real nature of one's own self is realized.

As the soul, according to St. John of the Cross, is essentially different from God, and has a nature of its own, it can never become identical with God. However, as the soul is created by God in His likeness, which the soul has lost because of sin, in recovering its original image or Divine likeness, the soul is united with God. This it achieves by transforming itself into the nature of God. Thus the soul's relation with God is unity through transformation.

According to Rūmī, the soul has descended from the state of Divine union into the world of forms and multiplicity; and in regaining its original state of union with God, the soul's ascending spiritual evolution is consummated. According to him, the soul is neither completely different from God, as it is a part of His unity, nor is it absolutely one with Him, for it has an essence of its own. It has no existence independent of God, but has an essence of its own by which it abides in the unity of God. In other words, when the soul is united with God, it ceases to have an independent existence and exists in and through God. Thus Rūmī distinguishes "becoming one with the light of God" from "infusion" or "incarnation" which involves homogeniety and "homogeniety (between soul and God) is not in respect of form and essence".[45] It is like water

[45] *Rumi: Poet and Mystic,* poem CXI, p. 178 and footnote thereon by Nicholson.

becoming homogeneous with earth in the plant. To quote Nicholson, "the perfect man though invested with all the Divine attributes is not God absolutely: he is real, but not the Real".[46]

Means to attain the highest

While, according to both St. John of the Cross and Rūmī, the supreme state of spiritual perfection is through the union of the soul with God, it is, according to Śaṅkara, through the realization of the Self which is not different from *Brahman*. Though the nature of spiritual perfection is different in all the three, there is something substantially similar in all the three regarding the way by which it is attained. All the three have emphasized that ethical perfection is essential for the attainment of the highest end of man. According to Śaṅkara, its value lies in purifying the heart or intellect, the seat of *Brahman*-knowledge. Union with God, says St. John of the Cross is not possible without perfect purity which is "perfect resignation and detachment from everything for God's sake alone".[47] According to Rūmī also purity of heart is essential for the union of the soul with God.

There is another point on which there is more agreement among the three. All of them say that the path leading to highest spiritual perfection consists in negating from the soul all that is not in conformity with the nature of Reality or God. As the Self by its nature is ever attained, Śaṅkara says that nothing need be done to attain it. Nevertheless, as its real nature is veiled, as it were, by ignorance, to realize the Self, one should liberate oneself from the veiling power of ignorance, and the various spiritual means are helpful in achieving this. Just as when darkness is dispelled the nature of the rope is revealed, the Self in its real nature becomes self-revealed when all that is

---

[46] *Rumi: Poet and Mystic*, footnote by Nicholson on p. 178.

[47] *Complete Works*, vol. I, book II, ch. V, p. 78.

superimposed on it due to ignorance is negated. Therefore, in *brahmānubhava* there does not emerge any new awareness; only the wrong understanding concerning one's Self is shed. Nothing new is attained thereby, but what is there already and eternally is discovered or realized. Therefore, the words like attainment, union, merger and reaching are inadequate to express it, and when used they will have only a figurative meaning. Negation is possible through scriptural knowledge which enables us to discriminate between the Self and the non-self. Thus the path leading to Self-realization is through negation based on scriptural knowledge.

According to St. John of the Cross, spiritual perfection of the soul does not consist in its attainment of something which is entirely new, or to see this or that form of God. It is to attain that which being natural to every soul is already there within every soul. Every soul in its original state is a perfect image of God and entirely free from sin, but the soul has lost it because of sin. So in being united with God, the soul simply regains what it had lost. The spiritual perfection of the soul, therefore, does not consist in understanding or remembering or feeling or imagining anything about God or anything else. In supernatural union, nothing that is not already there in the depths of the soul is added to it, nor is there any increase in its substantial union with God. "All that is capable of coming to it anew it has already had."[48] The soul then enjoys the riches which it already possesses; but these riches come to be revealed when the soul is illumined by Divine light, just as when the sun shines fully upon the sea, it illumines even its in-most depths and reveals the pearls, etc.

> So this Divine Sun, the Spouse, turns to the Bride and, as it were, bring to light the riches of the soul.[49]

---

[48] *Complete Works*, vol. II, stanzas XX and XXI, p. 287.

[49] Ibid., p. 288.

> In this illumination, great as is its excellence, the soul has no increase, but there is simply revealed that which she already has, to the end that she may rejoice therein.[50]

Let us quote Gilson in this context:

> He (man) has only to turn to God, by the aid of grace, to recover at once the Divine likeness and that conformity with his own nature which he had lost by sin.[51]

Thus in regaining its likeness of God, the soul undergoes a "cure" and recovers its Divine health. "To confirm the unity of the whole Christian tradition on this point", to quote Gilson again, "we have but to express in metaphysical terms, that to seek God is to have found Him already".[52]

To regain its lost perfection or the image of God, everything that is not of God should be emptied from the soul. The soul should become as void as possible, so that God can fill that void completely. If a log of wood is to be transformed into the nature of fire, all that is contrary of fire is to be burnt away from the log of wood. When everything that is contrary to the nature of fire is annihilated from the log, fire kindles it and changes it into its nature completely.[53] Similarly the soul should die to itself to have eternal life in God. It should pass through what St. John of the Cross calls "dark nights" and be stripped of all that belongs to it and opposed to God's nature, reserving nothing, to become fully transformed in the nature of God.

---

[50] *Complete Works*, p. 289.

[51] *The Spirit of Medieval Philosophy*, E. Gilson, London: Sheed & Ward, 1936, pp. 287-88.

[52] Ibid., p. 276.

[53] *Complete Works*, vol. I, book II, ch. X, pp. 403-04.

According to Rūmī also, ultimate spiritual perfection does not consist in reaching a region or acquiring something new. Union of the soul with God is not like the ascension of vapour to the sky or like a mortal reaching the moon. It is like an embryo growing to rationality, or like the sugar cane becoming sugar.[54] To regain its lost unity with God, the soul should negate from itself everything that is alien to God, or that because of which it is individualized. The same idea is well conveyed through a parable by Rūmī. When a sūfī was singing the glory of God and of the soul's union with Him in negative terms as "I know not", "I know not", a Turk approached him and demanded from him something positive about God. To him the sūfī replied thus:

> Until you deny all else, the affirmation of God escapes you: I am denying in order that you may find the way to affirm. I play the tune of negation: when you die, death will disclose the mystery. Not the death that takes you into the dark grave, but the death whereby you are transmuted and enter into the light.[55]

All the three have pursued negation not as an end in itself, but as a means to affirm and realize the highest ultimately. But what is negated and what is realized thereby are different in each of them. In the case of Śaṅkara, what was first superimposed on *Brahman*, because of ignorance is latter negated, and the highest end achieved thereby is the realization of the Self or to abide in the true nature of one's own self. According to St. John of the Cross, what is to be negated is the sinful nature of the soul and its self-centredness, to attain thereby its real centre, that is, God. It is alienation from God that is to be negated. And by negating all the

[54] *Rumi: Poet and Mystic*, p. 186.

[55] Ibid., pp. 104-05.

attributes that are natural to the soul and are alien to God, the soul regains its lost image or is united with God.

Although all the three have pursued the method of negation to affirm the truth in the end, in the case of St. John of the Cross and Rūmī, it is not carried out to its legitimate end. In this connection it may be argued as follows: One may negate from oneself all that is not of God, but so long as one fails to negate one's individuality, the negation is not complete. If it is asked as to what remains if one negates oneself as empirically known, it should be replied that though what remains is really incomprehensible, something which cannot be negated remains. That is the real Self or pure consciousness.

In this context a counter question may be asked as to why anything should be negated at all? If the process of negation has to be started at all, why should it not be thoroughgoing? St. John of the Cross and Rūmī talk of stripping the soul of everything — memory, understanding and will — and making it as void as possible. But they think that it still retains its individuality. If the negation or stripping of were to be carried out to its legitimate end, individuality too would be stripped of. Pure consciousness or the real Self alone will then reveal itself. Why should those who talk of negation stop short of this? It may be that they want to terminate the process of negation at a point which is acceptable to them or which is in accordance with the basic religious convictions they cherish. In the case of Śaṅkara it is thoroughgoing. He could negate everything till what by its nature cannot be negated remains. Thus what he negated includes all that a man can think of Reality either in terms of reason or on the basis of revelation. If at all we are to follow the method of negation, it logically leads to the realization of the Self which is neither conscious of itself nor of something other that itself. Since, at the empirical level, the Self is known in relation to various functions it performs, such as thinking and willing, its knowledge is relative to them. And when it is stripped of all its functions and attributes, then it cannot be aware of Itself as this or that. In other words there can be no individual awareness on the part of the Self. Only pure consciousness devoid of all distinctions and of which there can be no awareness reveals itself. It cannot be known in any way other than by being it. On the other hand, one can be aware of God only when one is conscious of oneself, whereas self-consciousness is not the ultimate nature of the Self. One may refuse to realize the ultimate unreality of individual self so as to find place for God, but so long as one is occupied with the idea of God, one cannot realize one's true Self.

To realize one's Self as God or *Brahman* is neither blasphemous nor does it mean simple arrogance on the part of an individual self. It can be so only when the self being aware of itself and its finiteness still thinks of itself as God or *Brahman*. But in Self-realization there is no awareness either of itself or of some object. But when such realization is to be presented in language all misunderstanding concerning it crops up. Absolute truth, which is free from all relations and distinctions cannot be presented in a language which by its nature can operate only by presupposing them. Therefore, as conceived by Śaṅkara, the function of language in relation to truth is not descriptive, but indicative. All that is said of Reality cannot be literally true; it can only suggest or point out to it.

The subject and object are interdependent and reveal each other, and if one is to be negated, the other too stands negated. At least one will not be aware of oneself when one is not aware of something, which may be an external object or an internal idea or feeling. Even self-consciousness involves such duality. In it the object may be some notion or idea of oneself or the very fact that one is trying to think of oneself. When no such object is present or when all the faculties of the soul are emptied, the very notion of an individual self becomes unintelligible. Thus in realizing its relative nature, one also realizes that the distinctions made by or based on it are unreal or relative. But at the same time, the empirical self and its activity indicate the Self. The Self is the ultimate ground of what all we know and do. It is beyond everything we experience and there is nothing besides it to experience it. It is really transcendental and ultimate. No one is as sure and certain of anything as the Self. Every conception of Reality may prove to be relative and may also be contradicted, but not the Self which is the basis of all such conceptions and contradictions. Therefore, to realize it is to break through all the conceptions of it, whether conceived by the human mind or presented by the scriptures. Thus to realize the ultimate reality one has not only to become free from what one thinks of it, but should also transcend the limitations imposed on it by revelation.

In the light of this discussion we may venture to say that though St. John of the Cross and Rūmī could transcend their empirical limitations, they could not transcend the limitations of tradition or revelation. They conceive the process of emptying the soul only as a preliminary to its being filled up by God. God, so to say, occupies this emptiness in the soul. Since the soul will then experience the presence of God and will be conscious of its union with God, it must also have an idea of its own individual existence. It experiences God as filling up its emptiness, conferring perfection on it and as possessing it. Or the case may be other way round. Since the soul accepts the existence of God and considers the experience of God as ultimate perfection, it refuses to see its own unreality, so that it can think of God, see Him and attain union with Him. All this, no doubt sounds meaningful within the framework of an individual self, but not when it is transcended. In such a union duality persists. The God of St. John of the Cross and Rūmī is not the one total and absolute reality, for over and against it are the souls and the world.

A really all-inclusive and infinite reality should exclude nothing from itself; anything other than it cannot be the ultimate reality. To see the ultimate reality or God as an adorable "Other" and an object of ultimate union may seem to satisfy the needs of religious life, but thereby Reality in its absoluteness is not realized, finitude is not abolished and liberation not attained. Further, a reality of that sort would be limited by the conditions of human understanding, as the latter has to superimpose its own categories on Reality while trying to comprehend it. Stace says:

> The pantheistic interpretation of mystical experience which is found in the major Vedāntist tradition and in Plotinus is not only natural, but constitutes the more perfect type of mysticism, while its dualistic interpretation — as expressed, for example, by Ruysbroeck and St. John of the Cross — is relatively undeveloped. The essence of the mystical experience, since it transcends all multiplicity, must transcend the dualism of subject and object. Dualistic interpretations, consequently, do violence to the experience.[56]

Setting aside the question whether Vedānta is pantheistic or not, I am inclined to agree with Stace.

Finally, let us consider the status of the world for these mystics. Generally speaking, when the highest reality is realized, the status of the world becomes reduced either to that of a contingent reality or to that of an illusion and also loses its old significance and validity in the eyes of a mystic. It

---

[56] *The Teaching of the Mystics: Selections from the Great Mystics and Mystical*, New York: American Library, 1960, p. 202.

no longer appears to be as real as it was before the attainment of the highest.

For a *brahmajñānī*, the world as world is just not real, just as for a waking person what he dreamt is unreal. Yet it is in and through the world we realize the highest. The world which is an appearance of *Brahman* helps us in realizing *Brahman*, the substratum of the appearance. It is a pointer to Reality. But for the fact that there is the world and we are in it, there would be no question of *Brahman*-realization. But all this is meaningful from the empirical standpoint only. Advaitic realization is not pantheistic. World is not identified with *Brahman* as it is not identified with the individual self, for in *brahmānubhava*, there is nothing besides *Brahman* with which it can be identified. The question of seeing the world as *Brahman* or identifying the self with *Brahman* arises, only when the world and the self exist in reality.

For mystics like St. John of the Cross, after attaining the highest mystic state, there is a devaluation of the world. He says that the wisdom of men concerning the world is profound ignorance when compared to the infinite wisdom of God, because when God is not known nothing is really known. As the creator of everything, God is the One principle in knowing which all things are known in their true nature. For this reason, things are not truly known if God is not known. Conversely, to a man of worldly wisdom, the wisdom of God and the wisdom of a mystic may seem to be utter foolishness.[57]

When the unity of God is realized, says Rūmī, things cease to exist independent of God. He is One and the only reality which has real existence and everything else is contingent, soulless, a mere shadow; and the process of ascending spiritual evolution culminates in realizing His unity. In this process,

---

[57] *Complete Works*, vol. I, book I, ch. IV, p. 26.

the lower states in the evolution lead to the higher states, and this continues till the highest state of Divine unity is realized.[58] The lower states help us as means to attain the higher states and thus the whole world becomes an instrument to realize the highest truth, that is, the unity of God. The world, like a mirror, reflects the unity of God and by gazing on the reflection of God one is able to contemplate on His essence. Rūmī says that as we have for long seen the reflection of God in the mirror of the world, we will be able to know His essence through the former.[59] Thus conceived, the world acts as a bridge between the soul and God.

We shall consider another point. The soul's union with God is through love, according to St. John of the Cross and Rūmī, while *brahmānubhava* is through knowledge, according to Śaṅkara. Here, if overemphasis is not placed on the literary meaning of the words "love" and "knowledge", and if sufficient care is taken to understand their content or what they mean to a mystic and how they express themselves in the lives of mystics, we may find out some close similarity between them.

---

[58] *Rumi: Poet and Mystic*, p. 103.

I died as mineral and became a plant,
I died as plant and rose to animal,
I died as animal and I was man.
Why should I fear? When was I less by dying?
Yet once more I shall die as Man, to soar
With angels blest; but even from angelhood
I must pass on: all except God doth perish.
When I have sacrificed my angel-soul,
I shall become what no mind e'er conceived.
Oh, let me not exist! for Non-existence
Proclaims in organ tones, "To him we shall return". — Poem LXI

[59] *Rumi: Poet and Mystic*, p. 139.

Brahman is pure knowledge and the nature of God is pure love. As "love" in the sense in which it is ordinarily used and understood is not the love that is God, "knowledge" with which everyone is familiar is not the pure knowledge which is *Brahman*. They are only manifestations or expressions of pure love and pure knowledge. Pure knowledge is objectless consciousness and it does not belong to any individual subject. Similarly, love that is God is not the worldly love that exists between two persons on earth. Real love is a gift of God and the soul will be able to love God only if the latter reveals His love to the soul. That means, the soul loves God with the love which it gets as a gift from God, or in other words, God loves Himself with the love which is His nature. As Gilson puts it, "there is a circulation of love that starts from God and finds Him again".[60] Thus while love is a gift of God, pure knowledge is somehow reflected in and through the individual self.

If we look at these concepts from the standpoint of their influence on a mystic's life and behaviour, their similarity becomes more evident. While a Christian loves the whole creation, not because he as an individual is capable of doing that, but because of his participation in the love of God, an Advaitin loves the world because it is not different from his Self. In Self-realization, the individual identity is completely transcended and the identity of all with the Self is realized. Thus in loving or realizing one's Self one transcends the limitations of the individual self and loves all, as all is one with the Self. As we have discussed earlier, to realize *Brahman* is to realize *Brahman* as everything. Self-realization cannot be understood without understanding the all-Self identity realization. Thus in terms of one's behaviour, Self-realization means loving everything as one's Self. A sūfī loves the world through his realization of God's unity, as everything in its

[60] *The Spirit of Medieval Philosophy*, Gilson, p. 276.

essence is one in God, and in realizing the being of his being, a sūfī comes to realize the essential unity of everything, that is, God.

Although the love that is God finds its expression in His creation, before the creation, it is objectless, for we cannot say that God loves Himself, as if God becomes an object of His own love. Because it is His nature, there is no point in thinking that God loves Himself. It is only in terms of human understanding that love cannot be conceived without an object. If God can exist without His creation, His nature can also abide in Him without depending on its expression. Even if there were to be nothing to reveal, the sun's light would be shining. Whereas, in the context of human life, love reveals itself through its various manifestations. Likewise, pure knowledge, which is *Brahman*, exists in itself eternally self-revealing, and manifests itself within the empirical realm as that through which things are known. While by His nature God is pure love, the soul becomes so by virtue of its participation in the nature of God. Likewise, the individual self is known by knowledge or knowledge is its being, while pure knowledge is the being of its being.

The concept of Advaita

Non-duality can be understood in two different ways.

1. In the state of *brahmānubhava* everything becomes naught and all the differences are literally abolished. *Brahmānubhava* may accordingly be identified by some with the *nirvikalpa samādhi* of yoga in which there is no awareness either of oneself or of something other than oneself. It is simple unconsciousness. This state, which is similar to the states of deep sleep and swoon, may seem to be the highest state of spiritual realization for those who want to escape themselves from the

limitations and suffering caused by the experience of differences. It has a beginning and an end, and so it is possible for one who has it to interpret everything in terms of non-duality even after passing from that state into normal consciousness of differences. As such, according to this view, non-duality is only an interpretation of an experience of which nothing positive can be known while one was in that state, but not a well-established truth while one is in normal waking state. What that unconscious state signifies is later interpreted. Thus in terms of an indeterminate experience of which nothing can be said, except in recollection, as in the case of deep sleep, everything is interpreted non-dualistically. Some of Śaṅkara's writings may seem to provide a basis for understanding Advaitic experience in this way, or he himself may appear to explain Advaita in such terms at times.

If *brahmānubhava* is such a short-lived and indeterminate state of experience, there seems to be no valid reason why similar states of experience like swoon and such other states that can be induced by drugs, should be rejected as having nothing to do with Self-realization. In all these states, there is no freedom from ignorance, the fragmentary and conditioned knowledge of things, nor does one feel that one is liberated. In the case of *yogīs*, the sense of liberation may be due to their belief. Non-duality is literally attained in all such states, whether one is aware of it or not. Moreover, the attainment of such an experience need not depend on a sound understanding of Advaita doctrine, but can be induced by drugs. Whereas, it seems to be sounder to maintain that if non-duality is not a subjective truth or based on interpretation, but an established and objective truth, its realization should not be short-spelled, but must be unintermittent and one should be aware of it always.

2. But the spirit of Śaṅkara's approach to spiritual problems and the major part of his writings are more favourable to an interpretation of Advaita which fundamentally differs from the above. This, in my view, is the right understanding of Advaita and that may be the standpoint of Śaṅkara also. According to this view, non-duality does not consist in the actual disappearance of distinctions and multiplicity, but in the realization of their ultimate unreality or illusory nature, because of the realization of *Brahman* which is everything or besides which there is nothing.

In *brahmānubhava,* there is no absence of awareness. When once the awareness of non-duality arises, there is no end to it. It is eternal and there is no return from it into a state of ignorance. In other words, it is not an interpretation of a momentary state of unconsciousness. Whereas, the scope for interpretation is present in all such experiences which lost for a short period or in which the individual experiences something other than himself. In *brahmānubhava,* differences and multiplicity do not actually disappear; only their unsubstantiality is realized. They are not absolutely true and ultimately real, as *Brahman* is. A *brahmajñānī* will be aware of things such as the universe and other selves, but not as different from the Self or *Brahman.* He realizes their oneness with the Self. Similarly, his awareness of himself is not annihilated; only the sense of individuality or the wrong knowledge that he is not one with Reality is discarded. To experience an all-inclusive and non-dual reality is to see it everywhere, that is, to realize that things, which appear to be different from one another and also from *Brahman*, are not really different from *Brahman* and are of one nature. Such a realization will be incomplete if one does not also realize one's identity with Reality. Thus the purpose of Vedānta, according to Śaṅkara, is twofold.

> The Vedānta passages have a twofold purport; some of them aim at setting forth the nature of the highest Self, some at teaching the unity of the individual self with the highest Self.[61]

Before or after anyone's realization, Reality remains what it is, as a rope remains as such during and even after the removal of its illusion as a snake; only there will be a change in our understanding of it. Other examples may be given. For a man in high fever sugar may taste bitter, but he knows it is not. A jaundiced man may see all things to be yellow, but he knows and believes that they are not. Similarly, a *brahmajñānī* does see multiplicity, but he knows that it is not real; that *Brahman* alone is. Thus what to an ignorant person appears as the world, which is full of differences, and as the source of bondage and suffering is the absolute reality, complete and perfect to a *brahmajñānī*.

The differences are due to one's wrong understanding of Reality and when that wrong understanding is completely destroyed, there will be no scope for seeing it as many. Many is the distorted view of the One. Thus, it may be said that *brahmānubhava* means a complete change or transformation of one's outlook. The vision of differences and distinctions is discarded and an integral vision of oneness is attained. In the words of Śaṅkara, "one should see the universe as filled with *Brahman* (*brahmamayam*) by way of transforming the vision of differences into one of perfect knowledge".[62] This does not

---

[61] *SūB*, I.3.25, tr. Thibaut, vol. I, p. 198.

[62] *Aparokṣānubhūti*, *śl*. 116.

mean ignoring or being indifferent to all that is empirically experienced or giving a value to it, but to realize that non-duality is the nature of Reality. In realizing this nothing is imposed on Reality, but the superimposition on it is removed.

It is not possible and at the same time highly inappropriate to determine the nature of such an all-inclusive and non-dualistic experience. It is not an intellectual understanding through which universals and abstract ideas are intuited. Although intellect plays an important role up to the moment of *brahmānubhava*, it is transcended the moment *Brahman* is directly experienced. It is not a mystic experience, in the sense of experiencing a divine object intimately and intuitively, nor is it an emotional and subjective state of imagination. In so far as it is inward, it is similar to the experience of pain and pleasure, sure and certain to the individual who has attained it. It is the realization of an eternal and objective truth by being it. It is wisdom, as Louis Renou puts it, as opposed to intellectual understanding.[63] It is liberating enlightenment having its basis in scriptural knowledge. It is realization (*anuvedana*) which means the supreme consummation or ripening (*paripāka*) of scriptural knowledge. It is freedom from ignorance, the fragmentary and conditioned knowledge of things. It is an integral experience in which the whole personality participates and gets transformed.

Criticism of Brahmānubhava

Śaṅkara's position may be criticized in two ways. First, if the individual self is ultimately unreal and is annihilated in realizing *Brahman*, it may be asked, what will be left to experience and enjoy the bliss that is *Brahman*? Second, if *Brahman* is attributeless, undescribable and actionless, why should anyone take the trouble of attaining such a void like Reality ?

---

[63] *Hinduism*, ed. Louis Renow, London: Prentice Hall International, pp. 56-57.

It is true that in the state of *brahmānubhava*, there is no distinction of an experiencer and the experienced, for then there will be no individuality. But this does not mean that the Self loses its existence and consciousness. The Self is pure existence and pure consciousness and remains so eternally. In *brahmānubhava* also, the Self remains as such; only the differences and distinctions which are superimposed on it are negated. It is then freed from the limitations of individuality, falsely imagined, and its true nature — absolute consciousness — shines forth. Since individuality does not at all constitute its real nature, the Self does not in any way suffer by its removal. There will be none to experience the delight, that is, *Brahman*, and that is the final ontological truth, whether we like it or not. If at all, it can be said that the bliss of *Brahman* is experienced, it is so by being it.

This problem arises only when absolute experience is viewed and understood from the standpoint of individuality. The existence of bliss and awareness in the absence of an individual self may appear unintelligible, as bliss is meaningful at the empirical level only when it is enjoyed, and consciousness without individuality is difficult to be conceived at this level. But Advaita Vedānta affirms that absolute consciousness and pure bliss constitute the nature of ultimate reality and that it is known from the scripture and *anubhava*. Our logical understanding can at the best conceive of the possibility of such a state, but what it is like and what happens when it is actually realized cannot be understood in terms of it.

The second criticism may be answered in the following way. According to Śaṅkara, *Brahman* is not at all a void.[64] Nothing is positively affirmed of It because of Its non-dual and all-inclusive nature. There is nothing different from It in

[64] *BṛUB*, IV.4.6; *TaiUB*, I.1, Introduction.

terms of which something can be affirmed or denied about It. If so, it may be asked how the negation of what is superimposed on *Brahman* is possible? To this the reply of Śaṅkara would be that what is superimposed and what negates it are both ultimately unreal. Likewise, what is positively asserted of *Brahman* is also due to ignorance, but not real. Contrary to this, if assertions and denials about It are taken as real, the plurality of one who affirms, what is affirmed and that of which something is affirmed would also be real. Nothing particular can be said about an all-inclusive and non-dual reality, as it contradicts its completeness and disturbs its all-inclusive nature. Even to say that It is non-dual and all-inclusive presupposes the existence of one who asserts so, violating thereby the non-dual nature of *Brahman*. For these reasons, *Brahman*, though It is everything and not void, is best described through silence. But our inability to speak about It in positive terms does not prove that It is nothing. In attaining It, one does not enter into void, but attains completeness and perfection. To attain It is to know one's identity with It; this is the highest good and positive bliss.

Bibliography

Primary Sources (Sanskrit)

Śaṅkara: *Aparokṣānubhūti: The Works of Sri Sankaracharya*, vol. XV, Memorial edn., Srirangam: Sri Vani Vilas Press, 1910.

———, *Ātmabodha: The Works of Sri Sankaracharya*, vol. XV, Srirangam: Sri Vani Vilas Press, 1910.

———, *Bhagavadgītā Bhāṣya*, Madras: Vavilla Ramaswamy Sastrulu & Sons, 1953.

———, *Brahmasūtra Bhāṣya*, Madras: Vavilla Ramaswamy Sastrulu & Sons, 1937.

———, *Dakṣiṇāmūrtyaṣṭakam: The Works of Śrī Śaṅkarācārya*, vol. XVII, Srirangam: Sri Vani Vilas Press, 1910.

———, *Sarvavedānta Siddhānta Sārasaṁgraha: The Works of Śrī Śaṅkarācārya*, vol. XV, Srirangam: Sri Vani Vilas Press, 1910.

———, *Śataślokī: The Works of Śrī Śaṅkarācārya*, vol. XV, Srirangam: Sri Vani Vilas Press, 1910.

———, *Śivānandalahariī*, Madras: Vavilla Ramaswamy Sastrulu and Sons, 1958.

———, *Svātmaṇirūpaṇam: The Works of Śrī Śaṅkarācārya*, vol. XV, Srirangam: Sri Vani Vilas Press, 1910.

———, *Upadeśasāhasrī*, Madras: Sri Ramakrishna Mission, 1949.

———, *Upaniṣad Bhāṣyas: Ten Principal Upaniṣads with Śaṅkara Bhāṣya*, Delhi: Motilal Banarsidass, 1964.

———, *Vivekacūḍāmaṇi*, Advaita Ashrama, Mayavati, Almora, Himalayas, 1932.

Translations

Śaṅkara, *Aparokṣānubhūti*, tr. Swami Vimuktananda, Calcutta: Advaita Ashrama, 1955.

———, *Bhagavadgītā Bhāṣya*, tr. A. Mahadeva Sastri, Madras: V. Ramasvamy Sastrulu & Sons, 1961.

———, *Bṛhadāraṇyaka Upaniṣad Bhāṣya*, tr. Swami Madhavananda, Advaita Ashrama, Mayavati, Almora, Himalayas, 1950.

———, *Brahmasūtra Bhāṣya*, tr. George Thibaut, Delhi: Motilal Banarsidass, 1962.

———, *Chāndogya Upaniṣad Bhāṣya*, tr. Ganganatha Jha, Poona: Oriental Book Agency, 1942.

———, *Gauḍapādakārikā Bhāṣya* and *Māṇḍukya Upaniṣad Bhāṣya*, tr. Swami Nikhilananda, Mysore: Sri Ramakrishna Ashrama, 1955.

———, *Upadeśasāhasrī*, tr. Swami Jagadananda, Madras: Sri Ramakrishna Math, 1949.

———, *Upaniṣad Bhāṣyas* (*Aitareya, Īśa, Kaṭha, Kena, Muṇḍaka, Praśna and Taittirīya Upaniṣads*), tr. Swami Gambhirananda, vol. I (1957) and vol. II (1958), Calcutta: Advaita Ashrama, 1957.

———, *Vivekacūḍāmaṇi*, tr. Madhavananda, Almora: Advaita Ashrama, Mayavati, Himalayas, 1932.

Other Books

Allison Peers, E., *The Complete Works of St. John of the Cross*, 3 vols., London: Burns Dates and Washbourne, 1957.

Arberry, A.J., *Sufism: An Account of the Mystics of Islam*, London: George Allen & Unwin, 1956.

———, *Tales from Masnavi*, London: George Allen and Unwin, 1961.

Gilson, E., *The Spirit of Medieval Philosophy*, London: Shed and Ward, 1936.

Handland Davis, F., *Wisdom of the East: The Persian Mystics: Jalalu'd-Din Rumi*, London: John Murray, 1912.

Inge, W.R., *Christian Mysticism* (*Bompton Lectures 1899*), London: Methuen & Co., 1925.

Marquette, J. DE, *Introduction to Comparative Mysticism*, Bombay: Bharatiya Vidya Bhavan, 1965.

Nicholson, R.A., *The Mystics of Islam*, London: Routledge and Kegan Paul, 1963.

Otto, R., *Mysticism East and West*, New York: Meridian Books, 1957.

Radhakrishnan, S., *Indian Philosophy*, 2 vols., London: George Allen and Unwin, 1956.

Rumi, *Rumi: Poet and Mystic*, tr. R.A. Nicholson, London: George Allen & Unwin, 1956.

Stage, W.T., *The Teachings of the Mystics*, New York: The New American Library, 1960.

Swami Atmananda, *Śrī Śaṅkara's Teachings in His Own Words*, Bombay: Bharatiya Vidya Bhavan, 1960.

Zaehner, R.C., *Hindu and Muslim Mysticism (Jordan Lectures in Comparative Religion, 1959)*, London: University of London, 1960.

Index